Black Magic Woman

Women, Gender & Sexuality in German Literature & Culture

Helen Watanabe-O'Kelly, University of Oxford
Series Editor

Volume 23

PETER LANG
Oxford · Bern · Berlin · Bruxelles · New York · Wien

Barbara Hales

Black Magic Woman

Gender and the Occult in Weimar Germany

PETER LANG

Oxford · Bern · Berlin · Bruxelles · New York · Wien

Bibliographic information published by Die Deutsche Nationalbibliothek
Die Deutsche Nationalbibliothek lists this publication in the Deutsche
Nationalbibliografie; detailed bibliographic data is available on the
Internet at http://dnb.d-nb.de.

A catalogue record for this book is available from the British Library.

Library of Congress Cataloging-in-Publication Data:

Names: Hales, Barbara, 1962- author.
Title: Black magic woman : gender and the occult in Weimar Germany /
    Barbara Hales.
Description: Oxford ; New York : Peter Lang, [2021] | Series: Women, gender
    and sexuality in German literature and culture, 1094-6233 ; vol. 23 |
    Includes bibliographical references and index.
Identifiers: LCCN 2020039182 (print) | LCCN 2020039183 (ebook) | ISBN
    9781789976816 (paperback) | ISBN 9781789976823 (ebook) | ISBN
    9781789976830 (epub) | ISBN 9781789976847 (mobi)
Subjects: LCSH: Occultism--Germany--History--20th century. |
    Women--Germany--Social conditions--20th century. | Women
    occultists--Germany--History--20th century | Feminist
    spirituality--Germany--History--20th century. | Sex
    role--Germany--History--20th century. | Germany--Social
    conditions--1918-1933.
Classification: LCC BF1434.G5 H35 2021 (print) | LCC BF1434.G5 (ebook) |
    DDC 130.943/2241--dc23
LC record available at https://lccn.loc.gov/2020039182
LC ebook record available at https://lccn.loc.gov/2020039183

Cover image: Mary Wigman (1886–1973). German dancer, dance pedagogist,
and choreographer, pioneer of Expressionist dance. Collection Atelier J. Merkelbach.
Archive Amsterdams 1922.

ISSN 1094-6233
ISBN 978-1-78997-681-6 (print)   ISBN 978-1-78997-682-3 (ePDF)
ISBN 978-1-78997-683-0 (ePub)   ISBN 978-1-78997-684-7 (Mobi)

© Peter Lang Group AG 2021
Published by Peter Lang Ltd, International Academic Publishers,
52 St Giles, Oxford, OX1 3LU, United Kingdom
oxford@peterlang.com, www.peterlang.com

Contents

Figures

Acknowledgments

This project is the culmination of many years of research spurred on by lively discussions with colleagues. I am especially grateful to those scholars with whom I have had the pleasure of working, including Mila Ganeva, Sara Hall, Anjeana Hans, Barbara Kosta, Barbara Mennel, Ingeborg Majer O'Sickey, Mihaela Petrescu, Christian Rogowski, Philipp Stiasny, Regine Wagenblast, and Cynthia Walk. Irene Guenther's generous contribution of her father Peter Guenther's library on expressive dance (*Ausdruckstanz*) was essential in realizing my vision. I moreover thank my coeditor, and friend, Valerie Weinstein for her feedback and support. Her close reading and regular comments on the manuscript helped to refine my writing and enrich my thesis. I am also thankful to the anonymous peer reviewers and editors at Peter Lang for their valuable feedback. My thanks in particular go to Laurel Plapp for shepherding the book through all phases of publication. Additionally, I would like to thank my home institution, University of Houston Clear-Lake, for Faculty Development leave to work on the project, as well as financially supporting its production.

Some of the material used in the book first appeared in "Dancer in the Dark: Hypnosis, Trance-Dancing, and Weimar's Fear of the New Woman" *Monatshefte* 102.4 (Winter 2010): 534–49.[1] Aspects of the work herewith likewise made their first appearance in "Mediating Worlds: The Occult as Projection of the New Woman in Weimar Culture" *German Quarterly* 83.3 (Summer 2010): 317–32.

I would further like to recognize Louise Chapman for the editing help and indexing. She did an amazing job with the manuscript in preparation for publication. I would also like to thank my graduate students, James Dillard and Christen Symmons, for assistance with the images. For minting in me a love of learning, I thank my mother: Marjorie Hales.

Finally, I am grateful to my wonderful husband and colleague, Daniel Silvermintz, who has patiently read and commented upon several versions of the entire manuscript. Without question, his enthusiasm about the project has not only improved the manuscript in countless ways: he has helped to bring it to fruition.

The Occult Woman as Metaphor for Weimar's New Woman

If you are a woman and dare to look within yourself, you are a Witch. You make your own rules. You are free and beautiful. You can be invisible or evident in how you choose to make your witch-self known. You can form your own Coven of sister Witches (thirteen is a cozy number for a group) and do your own actions. [...] You are a Witch by saying aloud, "I am a Witch" three times, and thinking about that. You are a Witch by being female, untamed, angry, joyous, and immortal.

– Women's International Terrorist Conspiracy from Hell (W.I.T.C.H.) leaflet

Breitbart, the far-right online news outlet, cautioned its readers in December 2017 about the rise of feminist witchcraft in the wake of Donald J. Trump's U.S. presidential victory.[1] The story was prompted by reports from several sources of factions that had formed over the internet to perform a ceremonial hexing of the president. For instance, Vox Media reported that a group of neo-pagans, amounting to more than 13,000 members, had "come together each month since Trump's inauguration with one goal: to perform a spell – equal parts quasi-religious ritual and activist performance – to 'bind' the president, forming a collective known as the #MagicResistance."[2]

This newfound interest in the occult did not emerge out of thin air. It had, in fact, been brewing for some time, facilitated in large part by the internet, which enabled millions to access a trove of information regarding esoteric wisdom about pagan practices, arenas hitherto off-limits. This was especially true of young people, 63 percent of whom – as a 2012 Public Policy

---

1 "#MagicResistance: The Rise of Feminist Witchcraft" December 17, 2017, <www.breitbart.com/tech/2017/12/17/rise-feminist-witches/>.
2 "Each Month, Thousands of Witches Cast a Spell against Donald Trump" October 30, 2017, <www.vox.com/2017/6/20/15830312/magicresistance-restance-witches-magic-spell-to-bind-donald-trump-mememagic>.

Polling survey demonstrated – believe in demonic possession.[3] Indeed, it is young women in particular, contends Katie Fustich, who are drawn to the occult as a way to cope with growing social and cultural pressure. She writes, "Being a girl in 2016 can be frustrating, confusing, and lonely. For today's young digital witches, finding and exercising the very real magic they possess is a powerful act."[4]

The association of women with the occult has a long history – at least as old as the mythic account of Lilith, supposedly the first wife of the biblical Adam.[5] The myth purports that, immediately following their cocreation from the earth (Genesis 1:27), man and woman were engaged in an intractable power struggle: Adam demanded that Lilith assume a subordinate position during intercourse but she refused, decreeing their equality. When Lilith realized that Adam would not relent in his desire for domination, she pronounced the ineffable name of God, thereafter fleeing the garden; taking flight in the air like a winged beast. Lilith, who is described as having long, flowing black hair, would take eternal revenge by haunting men in their sleep: creating demonic spirits through the extraction of their nocturnal seminal emissions.[6] As Rabbi Hanina remarks, Jewish belief in Lilith's preternatural powers is attested to by the following legal restriction of the Talmud: "It is prohibited to sleep alone in a house, and anyone who sleeps alone in a house will be seized by the evil spirit Lilith."[7]

From the ancient myth of Lilith to twenty-first-century digital witches, the association of women with the occult has functioned as an enduring narrative in the continuing struggle to define women's identity. The myth of Lilith represents man's fear of woman as a beastly creature whom he cannot capably control. However, while man may be able to *physically*

3   "Most Americans 18–29 Years Old Believe in Demon Possession," *Huffington Post*, October 25, 2013, <www.huffingtonpost.com/bruce-wilson/most-americans-1829–years_b_4163588.html>.

4   Katie Fustich, "Why Is Digital Witchcraft So Appealing" posted on *The Social Justice Foundation*, October 28, 2016, <www.psmag.com/news/why-is-digital-witchcraft-so-appealing-to-young-women>.

5   For discussion, see Judith Reesa Baskin, *Midrashic Women: Formations of the Feminine in Rabbinic Literature* (University Press of New England, 2002), 58.

6   See Goldwurm 100B.

7   *The William Davidson Talmud*, *Shabbat* 151b, <www.sefaria.org/Shabbat.151b?lang=bi>.

dominate woman, she is possessed of supernatural powers, which amply compensate for any physical limitations, as suggested by Lilith's ability to take flight and transcend natural laws. Lilith – along with all other empowered women – threatens to upend the patriarchy while its gatekeepers lie prostrated and powerless. Laying claim to this spirit of emancipation, women from the Victorian era up until the #MeToo movement have been spellbound by the allure of the occult as a way to express their individuality, political liberties, and sexual emancipation.

Thus, *Black Magic Woman* investigates women's involvement in occult practices as an expression of Weimar's New Woman, who bore witness to unprecedented advances socially, economically, and sexually. Weimar physician, Walter von Gulat-Wellenburg, defines the occult in his *Der Physikalische Mediumismus (The Physical Art of the Medium*, 1925) as the theory and findings of the hidden (1). Whether fictive or historical, the occult woman's supernatural ability to tap into an unseen world serves to reconfigure female identity in a time of social and political crisis in the popular Weimar imagination: from its traditional conception of woman as a nurturing mother and demure housewife to a beastly monster, who threatens the enfeebled and emasculated post-World War One psyche. Each chapter is devoted to a historical and cultural analysis of specific occult practices. To this end, Chapter 1 explores the ghost; Chapter 2, the vampire and monster; Chapter 3, the witch and gypsy; and Chapter 4, the trance-dancer and medium. A full précis of each chapter is given toward the end of this introduction.

The Occult as a Response to Crisis

Corinna Treitel contends that the embrace of the occult in Wilhelmine and Weimar Germany was motivated by a need to bring order to an "anonymous, irrational world." She continues that "[modern-minded] men and women sought to rectify their suffering under modernity's burdens through an embrace of the new occult sciences" (246–47).[8] This interest

---

8   Treitel notes that the occult movement garnered support from all echelons of
     German society. It was often considered a path to a healthier lifestyle, akin to the

in the occult was already emerging at the end of the nineteenth century. In the period from the late 1800s to Nazism, there were over 200 clubs dedicated to occult practices, attracting tens of thousands of members (Treitel 57–59).[9]

If we are to understand the relationship between the occult and German modernity (1880–1930), then we ought to consider the various historical crises that Germany experienced throughout this period. According to Priska Pytlik, Germany's interest in the occult emerged in response to a series of scientific, psychological, and religious ruptures. Technological change in particular represented "eine Welle der Fortschrittseuphorie" ("a wave of euphoric advancement"), reordering the fundamental understanding of natural rules and methods (Pytlik 10). Within this period of radical, cultural upheaval, the synthesis of the scientific method with occult knowledge was looked to as holding the promise of bringing order to the world (Pytlik 13). Technological developments, including the camera and the telegraph, were moreover believed to offer a means for communing with the spiritual world (Gunning, "Der frühe Film" 559). In 1895, the German mechanical engineer and physicist, Wilhelm Conrad Röntgen, discovered electromagnetic radiation (X-rays), producing thereby the first radiographic image. Commenting on Röntgen's discovery, philosopher Karl du Prel noted that the ability of X-rays to detect hitherto invisible energy fields represented a landmark moment, whereby traditional science finally coincided with the occult. The once merely *alleged* capacities of highly sensitive people for detecting and diagnosing diseases (such as somnambulists and clairvoyants) thereafter enjoyed scientific vindication: "Die Physiker haben nun festen Fuß gefaßt an einer Küste, die ihnen unbewohnt scheint; aber es tönt ihnen der Gruß der Occultisten entgegen: Spät kommt Ihr, doch Ihr kommt!" (The physicists have just set foot on a coastline that seems to

---

Lebensreform movement (247). There were also occult groups that were völkisch in nature (Treitel 73–80).

9   For a discussion of the German occult as mass movement, see Treitel's chapter "The Occult Public" 56–80. In her Appendices, Treitel extensively lists occult clubs, presses, and other institutions (including bookstores, businesses, institutes, and schools) that were active during the Weimar (and Wilhelmine) period. She there also includes parapsychology and psychical journals.

be uninhabited: but they are greeted by the occultists who note: you are late, but at least you have come!) ("Röntgens Strahlen" 324). Science thenceforth had the promissory potential for vindicating religious convictions, which had previously been the sole purview of psychics. According to du Prel, the new science was even capable of proving the existence of God and the immortality of the soul (Ibid.), while photography in particular was believed to hold the key to making visible the presence of an intangible, not to mention unimaginable, God (Ibid.).

Ulrich Linse further contends that modern occult practices constituted a "working through" of dichotomies (Linse 21). Scientific ideas were placed side by side with occult phenomena in an effort to disclose invisible realities. In this way, electromagnetism was connected to magnetism; X-rays were coupled with clairvoyance; the telegraph was tied up with telepathy; and radioactivity was associated with alchemy (Henderson 15).[10] Weimar psychologist Richard Baerwald speculated about the scientific bases of occult phenomena. In his work *Okkultismus, Spiritismus und unterbewußte Seelenzustände* (*Occultism, Spiritism and Subconscious States of Mind*, 1920), Baerwald set out to establish a scientific basis for occult practices, for instance, modern psychology's ability to access the subconscious, thereby substantiating the mediumistic art of reading another's mind (Baerwald 5).

The relationship between the occult and science is moreover evident in the works of modern abstract artists, who sought to capture far-out phenomena including ethereal vibrations and the so-called fourth dimension. Before Einstein's pioneering work on relativity, many physicists (including Charles Howard Hinton and Victor Schlegel), as well as occultists (such as Helena Blavatsky and Rudolf Steiner), worked on the problem of the fourth dimension, which was believed to hold the answer to all of life's mysteries (Henderson 19). Artists including Marcel Duchamp and Wassily Kandinsky attempted to depict such phenomena by inciting "vibrations" in the souls of their spectators (Ibid. 25). For example, Duchamp's *The Bride Stripped Bare by her Bachelors, Even/The*

---

10 "Man verknüpfte damals nicht nur Elektromagnetismus und Magnetismus, sonder auch andere okkulte Phänomene und wissenschaftliche Ergebnisse miteinander, Beispiele hierfür sind Röntgenstrahlen/Hellsichtigkeit, Telepathie/drahtlose Telegrafie, gelegentlich auch Radioaktivität/Alchimie" (Ibid. 15).

Large Glass, 1915–23 was purposefully fashioned out of glass, wire, lead foil, and dust in order to depict the telepathic communication between a bride in an ether-driven, fourth dimension at the top of the artwork, and bachelors in their measly three-dimensional world at the bottom (see Figure 1). Juxtaposed with the depiction of the mechanistic chocolate melanger and waterwheel in the lower quadrant, the bride is bound to the ether in the top quadrant, while bullet holes at the top right of the piece suggest that the "bachelors" are shooting upwards (Ibid. 30).

Figure 1. Marcel Duchamp. *The Bride Stripped Bare by her Bachelors, Even/The Large Glass*. Glass, wire, lead foil, and dust. 1915–23. © Association Marcel Duchamp / ADAGP, Paris / Artists Rights Society (ARS), New York 2020.

Yet more emphatically than visual artists, many occultists of the period believed that moving images had the ability to evidence the preternatural sphere. Although film was originally employed by scientists (such as the physiologist Etienne-Jules Marey in his documentation of various natural laws), it quickly became a vehicle for disseminating knowledge about the occult world: ghosts appeared on-screen, and hypnotic energy was unleashed onto film audiences through the dynamism of moving images (Gunning, "Der frühe Film" 560–61).

Modern dance further synthesized science and spirituality. For Rudolf Steiner, modern dance grew out of the concepts of anatomy and geometry – the astral part of the human body was believed to be the repository of the soul. Steiner's choreography for his new dance form *Eurythmie* was based on charts depicting the planets, stars, and the zodiac, whose celestial rotations were to be imitated through various gestures and gyrations. Shapes such as circles, spirals, and triangles supposedly made up the body itself and dictated its movement (Witzmann 609). Other modern dancers, who also depicted science and spirituality, included Rudolf von Laban and Mary Wigman.

Furthermore, there were literary figures, including Max Brod, Franz Werfel, Thomas Mann, Alfred Döblin, and Franz Kafka, who evinced a profound fascination with occult practices (Pytlik 90). Passages in Rainer Maria Rilke's novel *Die Aufzeichnungen des Malte Laurids Brigge* (*The Notebooks of Malte Laurids Brigge*, 1910) and Thomas Mann's *Der Zauberberg* (*Magic Mountain*, 1924) treat the existence of ghosts as central to their narratives (Ibid.). At the same time, Sigmund Freud was reading du Prel's *Philosophie der Mystik* (*The Philosophy of Mysticism*, 1886). Indeed, he took it so seriously that he ended up citing it in his magnum opus, *Die Traumdeutung* (*The Interpretation of Dreams*, 1900) (Ibid. 91).

Many individuals in Weimar were enthralled by the idea of being able to communicate with the dead. In addition to consulting mediums, people looked to astrology (and even simple luck-of-the-draw games) as ways to tap into this hidden reality. Evidence of the legitimacy of astrology in Germany is suggested by figures including Paul von Hindenburg, Heinrich Brüning, and Adolf Hitler who all consulted astrologers for personal guidance. The use of clairvoyants by the police to help solve crimes is also documented (Hellwig, "Hellsehen als strafbare Gaukelei" 125). Weimar's obsession with the occult is further evidenced in the journals and newspapers of the day, with titles such as "Querschnitt durch ein okkultes Zeitalter"

(Cross-section of an Occult Age), "Wissenschaft und Spiritismus" (Science and Spiritualism), "Besuche in der vierten Dimension" (Visits in the Fourth Dimension), and "Die Konjunktur der Wünschelrute" (The Boom of the Divining-rod).[11] Indeed, popular print journals, such as *Der Querschnitt* (Cross Section), *Die Woche* (The Week), and *Süddeutsche Monatshefte* (South German Review) published entire issues dedicated to the occult. Thereafter, in the arts and culture more generally, the commingling of science with the occult had reached a "crisis" point. This caused uncertainty in the overlapping spheres of science and culture, the floodgates of change having been opened with both propitious and perturbing developments.

Occult Practice and the New Woman

Women's involvement in occult practices was bound up with a move toward emancipation in the early twentieth century. Tatiana Kontou notes in the introduction to her edited volume, *Women and the Victorian Occult*, that women's "empathy, sensitivity and passivity" bound her to the occult: women were either investigators or subjects of occult examination from clairvoyants to telepathists (3). Victorian occult women were depicted in "sensation novels, ghost stories, autobiographies, séances and fashionable magazines" (3).

Diana Basham in her book *The Trial of Woman* notes that the cultural associations between the occult revival and the "Woman Question" of Victorian England fostered an atmosphere whereby women who engaged in occult practices were regarded with hostility (vii). The literature depicted the occult woman as an "inspired prophetess, mesmerised somnambule, spiritualist, medium, [or] revamped witch" (x).[12] Such fears about female

---

11   *Der Querschnitt* 12.12 (December 1932).
12   In the medieval work *Malleus Maleficarum* (*Witches' Hammer*, 1486), women *qua* "witches" are considered dangerous, especially those who seem especially ambitious: "ambitious women are more deeply infected who are more hot to satisfy their filthy lusts."

witchery were only allayed by the development of a "scientific control" over occult practitioners.

In the early twentieth century, Social Darwinism increasingly informed the definition of the modern woman as "vampire": Bram Dijkstra posits that the fear of women was inherent in the drive to protect male bodily fluids from bloodthirsty, Lilith-like females. European scientists and artists speculated that, just as males in the animal kingdom could be drained by females, so too could women – in the manner of Lilith – drain men of their vital powers (50–55). This depletion of seminal fluid, and sexual prowess, by female sexual "vampires" would both undermine and eviscerate the essence of man, thereby laying waste to his native vigor. These beliefs were undergirded by the idea that a person's blood constituted the "conduit" for the dissemination of his vital powers. As Dijkstra writes, "[physicians] of the day had no doubt whatever that the human generative fluid was an almost pure distillate of the vital essence stored by the blood" (Ibid. 56–57). In other words, sperm was a pure extract of blood – "loss of semen is loss of blood" (Ibid. 86).[13] Sexual women were supposedly driven to go after male vital fluids and, in so doing, would create genetically contaminated blood that could degrade the male and his bloodline (Ibid. 91). Perhaps the most famous example of the sexual vampire is Lucy Westenra in Bram Stoker's *Dracula* (1897), who is portrayed as a beast waiting to prey on men in order to suck their blood (Stoker 217). Nevertheless, this diabolical nymph ends up paying for her sociopathic urges, being staked and beheaded.

There further existed numerous academic and popular accounts from the early twentieth century documenting women's occult powers. Treitel, for instance, states that bourgeois women comprised a significant majority of audience participants at occult events in the Weimar period (65). We furthermore have evidence of women's participation in astrology, prophesy, and clairvoyance. Weimar Doctor of Medicine, Wolfgang von Weisl, discusses some examples of women's involvement in occult practices, including Frieda Weißl, whom we are told was able to initiate the movement of gramophone

13   "Certain arteries brought 'fresh blood' to the sexual organs, which distilled the seminal fluid from the blood. Other arteries carried away the blood that had 'been drained of its vital essence' and was therefore no longer of use" (Ibid. 57).

records through solid walls (847). Weimar writer Rudolf Grossmann moreover provides reports of women with supposed abilities to read the past and
foretell the future: Anna Karlik through the Tarot and astrology, while
Frau Raschig read palms (Grossmann, "Wahrsager" 411–12). He further
comments on the methodical nature of their practices, noting that these
women were not the familiar witches of fairy tales (Ibid. 412). Women like
Hanna Vogt Vilseck formed their own spiritualist groups. For instance,
Vogt Vilseck's club, Die Sucher (The Seekers) covered topics of the day
including astrology and spiritualism (Treitel 64). In fact, several female
mediums were consulted by the police in order to help solve criminal cases.
Frau Wildhagen in particular was employed by the government to detect
toxic environmental elements using a dowsing rod (Treitel 143–54), while
scientists such as Baron von Schrenck-Notzing set out to prove the validity
of the supernatural abilities of women, further legitimizing these practices
in popular consciousness.[14]

Stories about women leading séances or reading palms inevitably made
for sensational reading in Weimar's popular press. Such accounts were
often accompanied by photographs, which sought to titillate readers with
images of women engaged in occult practices. In the most disturbing of
such images, readers were able to detect the faces of the deceased, cast in
a white substance (suggestive of ectoplasm) that oozed from their mouths
and noses (see Figure 2).[15] Schrenck-Notzing describes the phenomenon
of "teleplasma" in his 1920 *Phenomena of Materialization*. He grimly elaborates thus: "[a] substance emanates from the body of the medium, it ex-
ternalises itself, and is amorphous, or polymorphous, in the first instance.
[…] Its appearance is generally announced by the presence of fluid, white
and luminous flakes" (328).

14   Schrenck-Notzing's works (*Die Traumtänzerin Magdeleine G.*, *Phenomena of
      Materialisation*, and *Die Physikalischen Phänomene der Grossen Medien*) provided
      popular sources for a Weimar interest in the occult woman.
15   See *Der Querschnitt* 12.12 (December 1932) for several images of woman and
      teleplasma. The theme of woman and the occult was also evident in popular jour-
      nals, including *Berliner Illustrirte Zeitung*, *Berliner Leben*, and *Die Dame*.

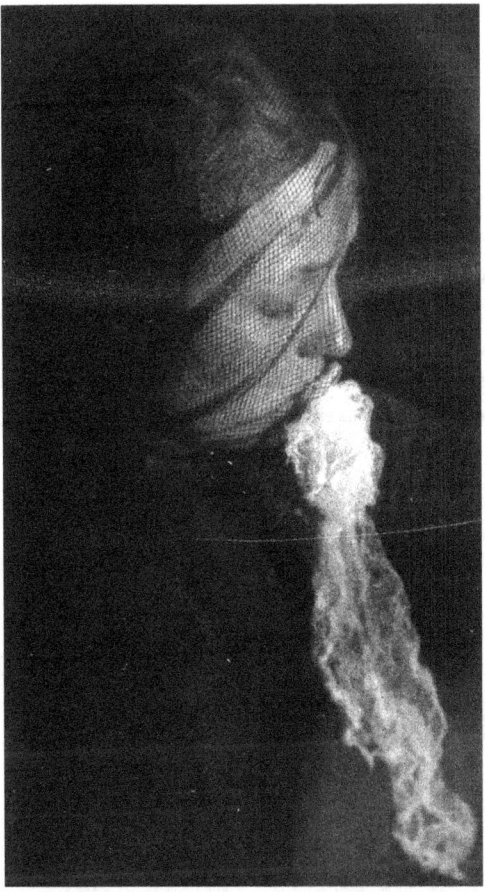

Figure 2. Teleplasma. Albert von Schrenck-Notzing. *Phenomena of Materialisation: A Contribution to the Investigation of Mediumistic Teleplastics.* Trans. E. E. Fournier d'Albe. London: Kegan Paul, Trench, Trubner & Co., 1923.

Popular literary and artistic works of the period further reflected an interest in the occult. In the poem, "Der Spruch der Kartenlegerin" (Maxim of the Female Fortune-teller), the poet affirms the inevitability of a prophesied event; the female fortune-teller's prognosis disclosing one's certain fate: "Was mich deckt / Was mich schreckt / Was mir zur Seite steht / Was mir gewiß ist / Und was mir nicht entgeht" (What covers me/What frightens me/What stands by my side/What is certain/And what does not escape me. 893). The poet describes woman as omniscient and aligned with the dangers of the unknown. In Fränze's Herzfeld's short story "Vierte Dimension" (The Fourth Dimension), the protagonist Miranda exhibits prophetic powers as she foretells the death of her brother – a somnolent apparition – and makes contact with her dead landlord who was murdered by his lover (169–70). Another such example can be found in Hanns Heinz Ewers's tale "Meine Mutter, die Hex" (My Mother, the Witch, 1922). There, occult practices are described as being so pervasive that the main character sees women engaging in necromancy on every street corner: "es gibt keine Straße in einer großen Stadt, in der nicht […] Kartenschlägerinnen […] und Wahrsagerinnen aller Art wohnen" (There is no street in a big city, where female card readers and fortune-tellers of every sort are not living. 349).[16]

Notwithstanding this burgeoning interest in the occult in the *Zeitgeist*, which brought various attempts to legitimate its use, there were of course concerns about its subversive side. Women were especially at risk of being singled out for their ability to unbridle their necromantic powers in these ways. Instances of this form were exemplified in clairvoyants' ability to foretell ominous political events. Writing for the magazine *Der Querschnitt*, Curt Corrinth relays a prophesy of a clairvoyant from Dresden, who predicted the inception of the World War One:

> Es war im Sommer 1912. Sie sah zunächst im wachen Zustande Bild auf Bild: mein Haus, meine Tätigkeit, meine Kinder, beschrieb alles bis ins kleinste hinein und gab mir Ratschläge, ohne wissen zu können, wer ich war. Aber das Seltsamste: sie sagte mir den Ausbruch eines großen Krieges für den Sommer 1914 voraus, seinen für Deutschland unglücklichen Verlauf und – den Untergang der Hohenzollern. Sie tadelte "den Vater, der nicht aufpasse, was oben links" geschehe (sie meinte den Kaiser und England!) und rief des öfteren sehr erregt: "Es ist furchtbar! Furchtbar!" Mittlerweile war sie in eine Art Schlafzustand verfallen. (879)

16   Noteworthy paintings depicting occult practices include Paul Kleinschmidt's *Bei der Kartenlegerin* (At the Fortune-teller, 1922), the whore with the cards, and Alfred Lomnitz's *Gespenstersonate* (Ghost Sonata, 1920). The latter features a woman, effortlessly flying through the night, terrorizing those who have taken refuge in their domiciles, as well as those who find themselves at her mercy on the street. In these images, women are not represented as benevolent but as flagrant dabblers in the malevolence of the spirit world.

> It was summer 1912. In a waking state, she saw picture after picture: my house, my occupation, my children, describing everything in the smallest detail, and gave me advice, without being able to know who I was. But the strangest thing: she predicted the outbreak of a great war for the summer of 1914, which had an unlucky course for Germany and – the downfall of the Hohenzollern. She blamed the father, who was not paying attention to what could happen (she meant the Kaiser and England!) and often shouted the phrase in a very agitated manner: "It is terrible! Terrible!" Meanwhile she slipped into a state of sleep. (879)

The clairvoyant not only accurately predicted the impending devastation of the war, but implicated the government as being responsible for the carnage. Here, the occult woman possessed superhuman knowledge of events, revealing both defeat in war and the government's downfall.

Although it was believed that women's occult powers could restore social order, supernatural activities were also regarded with suspicion. The ambiguous status surrounding occult practices mirrors that of Weimar's emancipated woman. The term "New Woman" (*die neue Frau*) was coined by populist media to describe the emancipation of women. Weimar women were forced to adopt a more independent outlook given their limited marital prospects, having lost two million potential suitors (i.e., German soldiers) in the World War One. By 1925, nearly 36 percent of the German workforce were women, of whom 12.6 percent were employed in white-collar jobs (Grossmann, "Girlkultur" 65; Frevert 177).[17] Other notable characteristics of women's emancipation included suffrage and a significant decline in the birth rate, coupled with an increase in marital age.[18] Weimar women continued to maintain their economic emancipation, holding positions as white-collar workers, civil servants, and being tasked with more traditional

---

17 While the percentage of German working women did not rise significantly from 1907 (34.9 percent) to 1925 (35.6 percent), there were three times as many female white-collar workers in 1925 as there were in 1907 (Frevert 177). Female white-collar workers (such as secretaries, typists, and shop assistants) caught the attention of the Weimar public (Ibid.).

18 The number of children per family decreased as the Weimar Republic progressed: the early 1920s saw 2.27 children per family, while in 1929 that statistic was 1.98 (Ibid. 186). In 1920–24, women married at the average age of 25.4 (Ibid. 201).

jobs, such as domestic work.[19] Many married women, moreover, served as home help, while others toiled without a wage in their family businesses (Boak 138).

However, in spite of being discharged to new roles, Helen Boak notes that women still encountered barriers to full participation in German life. In particular, they faced challenges in the political sphere. The revolution marking the beginning of 1918 was a "male" phenomenon, and political parties expected women to be contented with "children, the *Volk*, [and] the working class," rather than being advocates for themselves (Boak 71–72). *Doppelverdiener* (married working women) were actively *dissuaded* from paid work, especially during the Depression.

Weimar women were caught in-between the desire to take advantage of modern opportunities and the pressures to revert to the more traditional roles of wife and mother (Ibid. 297). Fears about the New Woman were expressed both in the popular media and in academic journals in light of her rejecting traditional gender roles. Indeed, there was a common reactionary sentiment across these wide-ranging publications, in particular that women had a duty to resume their traditional gender roles – as housewives and mothers – in order to restore the family unit and the identity of the nation.[20] The New Woman therefore straddled two seemingly incompatible identities; she was marooned in a liminal space whereby she was simultaneously seeking to defy traditional gender norms while also being compelled into their conformity. According to a certain Weimar journalist and writer, Heinrich Eduard Jacob, women who tried to attain the same economic rights as men were partly responsible for the country's cultural decline (Jacob 114–15).[21] The press broadly asserted that woman must not

---

19   Boak remarks on Weimar women's experiences from more rural areas. To this end, she provides an important corrective to other scholars who rely solely on the experience of Berliners, noting thereby that women from rural areas did not enjoy the same political, economic, and social opportunities as those dwelling in urban centers (Boak 292).

20   For more information on the perception of women in this historical context, see Atina Grossmann, "The New Woman" 153–71.

21   Jacob states: "Das Leben der Frau, wie sie heute lebt, ist wirtschaftliche Tatsache; unstürzbar, unabänderbar. Männliche Bedürfnisse spürend, erwarb die Frau die

play "ape" to the male intellectual world: she should provide succor, thereby finding satisfaction in her role as a "true woman" and mother (Thiess 138).[22]

Other discourses relating to this "in-between" state included the threatening *Mannsweib* figure, who was pitted against the traditional feminine woman in the Weimar press. This alleged trend of "masculinized" women – synonymous with the New Woman's androgyny – was decried by many critics who saw them as a threat to the stability of the family and state. Indeed, an article from the *Berliner Illustrirte Zeitung* comments on the garçon style: "[the] look of a sickeningly sweet boy is detested by every real boy or man" ("Enough is Enough!" 659). The grotesque masculine woman – donning her dress coat, bobbed hairdo, and career ambitions – was contrasted with her retiring, more feminine counterpart. Fashion designer Paul Poiret contrasts the maligned garçon style with the maternal image, thereby juxtaposing the modern woman's wiry silhouette with the more robust, matronly proportions of contented mothers and housewives (33).

Women in the Weimar period – particularly in urban areas – entered all areas of cosmopolitan life, which included regularly attending the cinema and theater. They were, in addition, able to participate in athletic events, going as far as engaging in male-dominated sports like hiking and boxing. These "gender-bending" activities were met with changes in women's fashion, which better accommodated her broadening sporting aspirations. The popular press of the day cast the New Woman as embodying a masculine persona, describing her as "sexually and intellectually potent" (Boak 279). Indeed, writer and painter Georg von der Vring was especially unsympathetic to the emergence of modern woman's masculinity, remarking: "Sie sucht die Norm der Männerkleidung zu erreichen und eignet sich eine brutale Handschrift an. Geistig zeigt sie gesteigertes Interesse,

---

Rechte des Mannes [...] Es nimmt [...] die heutige Frau an [dem] Untergang der Kultur unablässigen gründlichen Anteil" (114–15).

22 Thiess notes: "Denn so wie absolute Freiheit sinnlos ist, kann auch absolute Gleichheit nicht gefordert werden, weil die Welt nun einmal von Bestimmung her ungleich ist und aus dieser Ungleichheit allein die schöpferische Kraft des Menschen erwuchs" (145).

und seelisch gibt sie sich unsentimental [...] Liebe ist ein Begriff" (She looks to conform to the standards of male dress and has picked up a brutal penmanship. She shows increased interest intellectually, and emotionally she is unsentimental [...] Love is a concept. 57).

The critique of Weimar's masculine-looking woman, typified by such public personae as Anita Berber and Marlene Dietrich, was also intended to question the *duplicity* of the modern woman in her newfound "double identity" (see Figure 3). Journalist Leo Matthias wrote that woman was both the same as man in her struggle for equality and also received undue female rights ("anderswertig"), creating an unacceptable double standard (66–67).[23] Women were deemed devious for wanting to share in masculine occupations, dress, and sexual practices, while at the same time demanding gender-specific concessions. Frank Thiess noted that women, who strove to achieve "male freedom" in dress and job prospects, were also in fact looking to achieve a "female freedom," corresponding with preferential treatment, rights, and norms (144–45). These rights included special compensation for motherhood, as well as for gender-specific health concerns and modes of redress for her limited physical strength (Ibid. 145). In response to this ambiguity, the pursuit of an equalizing masculinity alongside exclusively *female* privileges sought to further divide the genders into two distinct realms. To this end, Heinrich Eduard Jacob noted that women should step out of the "world of men" and be the "keeper of secrets" ("Verwalterin von Geheimnissen"), refraining from meddling in the male world of automobiles and the like (116). On Thiess's account, women ought not practice free sex like their male counterparts, for women are naturally inferior – sexually, intellectually, and spiritually. Owing to this, he claims, she must forego her masculine pursuits and surrender to her proper feminine domain (146–48).

---

23   Matthias inadequately addresses the nature of these special rights (aside from the fact that he addresses – sarcastically – his independent daughter), implying that women are not prepared (nor fit) for the difficult life of men. His advice to his daughter reads as follows: "Sorg dafür, dass die Frauen wieder ihre Privilegien bekommen, ihr eigenes Recht, ihre eigene Moral. Sorg dafür, dass man diese armen Wesen nicht mehr wie die Männer behandelt. Ich kann das nicht mehr mit ansehen" (67).

Figure 3. Anita Berber. Production still, *Bitte Zahlen*, 1921. Anita Berber dressed as Eton-Boy in Rudolph Nelson's revue *Bitte Zahlen* (Please Pay!). Image by Ernst Schneider, 1921.

Weimar critics commented upon the interstitial state of woman as caught between masculine and feminine desires. Many felt that the masculine woman could only represent an "intersexual" type. According to Sigmund Freud, the girl who refuses to accept her castration exaggerates her masculinity in defiance (Freud 197–99). The intersexual woman is typified by a more aggressive personality and a tendency toward homosexuality.[24] Indeed, German sexologist, Magnus Hirschfeld, de-nominated the intersexual woman the "third sex."[25]

Contemporary scholars, such as Katharina von Ankum and Rick McCormick, likewise divide Weimar's New Woman, although this time, into two discrete camps. Von Ankum notes that while women were initially enthused by the promise of professional and political emancipation, they soon returned to traditional gender roles following the economic decline of the mid-1920s: "[the] dominant cultural discourses of the time sought to negotiate the acknowledgment of women's newly won independence with their desire to reconstruct traditional gender roles" (6). McCormick states that the culture of male disquiet regarding female emancipation was matched by women's own concerns about their new gender roles and the vicissitudes of modernity (Ibid. 4). These competing voices created a space of chaos, in which women – real and imagined – were permitted to operate. McCormick writes: "It would seem that the binary division be-tween what was clearly 'masculine' and what was 'feminine' was becoming especially blurred" (Ibid. 5).

The myriad, interstitial states ascribed to Weimar's New Woman, as noted by Von Ankum and McCormick, created a situation in which an in-fernal spirituality was ascribed to women. Although anthropologist Mary Douglas developed her theory of marginalization by studying small-scale indigenous communities, her theoretical framework is useful in under-standing a similar dynamic in modern European societies. Douglas, who covers such varied themes as Central African cosmology, Joan of Arc, and the Cold War, notes that when a social system assigns an ambiguous role to an individual or group, the community often attributes *spiritual* powers to the disenfranchised (99). According to Douglas: "[to] have been in the margins is to have been in contact with danger, to have been at a source of

---

24   Sigmund Freud's hypotheses were found in the popular press, specifically in the woman's magazine *Die Dame*, where Löbel noted that masculine and feminine sides of woman battled for dominance.

25   See McCormick's introduction (1–14) for an in-depth description of the New Woman and the various ideas of masculinity and femininity associated with this debate.

power" (97). The feminine is often accorded a liminal position, with woman possessing the power of "the Other," whose dangers must be held in check.

The threat posed by the occult woman highlights the inevitable backlash that tempered women's advances in the social, political, and economic spheres. The scientific and popular perceptions of occult practices mirrored the needs of the master narrative to cognize and constrain the irrational Other. As Douglas suggests, the ambiguous "Other" must be strictly demarcated in order to preserve social hierarchies (4). Just as the female spiritualist is both prophet and demon, the New Woman participates in the masculine order, nonetheless remaining a pariah within (or, indeed, *outside of*) the dominant discourse.

Theoretical Framework and Outline

Ulrich Linse claims that modern occult practice consisted in a "working through" of dichotomies, thereby constituting a kind of "crisis" (Linse 21), which informed the image of women in Weimar as being caught between traditional femininity and a perceived masculine desire. According to Mary Douglas, this interstitial position is met with fear and loathing, whose ultimate result is the marginalization of the individual (102–03). The problem posed by the New Woman is played out in the figure of the occult woman, whose powers are considered both awe-inspiring and awful.

In my analysis of the occult woman as an interstitial being, I respectively draw upon the work of Maria Tatar, Anton Kaes, Elisabeth Bronfen, and Barbara Creed. In so doing, I reconstruct the occult woman in popular Weimar culture as someone who posed a threat to masculinity. Tatar's *Lustmord: Sexual Murder in Weimar Germany* presents sexual murder as a matter of men seeking revenge against women, and, in so doing, "naturalizing rape and murder directed at women" (8). Across various films and artworks from the Weimar period, overtly sexualized women are carved up and violated. To this end, *Lustmord* is a response to a perception of sexually predatory women (10). Tatar notes that the art of the period juxtaposes the amputees and shell-shocked victims of World War One with intact female bodies, who thereby assumed the role of the "covert enemy" (12). Weimar artists and writers thereby expressed "economic, sexual, or psychological rivalries with women" (12).

Such vitriol toward women is sharply counterposed against the evocative backdrop of the returning German veteran. On this point, Anton Kaes notes that post-war cinema translated the "military aggression and defeat" on the battlefield into the betrayal, sacrifice, and injury of the characters on the filmic landscape (*Shell Shock Cinema: Weimar Culture and the Wounds of War* 3). He mentions popular post-war themes, which include the homeward-bound and traumatized veteran, the experience of mourning, the burden of the dead on the living, narratives of honor in defeat, and anxieties resulting from tumultuous changes brought on by industrialization and modernity, including, of course, fears about the modern woman. In association with the New Woman, Kaes discusses Maria, the evil robot from Fritz Lang's *Metropolis* (1927), whose icy demeanor and futuristic dress is "[indicative] of anxieties about the increased power of women as a result of the war […] there was hardly a Weimar film after the mid-1920s that did not feature early versions of the femme fatale – sexual, independent, and pitiless" (197).

Bronfen furthermore investigates the popular notion that this female body has a special connection with the realm of the dead (4). Both through the female medium, who, in a hypnotized state, can access the realm of the dead, and through the female corpse itself (understood as a gateway to "a knowledge about sexuality, death, and spiritual survival"), man may learn the secrets of the afterworld (Ibid. 5). Thus, the ephemeral body here sits at a juncture where the soul separates from the body (Ibid. 7). On Bronfen's analysis of nineteenth- and twentieth-century European culture, the liminal status of women's bodies can provide a route for "[dialoguing] with the dead": man is receiver of the knowledge of both death and sexuality, which the female body possesses (Ibid. 8; 10).

Finally, woman's relationship with death is explored in Barbara Creed's character of the "monstrous-feminine," which reflects male anxieties about women's sexuality (Creed 5, 7). Here woman inhabits the interstitial space between the dead and the living, viz. as vampire, ghost, and witch. Creed cites Julia Kristeva's *Powers of Horror* to situate the monstrous-feminine as "abject," and a being who disrespects borders and rules (Ibid. 8). On her account, a woman's body is abject insofar it bears a relation to nature, which is, of course, closely related to woman's fertility (Ibid. 59).

All of the various women investigated in this study evince a certain monstrousness. The medium, trance-dancer, and gypsy claim to possess abilities to commune with the dead or the spirit world. The female ghost, vampire-monster, and witch all inhabit a world between the living and the dead. They derive power by drinking men's blood, are able to shape-shift, and take flight to commune with the devil. The overt sexuality expressed by these black magic women marks them out as *femmes fatales*. Mary Ann Doane asserts that this woman is capable of destroying man through her feminine wiles. She thereby symptomatizes men's anxiety in the midst of a historical crisis (Doane 2–3). In addition, the characters listed above are more than fatale femmes: they wield magical powers that work in tandem with their forbidden sexuality. With this backdrop in place, I shall now provide an overview of the monograph.

Chapter 1 investigates various accounts of female ghosts. My analysis includes a discussion of how the visual media of photography and film seek to legitimate ghostly sightings through provision of material records. I also analyze the role of the female ghost in fictional works. These include Gerhart Hauptmann's *Hexenritt* (Witches' Ride, 1928), Hanns Heinz Ewers's *Das Mädchen von Shalott* (*The Girl from Shalott*, 1923), Claire Goll's *Jedes Opfer tötet seinen Mörder – Arsenik* (*Arsenic*, 1933), and Fritz Lang's *Der müde Tod* (*Destiny*, 1922). The end of *Der müde Tod* sees a pair of lovers bound in death, signifying the fate of a generation of German men in World War One, who had fought for a dubious cause. Wedded to the fate of the soldier is the aggression expressed toward the modern woman after the War. If the occult marks a way to acknowledge loss by capturing the lost object, then this loss is also punctuated by the novelty of the modern woman, as signified by the female ghost. Just as the ghost inhabits a realm between the living and the dead, the ghost – being a symbol of the ambiguity of women's new gender role – evinces both benevolence and malevolence.

Chapter 2 constitutes a study of Weimar's female vampires and monsters. I hereby read the bloodsucking woman as a cipher of the threat that the New Woman posed to social order. This symbolism is disclosed across several works of fiction, which include Leonard Stein's "Der Vampyr" (1918), Hanns Heinz Ewers' *Vampyr* (1921), and Robert Wiene's film, *Genuine* (1920), as well as Carl Theodor Dreyer's film, *Vampyr: Der Traum des Allan Gray* (*Vampyr: Allan Gray's Dream*, 1932) – all of which portray women as creatures of the night. In addition to examples drawn from the period's literary and filmic works, I discuss the idea of *Lustmord*, as presented in the Käthe Hagedorn murders. In Weimar, fictional female bloodsuckers combine with *Lustmörderinnen* to fuel a cultural discourse about the modern woman. Just as the female vampire is fueled by her need for blood, and is motivated by sexual desire, so too Weimar's New Woman was accused of being "ruled by hunger, love and a need for relaxation."[26] In the fantastical films of the Weimar period, viz. Robert Wiene's *Das Cabinet des Dr. Caligari* (*The Cabinet of Doctor Caligari*, 1920) and F. W. Murnau's *Nosferatu* (1922), the monster-woman jointly unleashes desire and danger; her dual nature fueling her portrayal as an androgynous monster. I claim that the powers accorded to the New Woman ultimately reflect male subjectivity in crisis – a cataclysm brought forth by the Great War.

Chapter 3 investigates figures of the witch and gypsy in Weimar culture. The witch is regarded as a sexual creature: a concoctor of poisons; teller of fortunes; and an arbiter of nature. In the Weimar context, the witch can either take the form of animals, or else she produces poison to work her magic. In this regard, I analyze Mary Wigman's dance, *Bilda, die Hexe* (Bilda, the Witch, 1921), "Meine Mutter, die Hex" (My Mother, the Witch, 1922) along with Leni Riefenstahl's film *Das Blaue Licht* (*The Blue Light*, 1932). I also discuss famous legal cases of female poisoners, notably Klein/Nebbe and Vukobrankovic. Mary Douglas holds that the witch lives in non-structure; as she crosses boundaries, she is imbued with power: "[witches] are social equivalents of beetles and spiders who live in

---

26   Otto Flake, "Die alte Aufgabe – die neue Form," in *Die Frau von morgen wie wir sie wünschen: Eine Essaysammlung aus dem Jahre 1929*, ed. F. M. Huebner (Frankfurt am Main: Insel Verlag, 1990), 136.

the cracks of the walls and wainscoting" (102). Like the witch, Weimar's New Woman crosses boundaries to enter a masculine world of culture, industry, and sexuality. The gypsy similarly forces male counterparts to bend to her will. This period's fiction, which includes A. Rosalie's *Rache einer Zigeunerin* (*Revenge of a Female Gypsy*, 1928), as well as films such as Ernst Lubitsch's *Carmen* (1918) and *Sumurun* (1920), showcases the power of the gypsy persona.

Continuing with the theme of the independent woman, Chapter 4 investigates the female trance-dancer and medium. My investigation of the female trance-dancer focuses on the hypnotic power of dance, as exemplified in the work of Anita Berber, as well as in Fritz Lang's 1927 film, *Metropolis* and Arnold Fanck's 1926 film, *Der Heilige Berg* (*The Holy Mountain*). The Weimar trance-dancer cannot be easily contained: transfixing her male patrons through her hypnotic gyrations, the trance-dancer casts a spell of death; her hypnotic powers capturing anxieties about the New Woman and her threat to male subjectivity. Many Weimar critics viewed the modern woman – with her overt sexuality and need to engage in the public sphere – as a threat to traditional gender roles. Woman's mobility through dance was found to be synonymous with freedom and was thus paired with eroticism. In this scenario, only occultic or otherworldly power could explain modern woman's sudden claim to social status.

Finally, the medium is regarded as both prophet and demon. To this end, I offer a reading of Albert Talhoff and Mary Wigman's poetry and dance spectacle, *Totenmal* (Call of the Dead, 1930), and Mary Wigman's 1934 dance cycle, *Frauentänze* (Women's Dances), in particular *Totenklage* (Lament for the Dead), *Tanz der Seherin* (Dance of the Prophetess), and *Hexentanz* (Witch Dance). In this context, I focus in particular on how occult elements of mediumism, prophesy, and magic can be read as a cultural bridge from the Weimar period to National Socialism. While the Nazis quickly shut down various experimental forms of art, dance – with its supernatural themes – was able to flourish from 1933 to 1936.

As can be seen in numerous depictions from the Weimar period, the occult woman is presented as a harbinger of danger and misfortune. Historical documentation – in the form of popular journal articles, scientific and legal writings, art, dance, and cinema – provides evidence of a preoccupation with women's roles in the occult. If woman is a marker of historical crisis as Kaja Silverman suggests, then the restoration of the civic order is predicated on understanding her secrets. This was, as the following journal excerpt attests, a failed effort: "You sphinx, you […] demon creature […] can you be revealed, you unearthly being?" (Bauer 339). The elusive Weimar woman remains unknowable: dangerous in her role as gatekeeper between this world and the next.

Images of the occult woman foreground new gender relations and set the stage for change. Promising to bring order through her engagement with the other world, the Weimar woman casts a spell of death through her witch's dance. Scrutiny of these self-oriented, overly sexualized, and masculine women thereby serves to reveal the reactionary backlash against the progressive women's liberation movement of the Weimar Republic.

CHAPTER 1

The Ghost

"Crisis as change" became an overarching trope within Weimar Germany (1918–33). While political crises were not unheard of, levels of distrust toward the Weimar Republic as an institution were totally unprecedented, not least owing to its being perceived as an imposition of the Allies after World War One and thereby as an ineffectual, lawless body. Following the loss of life from the World War One, in tandem with a slew of other encumbrances, including the constraining Treaty of Versailles, the inflation of 1923, and the unemployment of the Great Depression (beginning in 1929), a miasmic melancholia permeated Weimar culture. The stabilization period from 1924–29 reflected economic prosperity at home as well as political stability, as noted in the "matter-of-fact" artistic era of *Neue Sachlichkeit* (New Objectivity). The final phase of the Weimar Republic was wracked with economic and political turmoil; the avant-garde mirroring the doom and gloom of an alienated public. Indeed, as artist George Grosz noted in 1931, Weimar was in a crisis period, whereby all ideas had become volatile and liberalism was on the decline (499).

The political and economic crises of Weimar Germany were closely bound up with a perception of cultural crisis, beginning with the traumatic birth of the Weimar Republic. The beginning phase of the Republic (1918–24) was marked by revolution and inflation. With 10 million dead in World War One, the newly developed weapons of mass destruction thereby employed grew to symbolize the evils of scientific rationality in the popular consciousness.[1] Indeed, it is befitting of Sigmund Freud's "Mourning and Melancholia" to be read in the context of a generation coming to terms

---

[1]   See Zweig for a discussion of the ills of technology in Weimar.

with the trauma of mourning their war dead. At the publication of this work in 1917, Freud was working on diagnosing and treating so-called "war neurosis." In his essay on mourning, Freud asserts that what has been lost must be reconstructed in order to develop a healthy sense of self. Although we typically think of mourning as a response to the loss of a loved one, Freud refines this conception by considering a similar response to the loss of one's country, liberty, and ideals ("Mourning and Melancholia" 243). The cure for such losses requires a testing of reality in which the subject conjures up memories of the past in order to comprehend that the forfeited object ceases to exist (Ibid. 255). Freud notes how arduous a process this is for the mourner: "Each single one of the memories and expectations in which the libido is bound to the object is brought up and hypercathected, and detachment of the libido is accomplished in respect of it" (Ibid. 245).

On Freud's account, coming to see what has been lost through a moment of personal and cultural *anagnorisis* constitutes an essential part of reconciliation, through which one unceremoniously readjusts to a change of status. With regard to interest in the occult in Weimar, we might therefore conjecture that the desire to commune with the dead functions as a means of acknowledging loss in order to overcome it. There are, however, inherent risks in attempting a meeting of minds with the melancholic, whose pre-occupation with the lost object operates with no view to its relinquishment. As Tom Gunning notes, Freud's ideas about reconciliation depend upon our ability to forget the dead: "[letting] them leave our world" ("Scan a Ghost" 119). Moreover, in spirit photography, the individual seeks to cling on to the dead in an attempt to fasten them to this world. This denial of loss leads to an unending, cyclical pattern of the dead's preservation and grief's evasion (Ibid. 120). Giorgio Agamben likewise notes that the presence of the phantasm sustains loss; the melancholic refusing to move on and heal: "The phantasm generates desire" (Ibid. 129). The road to healing involves "laying the ghost," that is, putting the dead to rest. In capturing their image, we hold the dead near. Still, their newfound spiritual amorphousness is likewise elusive. In true mourning, we could "release them into the realm of pure imagery [...] of mourning and untimeliness" (Ibid. 120).

This chapter foregrounds images and representations of women as ghosts. Such depictions proliferate as forms of Weimarian cultural capital, embodying paintings, literature, photography, film, and occult writings. In particular, parapsychologists (such as Bruno Grabinski, Max Kemmerich, Otto Piper, and Albert von Schrenck-Notzing) proffered scientific accounts of female ghosts, while their fictional presentation was typified in works such as Gerhart Hauptmann's *Hexenritt* (*Witches' Ride*, 1928), Hanns Heinz Ewers' *Das Mädchen von Shalott* (*The Girl from Shalott*, 1923), and Claire Goll's *Jedes Opfer tötet seinen Mörder – Arsenik* (*Arsenic*, 1933), which respectively uphold the notion of woman as ghost. Additionally, ghost photography of the early twentieth century – and artistic works by Otto Dix and Paul Klee, as well as Fritz Lang's 1921 film, *Der müde Tod* (Destiny) – disclose the power of the spirit woman. Images of women as ghosts emphasize the similarly ambiguous status of Weimar's New Woman (*Neue Frau*). Just as the ghost is caught between the realm of the living and the dead, so too is the New Woman caught between liberation and a scolding, reactionary backlash, which seeks to frustrate her progressive ambitions, shackling her to an apparently more befitting, traditional gender role. As with other occultic women – whom this investigation shall champion – the ghostly or ghoulish woman demonstrates both benevolent and malevolent traits, thereby mirroring the kindred ambiguity of the New Woman in her newfound role in the German economy and wider society.

Ghosts and Weimar

Representations of ghosts date back to our earliest extant literary sources, not least Odysseus' legendary trip to the underworld. Ideas about being able to commune with the dead continue apace even today (especially in the New Age movement). Tom Gunning notes that ghosts in the modern era serve as harbingers of the future, for they both unsettle our worldview while threatening the prevailing social order ("Ghosts, Photography and the Modern Body" 10). Similarly, Herman Rapaport suggests that spirits return from the past when the world is in turmoil (417). Taking note of the gender implications accompanying this rupture in the social order, Sladja Blazan posits that ghosts "expose the often turbulent nature of gender relations," thereby challenging moral boundaries as dictated by tradition (4). Carter notes how belief in these spiritual beings holds the potential to initiate and facilitate broader psychic processes (including revenge and atonement), as well as illuminating the shadowy, repressed depths of the human psyche (Carter 46). In short, ghosts seek to shake up the world of the living.

The power of ghosts, to this end, is epitomized in phasmophobia. Such a fear of apparitions constitutes, in part, a recognition of their confused, shape-shifting status. In this regard, Gunning notes: "The essential aspect of a ghost, its terrifying presence, comes from this uncertainty, this problematic relation to the senses and therefore to our sense of the world" ("Scan a Ghost" 103). Gunning contends that ghosts throw human vision and powers of discernment into free fall; being detected without witness through the respective sensibilities of smell, touch, and hearing (Ibid. 102–03). On the psychic terrain, the inability to exorcise a dead spirit represents the return of the revenant (of repressed trauma that cannot be fully overcome). As long as the spirit believes it has unfinished business in this world, it remains incapable of accepting its status as deceased. As Gunning puts it, "laying a ghost or putting it to rest has always been a tricky business" (Gunning, "Ghosts, Photography and the Modern Body" 9). Carter likewise observes that ghosts often appear as harbingers of death, as well as bearers of a "spectral request" (Carter 46).

Belief in spirits was popular in Germany from 1900 to the 1930s, the definition of "spiritism" being the affirmation of life after death, and the communication of the living with the dead (as well as the dead with the living) (Pytlik 35–37). The end of the nineteenth century saw the founding of the *Psychologische Gesellschaft* in Munich and the *Gesellschaft für Experimental-Psychologie* in Berlin, both of which were dedicated to the study of occult phenomena.[2] Members of the *Psychologische Gesellschaft*, including Karl du Prel and Albert von Schrenck-Notzing, were committed to the scientific study of such beings. For his part, du Prel advocated for the notion of a separation of the physical and astral body – the latter existing after death (*Der Spiritismus* 21). By contrast, Schrenck-Notzing was

---

2   Both organizations would later merge, becoming the *Gesellschaft für Psychologische Forschung*, committed to the study of the theoretical foundations of occult phenomena.

interested in hypnotism and mediumism as feats of the paranormal. Indeed, Schrenck-Notzing eventually became a vociferous backer of the séance in the 1920s, whose attendees included such notables as Thomas Mann and Rainer Maria Rilke (Pytlik 43).

In Weimar, a range of interdisciplinary luminaries set out to prove (or, indeed, *disprove*) the existence of ghosts. These individuals included neurologist Eduard Aigner, psychologist Max Dessoir, psychical researcher Bruno Grabinski, philosopher and art historian Max Kemmerich, psychologist T. K. Oesterreich, historian Otto Piper, and physician and psychiatrist Albert von Schrenck-Notzing. In the Foreword to his 1921 book *Gibt es Geister?*, Aigner notes that the profound devastation of the World War One provided individuals with an intense curiosity about life after death (Foreword 57). For example, there was a fascination with séances in the Bavarian Allgäu following the War, as well as a mass movement in East Prussia to expunge the devil from the community. Aigner moreover sought to demonstrate that supposedly occult phenomena were amenable to rational explanation (Ibid. 4, 50).

Notwithstanding the proliferation of propagandists for the paranormal, a great many Weimar scientists were in the business of discrediting the validity of ghosts, which were being held up as actual spirits sent from another world. Dr. Böhm's strategy, to this end, involved attributing unexplained phenomena (otherwise adduced to ghosts) as evidence of telekinesis. In an article for *Psychische Studien* (1921) entitled "Der Spuk von Dietersheim," Böhm posits that telekinesis – the power to move things from a distance – was to blame for objects mysteriously moving around the house. The power to heave potatoes, shoes, and bread came not from an amorphous *Poltergeist*, but a living person whose gift – absent the assistance of hands or other body parts – consisted in moving objects (77–78).

By contrast with the skepticism of Böhm, Weimar occultist G. Groskopff argued that there exists indisputable evidence that many mediums have in fact made contact with ghosts (50). Repudiating Böhm's explanations of spirit hauntings, Groskopff writes to the same journal that practices such as telekinesis and telepathy cannot be used to rebut the soul's immortality or afterlife: there are simply too many cases to the

contrary (50–51). Additionally, Groskopff notes that ghost sightings tran-
spire without even a hint of fraud, having been recorded by unbiased witnesses as well as well-meaning members of the scientific community.

Just as Groskopff gave credence to the existence of an afterlife, so too
did many Weimar followers of the occult, who saw the figure of the ghost as
proof of life after death. In Grabinski's book, *Spuk und Geistererscheinungen
oder was sonst?* (1922), he notes that while there *could* be a coincidence of
mimic and transfiguration of an unconscious psychic human energy, it was
the ghost that in fact proved otherwise: "Wenn irgend etwas überhaupt als
Beweis für die Fortdauer der Seele nach dem Tode und für die Möglichkeit
ihres Hereinwirkens in die psychische Sphäre angesprochen werden darf,
so ist es der örtlich gebundene Spuk" (If anything may be mentioned as
proof of the continuance of the soul after death and of the possibility of its
interference with the psychic sphere, it is the local spook. 130).

Max Kemmerich supports Grabinski's belief in the spirit world, noting
in his 1927 *Die Brücke zum Jenseits* that the "spook" originates whence
that person last lived and died (640). Often, the ghost did not know that
it was dead; instead of striving for otherworldly goals and tasks, ghosts
were filled with memories and dreams of their recent earthly incarnation
(Ibid. 678–79). Many individuals who were unready for death were forced
to leave their earthly husk ("Hülle") while being consciously unprepared
for the change. This transitional existence – the inability to accept death
by the dead spirit – is taken to be the *essence* of the spook phenomenon
(Ibid. 680). Additionally, many ghosts were believed to have died unjustly,
and so sought vindication among the living for the injustices perpetrated
against them (Ibid. 691).

With regards to making contact with the dead, the conviction of the
Weimar people was that ghosts communicated through knocking on walls,
opening doors, being heard through footsteps, breaking things, and creating general noise (Ibid. 668–69; Grabinski 128–30; Schrenck-Notzing
531). There were also certain physiological states in which the living could
more easily encounter the dead, including sleep, somnambulance, near-
death experiences (including illness), telepathy, mediumism, and the travel
of the astral body (Kemmerich 655). Indeed, there are several reports of
female mediums observing apparitions, including a 15-year-old servant

girl noted in the Hopfgarten case ("Der Spuk in Hopfgarten"; Aigner 44, 47). Albert von Schrenck-Notzing states that female mediums may enjoy unrivaled access to spirit sightings, further speculating that girls in transitional biological states (for example, puberty), or women going through the menopause, can uniquely access the spirit world (531–32).

Female Ghosts and the New Woman

Thus, ghosts were dominant figures in Weimar culture. Among the most significant examples of this were the appearances of spirits of the war dead, whose return to the world of the living functions to both chide and caution those left behind about the dangers of war. About this in particular, George Mosse has examined a variety of examples drawn from Weimar culture. He explains how soldiers were depicted as rising from their graves in order to convince the living to restore order to a ravaged Germany (Mosse 5). Jay Winter has moreover explored how various forms of spiritualism were exercised with the aim of facilitating the mourning process (Winter 54–77).[3] Citing examples such as Abel Gance's 1919 film *J'accuse*, Winter submits that the myth of the return of the dead widely permeated European consciousness after World War One (Ibid. 18).

Amongst the images of male ghosts, Weimar culture is replete with images of their female counterparts. According to Penny Fielding, the female ghost signals an absence or lack, pointing to a threatening female sexuality, fearsome and wild (Fielding 765). The female ghost is present in various paintings from that time. For instance, in Otto Dix's *Beerdigung* (*A Funeral*, plate six from *Death and Resurrection* (*Tod und Auferstehung*) 1922), one may observe a ghostly female spirit who hovers over a coffin

3   Mosse lists several Weimar documents affirming that the dead have returned to communicate with the living. In *A Tribute to the Army and Navy* (1920), the fallen of World War One "roam Germany" in order to suggest a new path for the nation (Mosse 5). Mosse also cites an official guide to German war memorials, as well as the work of Walter Flex (*inter alia*), which illustrates this phenomenon (Ibid. 5–6).

during a funeral procession through the city (see Figure 4). Although the palm leaves held by the pall-bearers evoke the hope of Palm Sunday, this is undermined by the depiction of these men as corpses. Furthermore, in Paul Klee's *Botschaft des Luftgeistes* (The Sylph's Message, 1920), one witnesses a female spirit in flight with flowing gown and bloody hands. She clears the rooftops while coming into direct opposition with a male figure who is precariously perched atop a building (see Figure 5). The man with gray hollowed eyes and folded arms represents a somnambulist who is bewitched by the spirit. This painting's contrastive palette signifies movement – an omen given that, if the male even takes one step further, then he will find himself over the edge. The spirit, however, is free in this mid-air setting; flitting between heaven and earth. Her white eyes represent her capacity to see and maneuver in the air; her multicolored frock is dynamic in its drapery.

Figure 4. Otto Dix. *Beerdigung* (*A Funeral, plate six from Death and Resurrection*). Dry point on paper. 1922. © 2020 Artists Rights Society (ARS), New York / VG Bild-Kunst, Bonn.

Figure 5. Paul Klee. *Botschaft des Luftgeistes* (The Sylph's Message). Oil transfer and watercolor on chalk foundation on paper, mounted on cardboard. Private collection, South Germany. 1920. © 2020 Artists Rights Society (ARS), New York.

Like artistic representations, actually reported ghost sightings – averring the specter of ghosts in the realm of the living – similarly exhibit a kind of kinesis or dynamism. For instance, Max Kemmerich's feminine "otherworldly entities" ("jenseitige Wesenheiten") have the ability to shift objects, as well as speak, sing, and manifest themselves (Kemmerich, 637).[4] Statistics also reveal that the female spook often appears in connection with a death (Ibid. 640; Grabinski 125). Kemmerich provides an example of this phenomenon, in which a female ghost relives her death by replicating her

---

4   Kemmerich provides a background on the status of the ghost, quoting Bozzano with the following statistics: out of 532 spook occurrences, 491 are in spook houses and 41 are on spook locations ("Spukorten") (639). Additionally, out of 375 cases of ghosts that have been investigated, 180 hauntings occurred in the place of tragic happenings (639).

fall down the stairs through the use of a colored ball and handprints on the wall (Kemmerich 672). By reliving her death, the ghost can supposedly separate her body from her soul (Ibid. 672).

In the modern era, female ghosts are depicted as both benevolent and malevolent forces. In the Weimar context, they have moreover been associated with the domestic sphere: haunting their house of origin for the sake of advising and comforting the living, while, conversely, they are vengeful spirits who signal a conflict in the domain of male-female relationships. In this vein, a spurned woman may return as a ghost to haunt those left behind. Similarly, a woman slain by a suitor will come back to frequent those mortal purlieux.

The two versions of the Weimar apparition – the traditional domestic female, on the one hand, and the newly assertive female, on the other – recall the New Woman in her dual manifestations. In a 1932 article entitled "Die heutige Rolle der Virginität im Seelenleben des jungen Mädchens" (The Contemporary Role of Virginity in the Inner Life of the Young Girl), Mathilde Vaerting posits that certain young women seek to retain traditional values (such as the search for marriage), while others seek extra-marital rendezvous (Vaerting 247). This early standoff with men is coupled with a desire to get ahead in the workplace, for many women prioritized work over marriage (Ibid. 248). This "large differentiation" ("große Verschiedenheit") in the attitudes of women with respect to the opposite sex signaled a brazen affront to tradition.[5]

Moreover, in his article on the virgin, Emmanuel Berl points to the difference between the working woman, who assertively assumes her role alongside men in the public sphere, and the domestic girl, who yearns for marriage. Berl sees a new majority of aggressive women as a signal of social crisis. On this view, women who do not take on the traditional path of marriage and family will remain Amazons in society: "boshaft, herzlos und glücklich" (mean-spirited, heartless and happy, 234). For Berl, it is a

5   Vaerting's article is also accompanied by a drawing that underscores the divided nature of the Weimar woman. The image features two women discussing their figures. As one undresses, the other compliments her on her athletic physique. In turn, she notes that her lean stature will do her no good with the return of the "new Biedermeier" style (248).

difficult task to change the modern, young woman into a devoted trad-itional wife (Ibid. 234).[6]

Weimar ghost enthusiasts, Kemmerich and Grabinski, offer examples of these female types in their various discussions of the ghost – the devoted family woman, as well as the aggressive femme fatale. The first category – the ghosts of mothers, wives, and dutiful servants – are not dissimilar from Weimar's archetypal woman. The spirits of mothers often come to aid, warn, or comfort family members (like the deceased spirit who came from the dead to provide information about an impending fraud). In this instance, a motherly spirit, who had accidentally met her death, returned to warn her daughter of bank fraud. The daughter then withdrew her money before the bank went bust (Kemmerich 643). Often appearing in the early hours of the morning, when connecting to the spirit world is most propi-tious, or at the stroke of midnight, mothers return to their children in an attempt to uphold family connections. There are numerous cases recorded including a spirit mother who refused to stop visiting her children in her mistaken assumption that she was still alive (Ibid. 678). Ghost lore also tells of a mother who appears to her family on the side of the road, offering a warning sign (Grabinski 297).

The staunch loyalty of mothers is matched in a report by Grabinski of a dead wife who evinced devotion toward home and hearth. She could be heard at her writing desk, in her bedroom, and on the stairs (Ibid. 125). She even tried to creep into the bed to make contact with her husband's body. Such attachment to place and family is further attested to through the example of a deceased female servant, who thereafter haunted a cer-tain bedroom in a castle. Having come into contact with a niece of her previous mistress, the servant spirit confided that she had stolen silver in her previous life and wanted to let the mistress know what had happened (Kemmerich 645). Thanks to this proactive honesty, the ghostly servant received forgiveness for her deeds. Devotion is similarly shown when a ghostly sister announced her death to her family (Grabinski 302). These "death visits" occur frequently in the ghost literature of the period, signaling

6   Berl notes: "Das junge Mädchen ist nicht sentimental, nicht romantisch. Geradlinig und stark wie eine Maschine in Ruhe" (234).

the desire to pass on the news that a loved one or friend has crossed over to the other side.

Just as the traditional female ghost comforts and strives to inform the haunted about important news, the second category of feminine spirit either seeks revenge or simply demonstrates a lack of interest in the welfare of her family. An initial example consists in Kemmerich's case of a dead wife who terrorizes her former husband and his new spouse. Appearing in costume as the woman in white, this female spirit terrorizes her husband's second wife through noises in the house, including working at her desk and rattling coins (Kemmerich 674–75). Over many years, this "woman in white" haunted the new couple's house, trying at one point to throw the second wife out of her bed. When the second wife asked if the ghost was angry that the husband had remarried, there was no reply (Ibid. 676). A further example involves a young woman who dies and then returns to count her money, harboring concerns about her business with little regard for her family (Ibid. 677).

The trope of "the woman in white" is commonly invoked to manifest a spirit who is committed to avenging some form of injustice. On this point, Piper notes that the woman in white often takes the form of a beautiful virgin spirit, appearing in castle ruins (86). Included in this category would be the white woman from Neuhaus, who appeared in a burned-out castle near Bohemia (Ibid. 88). The white figure may evince unnatural strength, as in the story of the white ghost who accosted a galloping horse and rider (Ibid. 12). Legend also notes that the widow Gräfin Agnes von Orlamünde was murdered by her two children in an effort to stop her marrying the Burggraf von Nürnberg (Ibid. 87). The Gräfin then became a vengeful spirit in white, hellbent on rectifying the injustice. Houses in which white female spirits have been supposedly sighted include castles in Cleve, Darmstadt, Altenburg, and Karlsruhe (Ibid. 87).

Ghost enthusiasts such as Piper, Kemmerich, and Grabinski cite stories of female ghosts who have been wronged and thereafter haunt the land of the living, seeking retribution. Many accounts discuss a murdered woman returning to haunt the family, such as the ugly female ghost who returns when a family member dies. One such case involved a rich woman who had been murdered by her nephew and cut into pieces (Piper 86). In another tale, a female spirit who placed her right hand over her heart was connected with her skeletal body parts found in the area; when the bones were thrown in the river, the haunting stopped (Ibid. 115). A final reported case is that of a mother and her three daughters who return to haunt her husband and their father after he allegedly murdered them by locking them in a hot room (Ibid. 110).

Kemmerich notes that the "Dauerspuk" (persistent ghost) haunts the site of a terrible crime by avenging the victim and establishing the culpability of the murderer (Kemmerich 689). In the story of the "small light" recounted by Grabinski, points of light seen by various inhabitants of the valley are supposed to signify the return of a young woman, who was seduced and murdered by a man. The woman transfixes the community with light, which cannot be extinguished until she is permitted to tell her story (Grabinski 330–31).[7]

By contrast with spirits that evidence concern for the families they left behind, many depictions show much more self-interested motives on the part of spirits, whose only concerns are with their personal finances. Similarly, spirits who are seeking revenge following murder or suicide (or simply owing to their being jilted wives) are characterized by their retaliation in the face of perceived injustices committed by men. Just as the New Woman is seen as a scourge on standard gender roles, these angry apparitions chronically afflict those whose wrongs they seek to avenge.

In Gerhart Hauptmann's play *Hexenritt* (1928), a vengeful female spirit haunts a ruined castle, unaware that she is deceased. In the story, the ghost of a famous witch (known as "the Generalin"), inhabits her ruined castle along with a ghostly admirer, Marquis Rene Seigneur de Bauvau-Craon. When two adventurers, Lars Andersdal and Peter Lerch, appear to avenge the name of Lars's uncle, the female ghost takes over their bodies, literally disassembling Lars into seven pieces. Just as the ghost possesses control over seven ghostly brooms, which symbolize her seven earthly husbands, she likewise seizes control of the explorers.

---

7   There is yet another recorded case of a female spirit light *qua* spook (Grabinski 331), whereby, owing to a perceived injustice, a young woman named Margarete, who is "unlucky in love," jumps to her death in a castle well, only to haunt the premises evermore with fiendish fervor (Ibid. 327).

The reputation of the Generalin is of one who robs and steals, and is capable of biting through men's throats (74). Lerch, the occult researcher, well-acquainted with the emerging field of parapsychology, is privy to a vision of this ghostly femme fatale: first as the "white witch" (76), and later as a "landed lady" (91). As a result of his dealings with her, he develops "sweet and soft feelings" toward her (77). In death, the ghost rides about on her broom, inhabited by the soul of her seventh earthly husband, Lars's uncle (77). After attempting to "fly" on the body of Lars, she is spurned by the explorer, fomenting her antipathy toward him (77–78).

The ghostly Generalin is a terrifying opponent. As seraph and demon (84), she is able to turn the water surrounding the island into a sea of blood (88–89). Referring to Lars, she threatens: "Ich wünsche höchstens einen widerspenstigen Esel abzustrafen" (I only wish to punish an unruly donkey. 92). This threat is realized as the evil ghost steals Lars's seven body parts after he attempts astral travel with the Marquis. Lars fears that he has been buried alive. Unable to find his body on return from his trip, he briefly meets a beautiful young ghost who helps him find his stolen body. In the end, Lars emerges black and blue, besieged by a deathly fatigue (98–99). Although he leaves with Lerch to continue his quest, there is a chance that he will be unable to recover his vitality.

In *Hexenritt*, a vengeful female ghost attacks her spurned suitor, with the brief appearance of the helpful ghost coming to his aid. As evidenced by the seven ghostly brooms, this wraithlike femme fatale is a threat even in the afterworld; she has taken her murdered husbands with her to serve in her ghostly lair and is a threat to the travelers who trespass on her island. Like the Weimar stories of Grabinski, Kemmerich, and Piper, which all involve a spurned lover, the feminine entity in Hauptmann's tale inhabits castle grounds and wreaks havoc on those around her. In the case of the Generalin, this ghost takes extreme measures against her male opponent. As with the cases relayed by the above-mentioned Weimar experts, the ghost in *Hexenritt* does not know she is dead. The Marquis begs Lars not to taunt the Generalin, for she has no idea that she is deceased. Thus, "real" and fictitious renderings of the feminine spirit coalesce in theme and scope.

A final example of lovelorn suicide emerges in Hanns Heinz Ewers' play, *Das Mädchen von Shalott: Sechs Theaterstücke* (1923). There, a young girl has committed suicide owing to a foiled love interest. As a feminine

specter, she has returned from the dead to offer sexual favors to her beloved. The ghost tempts the doctor with sexual advances, competing thereto
with the baroness, who has already won his love.[8] Such strange narratives
of suicide and spectral resurrection are punctuated in the second act of
Ewers' play that unfolds in the Middle Ages: stand-ins for the initial female
characters – viz. the young virgin in place of the young girl, and the experienced Guenivere in place of the baroness – compete for Lancelot's affection. When he returns to the castle following the virgin's suicide, a boat is
docked there ready to carry the dead girl down the river Styx. The young
ghost then takes the opportunity to visit Lancelot at night, expounding
her love for him: "Mein Leben war ein Sehnen nur nach dir" (My life was
a longing only for you. 40). As with the ghostly Weimar virgin described
by Grabinski (327), the female ghost who has taken her own life is compelled to haunt the site of the crime, which is here located in the castle
where Lancelot forsook her for Guenivere.

Moving onto the third act, we return to the baroness's castle, where
the tale of Guenivere and Lancelot plays out once again, albeit this time
in the present-day. The ghost of Shalott attempts to keep the doctor by
her side with promises of attending to him sexually (42–45). She tries to
replace the baroness as the object of the doctor's affection, noting that she
will be his lover "in wilde Sünde rot eingehüllt" (shrouded in red wild sin.
45). Ultimately, the ghost does not have her way. Scandalously, the baroness
and the doctor force the corpse of the dead girl off the bed in a reaffirm-
ation of their lust for one another (61). The lovers embrace: the girl from
Shalott's suicide has been in vain.

In the ghost literature of the Weimar period, there is evidence aplenty
that hauntings following a suicide bring little to no succor or recompense
for the vengeful spirit. Indeed, in cases documented by occultists like
Grabinski, the female ghost *qua* suicide victim is destined to haunt her
castle ceaselessly and without redress (327). Although she can make her
presence felt, the ills of her living years remain without remedy. The virgin

---

8   The baroness first sets up a scenario whereby the doctor must visit the young
     woman and her mother in order to be nursed back to health. When the young girl
     realizes that she has lost her doctor, she takes her own life and her body is laid out
     for burial at the baroness's castle (13, 26).

spirit, like the more terrifying ghost in white, attempts to rectify an unfair situation through confrontation. Her destiny, however, is to remain within the remit of the castle, evermore unrequited in love.

Sightings of the so-called "revenge ghost," as just documented in the works of Hauptman and Ewers, depict a feminine spirit who enjoins the living to acknowledge some committed injustice. In literature depicting ghosts, one often finds that the appearance of a specter is an omen of malaise or discord in an altogether different domain (Rapaport 417). In her novel *Jedes Opfer tötet seinen Mörder – Arsenik* (1933),[9] Claire Goll borrows from contemporary cases of female poisoners to establish a conflict between the victim and the perpetrator. Hania Siebenpfeiffer discusses Goll's novel in the context of Ernst Weiß's *Der Fall Vukobrankovics* (*The Vukobrankovics Case*, 1924), which depicts the poisoning of Milica Vukobrankovics, as well as Alfred Döblin's *Die beiden Freundinnen und ihr Giftmord* (*The Two Friends and Their Poisoning*, 1924), which features the case of Klein/Nebbe (141). In *Arsenik*, the ghostly apparition comes to haunt a female friend who murdered her over the love of a man.

In Goll's novel, a 23-year-old Susanne Amiel poisons her friend and neighbor, Gaby Thomas, after Gaby sequesters both Susanne's business and boyfriend, Otto Mary. After initially failing to poison Gaby with arsenic-laden liquor, she tries again (now successfully) using a higher dose (148). The novel builds upon the idea that both Gaby and Susanne are modern women who are interested in money and personal profit above all else. Susanne, the story's narrator, describes Gaby as cold, dishonest, and parsimonious (22, 58–60, 139). She demonstrates her business savvy selling felt hats to women who do not really wish to buy them. Susanne is likewise cold-hearted in her dealings, zealously counting her cash as she makes sales in her paper goods store (46, 84). Susanne's steeliness is evident in her murder of Gaby, which she accomplishes through certain demonic acts (57, 140–41, 156).[10]

---

9   The novel first came out in French in 1932, and a year later in German. In 1977, Goll revised the German version, considering this her finest work. She was a German writer and the wife of the poet Yvan Goll.

10 Susanne is referred to in the novel as a witch ("Hexe") – she is enchanting, but dangerous (Goll 19; 156).

The poisoning and eventual haunting is set into motion by Susanne's visit to a mystic, Madame Leyris, who is paid to bring ill unto Gaby (31–39). Promising Susanne that bad things should soon happen to her rival, the medium works her necromancy by appropriating several of the victim's belongings. When Susanne loses patience waiting for the medium, she takes matters into her own hands, procuring the poison and administering the fatal dose. After the murder, Gaby's ghost inhabits the narrator's nocturnal world. Susanne hears the ringing of a bell in the hat shop, senses that someone is following her, and has the sensation that someone – or something – is blowing on her neck (149, 157–61):

> Ein bekannter Schritt tappt im Nebenzimmer. Oh, so gedämpft hört sie den Rhythmus dieses Schrittes. Er nähert sich, jetzt ist er dicht hinter ihr, aber niemals nähert er sich ganz. Immer bleibt zwischen ihm und ihr eine Distanz. Manchmal spürt sie einen Atem hinter sich. Und jetzt dieser Geruch, der immer ein Unlustgefühl in ihr auslöst. Eine Stimme ruft sie bei ihrem Namen. Und doch, so lange sie wacht, geht die Erscheinung noch glimpflich mit ihr um. Aber wehe ihr, wenn sie einschläft. Dann erst bekommt die Tote Gewalt über sie. (158)

> A well-known step advances in the adjacent room. Oh-so muffled, she hears the rhythm of this step. It nears, now it is directly behind her, but never does it approach completely. There is always a distance between it and her. Sometimes she feels a breath behind her. And now this smell that always releases a dull feeling in her. A voice calls her by her name. And still so long as she is awake, the apparition only gently haunts her. But woe is she, when she falls asleep. Then the dead gains control over her.

The ghost of Gaby haunts Susanne, who eventually grabs her shoulders and digs her fingers into the narrator's body. When the shrill ghost asks why she was murdered, Susanne remarks that she could not bear to hear the ringing bell of the hat shop, conjuring up memories of Otto (159). At the end of the novel, all of Gaby's gifts haunt Susanne; she is finally forced to tear up Gaby's picture and flush it down the toilet before the dead woman can look at her (160).[11]

---

11   From these citations, we can detect a potent sexuality between Susanne and Gaby. The touching and breathing lend a sexualized feel to these ghostly encounters. The lesbian undertone is mollified, however, by Susanne's unending obsession with

In *Arsenik*, the reader is privy to the manifestation of the ghost who has been murdered not by her lover, nor a family member, but by her jealous friend and business rival.[12] The female ghost evinces aggression as she violently pursues and attacks her murderer. The depiction of the small metropole Lavallier, where the women live, is likewise notable in its ghost-like depiction: "Lebt dieser Ort? [...] Man kann [die Einwohner] leicht mit ihren Schatten verwechseln" (Do people live in this place? [...] You can easily confuse [the inhabitants] with their shadows. 7–8).

As modern women, both the murderer Susanne and her victim Gaby place their own self-interest above the good of the community. In spite of Gaby's being wronged by Susanne, she remains suspect of her ruthless business dealings. Even in death, Gaby continues to exhibit this vindictive behavior. Indeed, while there is some justice for Gaby – the local authorities solve the murder and send the murderess to prison – Susanne seems, in some ways, to bask in solitude behind bars, away from the city of Lavallier. Thus, the ghostly Gaby fails to extract the perfect revenge for the crime committed against her.

Female writers of ghost stories, notes Blazan, were not free to construct their narratives beyond the existing parameters of the patriarchy. Indeed, in many cases, the female ghost in such tales is meted out punishment rather than sweet, sought-after retribution (Blazan 5). While Goll depicts modern women in a contemporary context in *Arsenik*, these independent businesswomen are nonetheless both penalized for their desires. The ghost in particular does not profit, as the murderess feels that she has improved upon her situation in jail, thereby having no remorse for her actions. What's more, the victim leaves behind a female orphan about whose fate we have

---

Otto, and reminiscences about the tender times that they shared together. The last part of the book details her trip to visit him (166–71).

12   Susanne technically relinquishes her hat business to Gaby, who quickly makes the shop more innovative. In the process, Gaby also attracts Susanne's old suitor, Otto, who then begins visiting Gaby in the hat shop. Susanne quickly realizes her mistake and yearns to have her shop back, in order to preserve the memories of her time with Otto. Susanne then tries to acquire a new business in Otto's hometown. As she attempts to visit Otto's practice, she finds that he has moved to Paris, having gotten involved with another woman.

no cause for optimism, thanks to the unforgiving patriarchal structure in which the narrative is culturally unfolded.[13]

Weimar fictional works about ghosts – including the three works discussed – correspond faithfully to features of real women in the *Zeitgeist*. Myriad depictions of female characters as *femmes fatales*, thwarted virgins, and officious businesswomen, reflect the contemporary dilemmas of the liminal, modern woman. Because these women were pariah-like figures, sitting at the periphery of female acceptability – thanks to their independence and defiance in the face of the opposite sex – they serve as stark, mnemonic aids to the cultural reality faced by the Weimar woman herself.

Female Ghosts in Photography and Film

At the end of the nineteenth century, photographic advancements (such as double exposure) caused phantasmagorical lights and shapes to appear on film, which betrayed a ghostly translucence.[14] Further developments in image-retouching likewise enabled ghosts to appear, albeit staged in combination with their human counterparts. At this time, photographers took advantage of the public's interest in making contact with deceased family members, who were vying to receive signs from the afterlife. The World War One in particular ushered in a fascination with spirit photography, with mediums calling forth spirits that were supposedly caught on film. Evidence for these ghosts consisted in the goo-like substance known as "ectoplasm," which would emerge from bodily orifices. According to the cultural understanding of the time, this plasma-like substance could take the form of spirit faces, hands, and feet.

In his 1923 work *Phenomena of Materialisation* (*Materialisations-Phänomene*), Schrenck-Notzing reproduced photographs of spirit-formations

---

13 Gaby's husband died several years back, rendering her a young widow with a female child (Malou).

14 For more on spirit photography, see Gunning's "Phantom Images and Modern Manifestations," as well as Nancy Princenthal's "Willing Spirits."

that were complete with fingers and faces: "true phantoms" formed by the power of a being with a "slight metapsychic subtlety" (331).[15] The author used Gustave Geley's photographs of ectoplasm, which were taken during his observations of the medium Eva C., in order to provide evidence for one of these ghost sightings. The photographs – taken five years after Schrenck-Notzing's original work with the aforementioned medium – reveal a ghoulish female face, together with fragments of teleplasma, characterized by "rents, breaks and cracks" (334). In a series of 10 photographs collected by the author, a face of a woman materializes in a mass from the medium's shoulders and then from her mouth. Although at first scarcely apparent, the woman's spirit face gains in definition and form before dematerializing altogether (334–36).

Besides his own photographic documenting of female spirits, Schrenck-Notzing adduces other mediums who produced evidence of a female spirit, including Eusapia Paladina and the medium Countess Castelvicz of Lisbon (334). Those female phantoms seen in spirit photography were "luminous, transparent, and subsequently condensing clouds" (334). Schrenck-Notzing includes the photograph of a ghostly nun, produced by Castelvicz, bearing a flat, expressive face: "The face is veiled, the upper body is draped in white fabric" (see Figure 6; 334–35). The nun is wearing a long sheath with an affixed cross; her eyes are closed, suggesting she is dead. Schrenck-Notzing moreover displays the photograph of a Dutch medium, who, in her initial materialization of a spirit, produces a luminous cloud (335). Gunning points out a certain transparency in spirit photography, whereby bodies rendered optically illusive afford glimpses into another world ("Scan a Ghost" 99). Indeed, spirit photography's ability to hold onto the dead by capturing an image is considered an outright method of circumventing mortality (Thurschwell 22).

---

15   Schrenck-Notzing released the text initially in 1914, then again in 1920 with another 100 pages of new information. For example, his initial work with the medium Eva C. in 1913–14 has been enhanced by Gustave Geley's photography based on later sittings with the medium. He also has over 200 photographs of spirits and mediums, adding to the original work.

Figure 6. Picture of a nun ghost. Albert von Schrenck-Notzing. *Phenomena of Materialisation: A Contribution to the Investigation of Mediumistic Teleplastics.* Trans. E. E. Fournier d'Albe. London: Kegan Paul, Trench, Trubner & Co., 1923.

The technology of photography itself became a subject of discussion in Weimar, having been heralded as preserving the living after death. Photography was often seen not only as a way to escape death but as a metaphor for impending death (Ibid. 29). On Honore de Balzac's understanding, a ghostly layer of our being gets peeled away with every successive photograph; the "spectral" layer then being sustained through the image. For Balzac, the loss of these layers was tantamount to the erasure of *essence* ("Scan a Ghost" 110).[16] In addition, photography was eyed up as a method for resurrecting the dead. To this end, Pamela Thurschwell comments: "These images go about continually resurrecting the dead in a realm that hovers uncertainly between the terrifying and the consoling" (Thurschwell, "Refusing to Give up" 24).

Acknowledging the liminal status of the ghost, in his essay "The Uncanny" ("Das Unheimliche," 1919), Sigmund Freud expounds upon the idea of capturing an individual's duplicated image, stating that repeating the same thing brings about an uncanny feeling (236–37). Freud also took the duplication of an image or person as a sign of death; the "unintended recurrence of the same thing" evoking danger and fear (246–47). Freud's theories in this arena build upon the fact that during early times, the dead person is the living one's enemy (242, 248). In Freud's words: "Many people experience the [uncanny] in the highest degree in relation to death and dead bodies, to the return of the dead, and to spirits and ghosts" (241).

In his Weimar treatise "Photography" ("Die Photographie," 1927), Siegfried Kracauer unpacks the imagistic reproduction, or "doubling," to which Freud alludes, thereby elaborating upon woman's pictorial uncanniness. Kracauer notes that reproduction – as realized through the lens of a camera – affords the photographer and his subjects a sense of *outrunning*

16   Gunning provides a quotation from the nineteenth-century photographer, Nadar, to explain Balzac's dislike of being photographed: "[A]ll physical bodies are made up entirely of layers of ghost-like images, an infinite number of leaflike skins laid one on top of the other […] [Balzac] concluded that every time someone had his photograph taken, one of the spectral layers was removed from the body, and transferred to the photograph. Repeated exposures entailed the unavoidable loss of subsequent ghostly layers, that is the very essence of life" (qtd. in Gunning, "Scan a Ghost" 110).

death.[17] By producing the image, man's use of technology secures the apparent reproduction, or doubling, of the original, thereby introducing the possibility of the present's eternal preservation. In reality, however, the opposite is true. For, as Kracauer contends, reproduction in the form of images "chills" the observer. The photograph does not make manifest knowledge of the original: it offers only the *sum* of what is taken from the original then and there. Indeed, Kracauer goes on to claim that the image ultimately *replaces* its archetype: "[Photography] annihilates the person by portraying him or her, and were person and portrayal to converge, the person would cease to exist" ("Photography" 431).[18] Here, the conflation of original and reproduction – enabled through technology – serves to *negate* the individual: the image is but a husk with life blown into it; a ghost who usurps and inevitably *defiles* the original (Ibid. 430).

Kracauer's denouncement of the camera goes further yet, however, decrying the camera as a form of technology that is capable of cannibalizing the world (Ibid. 433). Like Balzac, Kracauer thought that the camera seizes and mutilates individuals; the image splitting its subject into infinitely many pixelated parts. Kracauer's critique then assumes a gendered slant, claiming that photography's ability to dismember its subject is the work of a technology that is framed as *feminine*. On Kracauer's analysis, examples of the grandmother and the diva, captured in images, exemplify the potential of photography to be uncanny in its destruction and spiritual possession.[19]

Kracauer begins his article on photography by looking at the contemporary film diva: his subject, a 24-year-old woman, appears on the cover of an illustrated magazine striking a seductive pose, the caption denominating her as demonic. Everyone is familiar with this diva: all and sundry have seen her on the big screen. One could not possibly confuse her with another woman, although she is only one member of the famous Tiller Girl dance troupe. Kracauer's diva differs greatly from the photograph of the

---

17 "[Die Welt] scheint dem Tod entrissen zu sein" (Ibid. 35).

18 "[Die Photographie] vernichtet [den Mensch], indem sie ihn abbildet, und fiele er mit ihr zusammen, so wäre er nicht vorhanden" (Ibid. 32).

19 The image as an outcome of the photographic process, made possible by the technology of the camera, links the image to technology.

grandmother. While her image – taken many years ago – is also that of a young woman, her story is not so easily reconstructed. Her grandchildren know that she lived in a small room overlooking the city in her later life, and that she was the progenitor of a vicious rumor. The grandmother in the photograph – complete with chignon, crinoline, and Zouave jacket – is ultimately an "archeological mannequin": a mere collection of parts and the cause of both laughter and horror for her grandchildren.[20] Here, the grandmother and her chignon, as depicted in the photograph, constitute metaphors for time that has run out and can never be recovered, while the contemporary photograph of the diva is a living, visual reference point. According to Kracauer, however, the photograph of the diva will likewise go the way of the grandmother's: "The photograph is the sediment that has settled from the monogram, and from year to year its semiotic value decreases" (Ibid. 429).[21]

Kracauer continues to articulate the dangers of photography by driving home the analogy of woman as a *proxy* for ghostly meaning. In the case of present-day photography, the photograph performs a mediating or signi-fying function: the photograph of the diva being a visual sign of the diva, who is easily recognizable. The diva's reputation as *demonic*, however, rests on her *mnemonic* image, which has nothing to do with her photographic image (for the demonic refers to her screen presence). The old photograph of the grandmother does not have such a reference point as this. She and her image are *ipso facto* emptied of life. The grandmother – reduced to the regalia of her generation like a punctuation point of time immemorial – is but a remnant, a ghostly apparition. As Kracauer notes:

> Ghosts are simultaneously comic and terrifying. Laughter is not the only response provoked by antiquated photography. It represents what is utterly past and yet this

20 Kracauer notes: "Vor den Augen der Enkel löst sich die Großmutter in modischaltmodische Einzelheiten auf […] [Die Enkel] lachen und zugleich überläuft sie ein Gruseln. Denn durch die Ornamentik des Kostüms hindurch, aus dem die Großmutter verschwunden ist, meinen sie einen Augenblick der verflossenen Zeit zu erblicken, der Zeit, die ohne Wiederkehr abläuft" (Ibid. 22–23).

21 "Die Photographie ist der aus dem Monogramm herabgesunkene Bodensatz, und von Jahr zu Jahr verringert sich ihr Zeichenwert" (Ibid. 30).

refuse was once the present. Grandmother was once a person – Now the image wanders ghostlike through the present like the lady of the haunted castle. Spooky apparitions occur only in places where a terrible deed has been committed.[22] (Ibid. 430)

In this passage, photography is synonymous with the manufacture of the undead. The image of the grandmother – and ultimately that of the diva – represents the doubling of the image, which freezes time and space, and reminds one that the past cannot be separated from the present. Woman, as a fragment and ghost of the past, causes the observer to shudder. A ghostly reality in the form of woman is released to confuse accepted social mores and to hamper newfangled ways of thinking. Like the playing of an old hit song, or the screening of a classic movie, the decontextualized photograph produces a disintegrated unity.[23] Photography is therefore associated with the foul stench of the past: the female ghost, who haunts the castle of the present, unfurls an aura of horror for those living individuals, who dare to delve into the photographic archive.[24]

In Kracauer's 1927 essay, photography *itself* is compared to the female ghost who haunts the castle. Instead of affirming life, the photograph is likened to the uncanny female spirit: betwixt and between, she wanders the halls of the present as a harbinger of death and violence. Similar to the work of other occultists and fiction writers of the Weimar period, Kracauer's depiction of the female ghost was that of a liminal and dangerous entity. Kracauer's diva, who is overtly sexualized in nature, and the figure of the grandmother both signal a state of the undead, threatening the stability

22   Das Gespenst ist komisch und furchtbar zugleich. Nicht das Lachen nur antwortet der veralteten Photographie. Sie stellt das schlechthin Vergangene dar, aber der Abfall war einmal Gegenwart. Die Großmutter ist ein Mensch gewesen […] Nun geistert das Bild wie die Schloßfrau durch die Gegenwart. Nur an Orten, an denen eine schlimme Tat begangen worden ist, gehen Spukerscheinungen um (Ibid. 31).

23   According to Kracauer, "[w]ir sind in nichts enthalten, und die Photographie sammelt Fragmente um ein Nichts" (Ibid. 32).

24   Hansen distils Kracauer's meaning thus: "The photograph thus in fact enables, rather than prevents, a momentary encounter with mortality, an awareness of a history that does not include us" (456). For more information about Kracauer's essay on photography, see Giles.

of the status quo. These figures also resemble Weimar tropes of the ghost in unsettling representations of the vengeful spirit.

We may summarize Kracauer's thesis, then, as maintaining that photographic images, which seek to *tame* the dead, instead resurrect them ("Photography" 430; Thurschwell 24). Like photography, film too is a ghostly medium. Gunning notes that film represents a type of "phantasm," which wavers between the material and immaterial. Speaking about the predator polyp in F. W. Murnau's 1922 film *Nosferatu*, Gunning equates this translucent image with cinema itself: "[the polyp] recalls for us the transparent nature of film itself, its status as a filter of light, a caster of shadows, a weaver of phantoms" ("Scan a Ghost" 98). Film is ultimately a "play between the visible and the invisible, reflections and shadow, on- and off-screen space" (Ibid. 97). Cinema is in the business of creating uncanny images (Ibid. 97); "phantom-like" in the shadows that move on a white screen (Kaes 140). Anton Kaes elaborates that silent film in particular lends especially to "unfamiliar, ghost-like, shocking subjects" (Ibid. 140).

Fritz Lang's 1921 film entitled *Der müde Tod* employs cinematic elements such as light, shadow, and stasis to recreate the interstitial region between life and death. Lang, in collaboration with Thea von Harbou, created *Der müde Tod* (premiering in 1921), which was then imported to England and the U.S. in 1924. The film features the character of a young maiden who enters the realm of the undead to bargain for her loved one who had perished. Virtually the entire film takes place between the world of the living and that of the dead, featuring a walled city full of flickering candles representing souls and spirits who must make their way into the afterlife. It is in this transitory state that the woman becomes a ghost-like entity in order to bargain with Death to bring her loved one back to the world of the living. In taking a poison that should end her life, the maiden instead meets Death in his own liminal space. Instead of ushering her directly to the afterlife, Death gives the maiden four chances to rescue her lover. She is brought back to life at the end, only to renounce life entirely in exchange for death alongside her betrothed.

Lang's narrative revolved around a young maiden (Lil Dagover) who is given three scenarios in which to rescue her beloved (Walter Janssen). The first takes place in ninth-century Baghdad, where a Frank is having an affair with the Caliph's sister and is discovered in a holy place. The second tale is staged in Venice during carnival where a young woman – betrothed to the powerful Girolamo – is tricked into murdering her lover. The third story involves a Chinese Emperor who pursues his magician's daughter; the daughter and her lover flee using a magic wand, but ultimately remain trapped by the Emperor's archer. When the maiden cannot rescue her lover in any of these tales, Death offers her one last chance: he will accept a life that has not been spent.

The supernatural permeates the entirety of the *Der müde Tod*. The figure of Death (Bernhard Goetzke) leases land next to a graveyard and surrounds it with a high wall; neither doors nor windows can be found in the structure. When the maiden has no luck breaching the wall in her search of her beloved, she is aided by an apothecary (Karl Platen) who is looking for mandrakes in the moonlight. The intertitle states that the herbs drawn from the full moon boast mysterious powers, including "touch-me-not, balsam and Solomon's seal, wolfberry and centaury." Other supernatural symbols include the cross with alpha and omega, and the hourglass and skeleton featured at the inn, which symbolize that life is running out.

In portraying these supernatural elements, Lang eschews quick editing "in favor of photography and set decoration" (Jensen 27). Hermann Worm and Walter Röhrig, who created the sets for the 1919 expressionist film *Caligari*, also manufactured the dream-like sequences for Lang's work. Paul Ickes commented on *Der müde Tod* in the *Film-Kurier* 1921: "Bild an Bild reiht sich in einer fabelhaft anmutenden, nahezu unüberbietbaren dramaturgischen Technik" (Image after image joins in a fabulous, almost unsurpassable dramaturgical technique). The *8 Uhr-Abendblatt* also recognized the beauty of the mise en scène: "Einzelne Bilder überraschen durch malerische Schönheit" (Individual pictures surprise by picturesque beauty).[25] In addition, Anton Kaes notes that films of the early Weimar era regularly present motifs of the supernatural, complete with "apparitions, hypnosis and sorcery, vampirism and clairvoyance" (140). In so doing, these films display a lack of movement in dwelling on the image.

---

25 Gunning believes that Lang's work is among the most perfect creations in Weimar cinema (*The Films of Fritz Lang* 15). Paul Jensen notes the film's slow pace, which can be divided into three dream-like sequences (24).

As the film *Der müde Tod* commences, a feeling of stasis is evoked through the presentation of a medieval town that has been frozen in time ("some time and some place"). The film begins with a scene at a crossroads, while a large Christian monument is shown bounded by tall trees. This sepia-toned tableau bespeaks the stillness of death, enhanced in turn by a widescreen shot of Death's forming shadow, complete with walking stick and a propped-up skeleton. The town itself features a square as well as an inn. The town square at night is a relic bereft of inhabitants, standing still and uncanny, as if the buildings with their glowing eyes take on a life of their own. The sole individual on the street is the town crier, who presents his solitary message of caution with respect to the dangers of the night. The image of Death is further portrayed in the three tales' cinematography. The photographic stillness of the final moments of each story speaks to a deathly outcome. In all three, the male body lies supine on the ground, the female positioned beside it. In the case of the Chinese tale, the maiden appears as a stone statue; as immovable as the corpse of the lover. In the third tale, the strange bamboo-like forest encases the statue and her lover, not unlike the enveloping nature of the candle forest in the "Hall of Flames." Common to all these endings is the personification of Death positioned vertically as gravedigger or archer.

In the latter tale, the maiden's encounter with Death takes on a ghostly form as she searches for her beloved. Looking for an entrance, she respectively sees cresting over the hill a king, a soldier missing a leg, the elderly, and the young. The figures move past and through the maiden on their journeys into the underworld. Some of these unearthly figures hold candles, crutches, and walking sticks as they proceed through the wall. When the maiden sees her beloved amongst the dead, her pleading is met with resignation. The intertitle featuring "Song of Solomon 8:6" notes that "Passion is cruel as the grave." As the maiden drinks the poison, she is transported to the wall, where she begins her long, slow climb up the stairs; the screen is black except for the light of the staircase emanating from the Gothic arch. The maiden meets Death, whereafter the scene dissolves into a room with tall candles (see Figure 7). This slow-moving scene, featuring a stark black and white contrast, is juxtaposed with the architecture of the grotto with its sea of vertical candles. Here, the mise en scène provides a simple statement, as well as a sense of permanence; the substantial candles mimicking and mirroring the tall trees from the film's opening scenes. Additionally, the lack of quick, filmic cuts, coupled with the use of dissolves as transitional elements, allows Lang to showcase the protracted and ponderous march of Death.

Figure 7. Bernhard Goetzke and Lil Dagover in *Der müde Tod* (Destiny). Producer Erich Pommer; director Fritz Lang, 1921.

The maiden joins Death in this in-between realm as they climb the otherworldly staircase, arriving in the "Hall of Flames." There, Death asks her why she has entered his realm unexpectedly. Unlike the dead who enter the wall, she is not translucent. Having taken the poison, she has passed on – albeit incompletely. Gunning speaks of two realms in the film: one of time measured by the village clock and the night watchman (designated as the realm of the living); and the other realm, outside the living, which is designated by the stopping of the clock (*The Films of Fritz Lang* 20–21). Weimar occultist Otto Piper likewise describes the world of the ghost as an in-between place; here, the dead may remain for a certain amount of time until they pass on to another space (108). In this netherworld, the maiden attempts to fight Death, reminding one of the female ghosts of Weimar lore, who similarly refuse to acknowledge their own death. In the film's reference to the "Song of Solomon," the female protagonist finds her inspiration in the words: "set as seal upon thine heart […] love is stronger than death."

Der müde Tod's female ghost, unlike other such Weimar representations, has the opportunity to return to the land of the living: "Time has in effect, hiccupped and run backwards slightly, like a scratched record" (Gunning, *The Films of Fritz Lang* 21).[26] The maiden, alive again, has a chance to find another life from amongst the townspeople to exchange for the life of her lover. Rejecting a new-born infant to trade for her lover, she instead decides to return the child to the mother, who has escaped the flames of the burning building. As she lowers the child out the window, she realizes that she herself will not be able to escape the flames. Moreover, in the film's final scene, death is again signified through the mise en scène and its lengthy shots. Tints of blue and red permeate scenes of the village and the burning hospital; these shots move to one last image of a Gothic archway, where Death presents the maiden with her dead lover. Death briefly touches the maiden's head; he then animates the translucent maiden and her beloved, all the while their bodies lie in the stone alcove. The lovers pass through the Gothic arch (mimicking the fated arch at the beginning of the film), thereafter walking arm in arm – together with Death – up a hill of flowers. The lovers face one another – hands clasped – as the town clock freezes at midnight. The town crier makes a final plea to the populace. By this time, the lovers have passed out of time and space.

Like the female ghosts of Weimar, Lang's maiden is incited to act thanks to her relationship with a man. She essentially commits suicide to be united with her beloved, not unlike the young maiden in Ewers'

---

26   Death has told the maiden to "go to the living and live."

Girl from Shalott. Lang's character seeks to right a perceived wrong with respect to her romantic relationship. Like the girl from Shalott, she is active in death, seeking to redress a love that has been torn asunder. The maiden takes on dynamic character traits in *Der müde Tod*'s three tales as Zobeide, Fiametta, and Tiao Tsien. On each occasion, she transcends gender barriers in an attempt to rectify an injustice. These scenarios range from defying religious edicts in the first tale, to fighting an arranged marriage and defying authority in the final two narratives. Her reenactment of power relations between men and women, as presented in the vengeful ghost scenarios in Weimar, is plain to see. The maiden's attempt to best her male rivals is thwarted by the character of Death. Again, as in the ghost tales of Weimar, the female spirit is guaranteed neither justice nor closure.

Conclusion

Weimar's traditional woman and modern woman, respectively characterized in the period's benevolent and malevolent ghoulish figures, are given voice in *Der müde Tod*. The maiden, at once a helpful and vengeful ghost, is permitted to voice her grievances with regard to perceived injustice. Like her sister spirit, however, she is not allowed to experience the succor she seeks. Neither the maiden nor her beloved will again experience life, whether in the living or the ghostly realm. The film's reoccurring theme "Not one day, not one hour, not one breath" becomes her fate. Although the call of the female ghost in Weimar is disruptive and solicitous, *Der müde Tod*'s female spirit is forced to reject life altogether. The town's crier delivers his final advice to the populace: "Defend you all from specter and sprite / That no evil imp your souls affright!" It is best to lay the troublesome female ghost to rest for the good of the community.

The Vampire and the Monster Double

The fearsome traits of the female vampire – and her counterpart, the menacing "monster-woman" – can be understood as cultural metaphors for the newly liberated, sexualized Weimar woman found in the aftermath of World War One. Thereafter, an entire generation was saddled with the psychological toll of 10 million war dead (Winter 15–53; Keegan 3). This trauma was felt particularly acutely in Germany, where two million soldiers were killed and another four million left with disabilities ("The Legacy of War" 5). In the battles of Verdun and the Somme, as well as trench warfare more generally, German soldiers were killed in close combat. Even in the trenches, the Germans were subjected to shelling from guns, projectiles, and air attacks (Ferro 85–97). The formerly freakish sight of blood became a battlefield banality, the loss of life accrued in World War One being utterly unprecedented (Keegan 3; "The Legacy of War" 5). Indeed, in his novel *Vampyr* (1921) Hanns Heinz Ewers notes that man needed blood to thrive following his wartime experiences: "They all want blood, blood! [...] Humanity had become stricken with a wild fever and had to drink blood to make themselves well and young again" (361–62). How, then, did the bloodshed of the War bear on the perception of Weimar's new independent woman? Scandalous numbers of male casualties incited an air of indignation toward women, who were seen as having had a comparatively easy time during these extraordinarily dark years. Their newfound emancipation was judged as an affront to untold measures of male sacrifice, whose legacy was that of a "skeleton" bereft of vitality (Bronnen 69). The woman who was supposed to help him integrate back into society had herself departed that now-elapsed part of the cultural narrative.

What remained of her in cultural consciousness had now assumed an altogether *vampiric* guise.

The independent woman in the semblance of a vampire is one fraught with sexual desire. Hans Richard Brittnacher contends that the Weimar female vampire is a paradigmatic figure of the *femme fatale*, who threatens to overwhelm and sexually eviscerate man (168).[1] The sexually motivated female criminal (*Lustmörderin*) strives to suck the blood of her male victim as the ultimate statement of her freedom from male dominance. In this chapter, I appraise and unpack various depictions of female vampires in cultural works from the Weimar period as a cipher of the New Woman. This symbolism is explicit in several literary and filmic works, which depict women as bloodsucking monsters, including Leonard Stein's "Der Vampyr" (1918), Hanns Heinz Ewers' *Vampyr* (1921), Robert Wiene's film, *Genuine* (1920), and Carl Theodor Dreyer's film, *Vampyr: Der Traum des Allan Gray* (*Vampyr: Allan Gray's Dream*, 1932). In addition to analyzing these works, I provide a historical account of the role of sexually motivated crime (*Lustmord*), as given grim expression in the Käthe Hagedorn murders.

I shall also analyze fantastic films of the Weimar period, namely Robert Wiene's *Das Cabinet des Dr. Caligari* (*The Cabinet of Doctor Caligari*, 1920) and F. W. Murnau's *Nosferatu* (1922). Through these studies, I track the monster-woman's twofold talent for terrorizing man, jointly unleashing desire and the dangers thereby. A vociferous debate on the supposed double nature of the "masculine woman" (the biological woman with alleged masculine characteristics) informs the uncanny nature of the double, through which her sexuality evinces various eerie distortions. The rhetoric of the double nature of woman, as depicted in the Weimar press, presents an image of an aggressive woman, who is adamant about infiltrating traditionally male bastions of power. In Weimar fantastic films, fears regarding female sexuality are epitomized in monstrous form, her infernal analogue serving as a proxy for a female sexuality deemed to be out of control.

---

1   There has been extensive research on the topic of the vampire. For more informa-
     tion, see Prins, Noll, Oinas, Cella, and Bertschik. Brittnacher has an excellent
     essay on female vampires in twentieth-century German literature and culture.
     Meanwhile, Perhold unpacks the vampire as lesbian lover.

Female Vampires and the New Woman

The vampire *qua* sexual predator is well-attested in the literature. For instance, Elisabeth Bronfen notes that the vampire escapes the realm of the dead thanks to imbibing vitality by enervating the living, namely through the sucking of blood (294).[2] Through this act, the vampire's corpse is rejuvenated, after which she needs to die a second death to guarantee that she ceases to pose a threat to the community.[3] For Bronfen, as for Brittnacher, the female vampire constitutes a special challenge to men in her capacity as "instigator and object of desire" (Ibid. 315). The construction of the vampire as the radical "Other" positions her as a threat to the social order, which demands that she is extinguished and purged in order to preserve male subjectivity (Ibid. 314–15). Just as the vampire's kiss is at once both titillating and repulsive, so too the liberated woman represents both a site of expanded gender relations and a reactionary backlash that hankers after traditionally patriarchal roles (Ibid. 315).

The female vampire is a border-crosser: she breaches the bounds of the living and dead, as well as the human and the beastly (Creed 61). Her beauty is ageless, empowering her to seduce helpless men to their deaths (Ibid. 72). Barbara Creed well notes the female vampire's association with bodily fluids – not only blood, but also her victim's tears (10–11). She further observes recurring facets of the vampire narrative, which include "womb-like coffins, the full moon, snake-like fangs, two bite marks, dripping blood, transformation" (Ibid. 63). Indeed, given that menstruating women are seen as being in a state of unabating blood loss, her condition encourages an interpretation that naturally associates her with a drive toward restoring her deficient state. Indeed, in spite of its mundanity, Creed notes that we are repulsed even by the sight of our *own* blood, which leaves the subject with a sense of lacking wholeness or its proper state of being (Ibid. 13). In

2   Barber believes that there exists a fear of contagion, as the intact body begins to decompose. The dead cease to be dangerous when the body is no longer undergoing change (Bronfen 296).

3   The female vampire also represents the *vagina dentata* (the "toothed vagina," with open mouth, pointed teeth, and bloody lips) (Creed 72).

its association with fertility, blood is abject in its connoting both life and death (Ibid. 59).

The female vampire, in all of her guises, can be understood as a metaphor for the ambiguous status of the New Woman, who must similarly pay the price for her radical transcendence. Weimar's New Woman possesses a duplicitous character: on the one hand, she helped to maintain social order as men fought in the trenches of World War One; on the other, her sexual and economic liberation posed a threat to male identity during and after the War. The writer and theater director Arnold Bronnen notes that women tried their hand at many "manly" pursuits during the War, as men fell in the trenches in their fight to protect traditional values (71).[4] Returning home, it was reported that man found a kind of woman he did not recognize. She not only participated in traditionally male lines of work, but furthermore pursued male leisure activities, including sexual pursuits, thereby usurping man's position (Ibid. 91). She was no longer interested in playing the virgin, breathlessly awaiting her lover. Now she flaunted her sexual currency with aplomb, baring her naked body at will (Berl 233–34). Otto Flake cautioned woman to prescind from frivolous, five-minute sex acts, decrying: "man erledigt es nicht wie das Huhn, das sich nach dem Überfall durch den Hahn schüttelt und weiter sein Futter sucht" (one does not do it like a chicken that shakes off the cock after the foray and continues to look for food). That is, woman ought to spend her sexual currency wisely, at the cost of its potential and irredeemable devaluation (139).

Weimar authors often depicted the modern woman as selfishly meeting her own needs and desires before those of her partner, so much so that Flake remarks that women's emancipation rendered them unromantic (135). The New Woman, who was ruled by hunger, love, and a predilection for leisure (136), undermined the idealized notion of the traditional woman, whose image was that of chastity and forbearance.[5] According to Flake, woman must retain her traditional gender role: "Die Frau von morgen hat keine andere Aufgabe als die von gestern und heute: die Liebe zu sublimieren,

4   Heinrich Eduard Jacob noted that it was a logical outcome for woman to change as a result of wartime pressure: "Der Mann hörte auf, sie zu ernähren; zog in den Krieg; zerschlug die Kultur. Kein Mann kann heute den Rücktritt der Frau ins Gestern fordern" (111).

5   "ein Körper, den Hunger, Liebe und das Bedürfnis nach Entspannung regieren" (136).

die Banalisierung zu vermeiden" (The woman of tomorrow has the same mission as the one from yesterday and today: to sublimate love, to avoid banality. 139).[6] Hans Ostwald further notes how the New Woman threatened the traditional family structure. In his 1931 work *Sittengeschichte der Inflation* (The Moral History of Inflation), Ostwald argues that women who appropriated traditional male positions during the War were unwilling to reoccupy traditional female roles following its conclusion. Ostwald goes so far as to claim that new expressions of female sexuality – including provocative fashion trends and participation in risqué theater culture – rattled the very foundations of the world (Introduction).

Many literary and artistic works of the Weimar period focus on woman's brazen oversexuality. For example, the artist Otto Dix would depict grotesque whores alongside war victims as if one were responsible for the other.[7] Dix's *Der Schützengraben* (The Trench, 1920–23), accorded acclaim from then-contemporary critics who commended its percipient social commentary (see Figure 8): "[Dix] scheut keine Brutalität des Ausdrucks" ("[Dix] does not shy away from a brutality of expression," Willi Wolfradt qtd. in März and Radeke 22).[8] Dix is no less harsh when portraying Weimar prostitutes. In paintings such as *Mädchen vor dem Spiegel* (Girl in Front of the Mirror, 1921) and *Drei Dirnen auf der Straße* (Three Prostitutes on the Street, 1925), Dix depicts lewd women with missing teeth and deranged expressions (see Figures 9 and 10).[9] These *femmes fatales* threatened a war-ravaged Weimar society with their all-consuming sexuality, Weimar critics denouncing these female images as bearing foul witness to an increasingly degenerate social system (März and Radeke 50).[10]

6 Flake includes motherhood in his criteria for the ideal woman (138).
7 Dada was a type of anti-art or philosophy that condemned art as aesthetic. Dada equated art with "arts and crafts," critiquing the middle-class need for an escape from reality.
8 Otto Dix, *Der Schützengraben*, destroyed in the War.
9 Otto Dix, *Mädchen vor dem Spiegel*, destroyed in the War; Otto Dix, *Drei Dirnen auf der Straße*, private collection, Hamburg.
10 A more sinister construction of Weimar's sexualized woman also stems from Dada proponents, Dix and George Grosz. At the same time as these artists were painting prostitutes, they also created an extensive *Lustmörder* series, portraying naked women hacked to pieces. In many of these works, fully clothed men flee the scene, leaving behind a mutilated female body. For more information about this phenomenon, see Lewis and Tatar.

Figure 8. Otto Dix. *Der Schützengraben* (The Trench) (*destroyed in the war*). 1920–23.
© 2020 Artists Rights Society (ARS), New York / VG Bild-Kunst, Bonn.

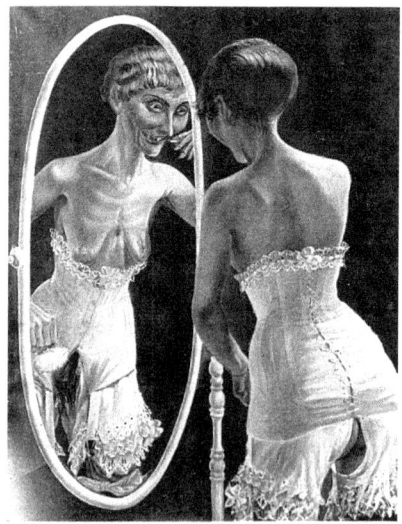

Figure 9. Otto Dix. *Mädchen vor dem Spiegel* (Girl in Front of the Mirror)
(*Destroyed in the War*). 1921. © 2020 Artists Rights Society (ARS), New York/VG
Bild-Kunst, Bonn.

Figure 10. Otto Dix. *Drei Dirnen auf der Straße* (Three Prostitutes on the Street). Private collection, Hamburg. 1925. © 2020 Artists Rights Society (ARS), New York / VG Bild-Kunst, Bonn.

In like manner to their prostitute counterparts, occult women were demonized for their apparently deviant sexual motives. Criminologist Erich Wulffen, in his *Woman as a Sexual Criminal* (*Das Weib als Sexualverbrecherin*, 1923), tenders an unequivocal condemnation of women practicing the occult arts. For Wulffen, the female spiritualist is an "artful defrauder," exploiting her victims by playing on their superstitions (Ibid. 115). In a chapter entitled "Female Swindlers and Cheats," Wulffen draws a comparison between the female spiritualist and the prostitute (Ibid. 116). He further notes that the art of prophesy has always been practiced by women on account of their native proclivity to deceive (Ibid. 116).

The sexual woman, as seen in Weimar's cultural critique (such as Dix's prostitute figures and Wulffen's criminal psychics), corroborates Doane's claim that the *femme fatale* is an emblem of historical crisis. Bronnen notes that women are somehow to blame for the crisis in male subjectivity following World War One: "wir erinnern uns noch des entsetzlichen Grauens [des Krieges] […] wir sahen selbst unsere Skelette, während die Frauen, blühend und ungefährdet, weiterlebten" (we still remember the ghastly horrors of war […] we saw our own skeletons, while women, flourishing and out of danger, lived on. 68–69).

The traits associated with the Neue Frau, viz. her apparent insouciance regarding her male counterparts, recalls Stephen King's notion of the vampire as a symbol of reckless and remiss sexuality (Noll intro. 16). The blood required by the War's returning soldiers was rebuffed by the greed of the New Woman, who was herself parasitic upon the male realm for her freedom and pleasure. Bronnen provides a summary of the situation, remarking: "Nichts ist trostloser als das Leben dieser Frauen und nichts ist gieriger" (Nothing is more desolate than the lives of these women and nothing is greedier. 71). In the following section, we will cover the vampire *qua* sexual predator and duplicitous being, as portrayed in the psychological and criminal treatises of the time.

The Female Vampire in Weimar Psychological and Criminal Treatises

New Woman's overtly sexualized propensities – bearing symbolic links to vampirism – resonated in the psychological and criminal investigations of the period. Indeed, over the foregoing century, vampirism gained recognition as a legitimate mental illness, consisting (symptomatically at least) in the "act of drawing blood from an object (usually a love object) and receiving resultant sexual excitement and pleasure" (Vanden Bergh and Kelly 27). Here, while sucking or drinking blood constitute *necessary* conditions for a diagnosis, it is not thereby sufficient for "clinical vampirism" (Ibid.).[11] Herschel Prins argues that blood has always enjoyed a unique position in history, upheld by certain cultures as befitting "dietary or immunological purposes" (for instance, drinking the blood of those defeated in battle, or to fertilize the earth, etc.), while, in others, such practices are utterly deviant. Take, for instance, the Jewish prohibition of physical contact with menstruating women and the eating of Kosher meat, characterized by having been drained of blood (Prins, "Vampirism – Legendary or Clinical Phenomenon?" 285).

The salience of blood as life-affirming (as well as damning) informs the contemporary discussion of the vampire. Vampiric activity, on its clinical construal, may be influenced by various beliefs, including blood's being a "vital life-giving symbol," the desire to be joined together with a deceased loved one, the sexual component of the vampire's "bite" or kiss as a sadistic sexual expression, and (most importantly here), the influence that Bram Stoker's novel *Dracula* (1897) had on Western society (Prins, 288–89).[12] Stoker used research material from the British Museum in London, as well as other sources, to construct the myth of the vampire. In so doing, he formed a link with the psychiatry of the period, associating the state of "insanity" with vampirism, as well as reaffirming the sexual frenzy attached to drinking blood (Noll intro. 10). *Dracula* then became a reflection of psychiatry's relation to the vampire, which was (by the end of the nineteenth century) now well-charted territory.

The psychiatric investigation of woman's relationship to vampirism is attested to in case histories of the nineteenth and early twentieth centuries. For instance, physician and psychologist Havelock Ellis wrote in 1903 that the person who practices the "love bite" has the ultimate goal of bloodshed, especially in the case of women, who, he claims, possess a "conscious desire, even if more or less restrained, to draw blood, a real delight in this process, a love of blood" (120). In a clinical example, Ellis mentions a girl that was sexually

---

11   According to Vanden Bergh and Kelly, vampirism has regularly been related to the "sexual desire for corpses" (27).

12   In Prins' study, thirty-three psychiatrists linked vampiric activities with "schizophreniform disorders, hysteria, severe psychopathic disorder and mental retardation" ("Vampirism – Legendary or Clinical Phenomenon?" 289).

stimulated by watching dogfights. She would also pierce herself libidinously to see and suck her own blood (Ibid. 122). Through this process, she would regularly reach orgasm, especially if she was thinking of an attractive man. Indeed, she would bite her own husband in the act of lovemaking, sucking his blood from him (Ibid. 123). Ellis hereby describes the act of drawing blood as overtly sexual, culminating in the girl's orgasm either from fantasizing about a man or by sucking the blood of her spouse.

Moreover, sexologist and psychiatrist Richard von Krafft-Ebing tackles another case study from 1892, whereby a married man, found with various scars and scratches, proffered an explanation pointing to his vampiric wife: "When he wished to approach his wife, who was young and somewhat 'nervous,' he first had to make a cut in his arm. Then she would suck the wound and during the act become violently excited sexually" (81). Krafft-Ebing notes here that the wife's act is similar to the actions of vampires, believing the motive to be some form of sadism (Ibid.). This act bears the hallmarks of vampirism's *clinical* definition, while also recalling Stoker's *Dracula*, in which Lucy – growing yet-more attractive in her undead state – feasts on blood to sate her libidinal hunger.[13]

Finally, American psychiatrist Benjamin Karpman cites bloody vampiric fantasies from 1934. Entertaining fantasies about male lovers, as well as her husband, the female patient expresses a wish to "chew the[ir] raw flesh but not swallow it, in order as she said, to get the taste of the blood" (605). This woman also longs to pierce the heart of a female victim in order to drink her blood:

> The patient asked herself anxiously what she might do if a young girl came into her power, docile and willing to submit. She said: "I would like most of all to kiss her breasts, then tear or bite them off and eat them […] I would at last find my way to the heart and then drink the heart's blood, then pluck out the heart and perhaps eat it." (Ibid. 604)

Here, the drinking of blood is surpassed by the desire to kiss and subsequently *eat* various body parts, thereby bringing to mind Sabine Perhold's

13   On this, see Bronfen for coverage of the vampire Lucy in *Dracula* (313–23). Also note the three female vampires in Dracula's castle, who want to "kiss" the male protagonist, Jonathan Harker (*Dracula*, Chapter 3).

contention that the act of kissing has its roots in cannibalism: "der Küssende will sich das Gute, Nahr-und Schmackhafte einverleiben" (The kisser wants to incorporate the good, nutritious and tasty. 12).[14] Clearly, homoerotic desire plays an important role in this patient's fantasy, as presented in various narratives involving the female vampire and her female victim. Creed notes that the lesbian desire of the vampire begets the most "abject of all vampire monsters" (72).

Vampirism and the act of sexual murder (*Lustmord*) are often paired up in criminal treatises of the early twentieth century. For instance, Erich Wulffen's *Woman as a Sexual Criminal* (*Das Weib als Sexualverbrecherin*, 1923) discusses female lust and a desire to harm. To this end, Wulffen reviews the case of *Karusselljule*, a woman with strong necrophilic urges. The accused from Kottbus supposedly "removed a corpse," as well as murdered her two lovers, thereafter roasting one of their hearts and subsequently eating it (437). In court, this woman appeared to be a mild-mannered and law-abiding individual, her hands folded as if attending Church. However, the face of the sexual murderess also boasted the eyes of a demon, which twinkled with depraved, ravenous intent (Ibid.). Elaborating upon the topic of necrophilia, Wulffen contends that women are generally disinclined toward these acts, explaining (somewhat concessively) that "lustful women cannot revive the organ of a dead man" (Ibid.). Thus, with regard to necrophagia (i.e., consuming the flesh of the dead), necrophilia, and other forms of *Lustmord*, Prins notes that these terms likewise fall under the rubric of vampirism ("Vampirism – Legendary or Clinical Phenomenon?" 289).

Wulffen further relays the case of a lesbian lust-murder in Graz, Austria, where the mistress of a brothel cut deep into the breast, heart, liver, and lungs of her female lover (*Woman as a Sexual Criminal* 473). Attempting to escape her assailant, who was wielding a kitchen knife, the girl – dripping in blood – ran into the courtyard. It was thereafter discovered that the brothel's mistress had also bitten off the girl's nose, further exacerbating the bloody spectacle (Ibid.). Here again, sexual tension

---

14 This patient had further fantasies about male lovers, as well as her husband: "She would like to suck the juices of the body, shell out or tear out the eyes and roll them around in her mouth so that she could feel their roundness and softness" (605).

is implied, for, as blood flows from one's victim, a state of arousal ensues, forging yet again a connection between bloodlust and vampirism (Noll intro. 17). We further observe the connection between lesbian desire and vampirism, topped off with a particularly violent murder.

The topic of sexual murder, as described in Wulffen's work, was a popular theme during the Weimar period. Murderers like Fritz Haarmann and Peter Kürten were said to bite their victims to death for sexual pleasure. Haarmann, the so-called "Hanover vampire," killed twenty-four young men, while practicing vampiric and necrophilic behavior (Prins, "Vampirism – A Clinical Condition" 75).[15] Kürten, better known as the "vampire from Düsseldorf," likewise participated in vampiric activities, killing numerous men, women, and children between 1929 and 1930. In his work *Geschlecht und Verbrechen* (1930), sexual researcher Magnus Hirschfeld defined sexual murder as "die vorsätzliche Tötung zum Zwecke des sexuellen Lustgewinns" (the intentional killing for the purpose of gaining sexual pleasure. 186). These high-profile murders certainly fit the contemporary model of *Lustmord*, as has been outlined by Hirschfeld. As Maria Tatar moreover notes, while these sexual "vampires" were male, their portrayal in the media was peculiarly feminized (55). Indeed, Weimar philosopher Theodor Lessing described Haarmann as having "feminine" characteristics (chest, back, and buttocks), while his body and voice too were like those of a woman (Lessing 59, 62). Haarmann's homosexuality also placed him in the remit of the feminine (Tatar 55). Here, then, we have a case of a male "vampire" morphing into a feminine analogue. Additionally, famous Weimar cultural vampires – such as those of F. W. Murnau's *Nosferatu* (1922) – possess *androgynous* characteristics, thereby marking a departure from the traditionally *male* figure of the vampire (Tatar 55–58). Vampires like Nosferatu have furthermore been associated with anti-Semitic tropes and stereotypes, viz. in their respective avariciousness and financial ambition, which supposedly leach the life out of well-meaning, stable communities.[16]

---

15   See Pozsár and Farin for historical accounts about Haarmann.
16   Vampires have often been connected to a rise in anti-Semitism. For German ex-
      amples, see Tatar 41–67. See also Bertschik 243.

The female sexual murderer *qua* vampire finds her apotheosis in the case of the child murderer Käthe Hagadorn. Her fascination with blood (epitomized in her vampirism), as well as necrophilia, were well known and keenly felt in the Weimar *Zeitgeist*, Hagedorn being convicted of obscene behavior with a child (unzüchtige Handlungen an Minderjährigen) and, subsequently, manslaughter (anschließender Totschlag). Indeed, various Weimar commentators deemed her the female "lust murderer" (*Lustmörder*) of her day (Wünsch 241),[17] one such reporter having this to say about her crime:

> Das gräßliche Verbrechen, daß in der Kriminalgeschichte der letzten Jahre einzig dastehend ist und in seiner psychologischen Unerklärlichkeit nur mit dem Fall Haarmann verglichen werden kann, hat seinerzeit in Duisburg eine Art Panik erzeugt. (qtd. in Siebenpfeiffer 160)

> The horrific crime that has stood out in the criminal history of the last several years and can only be compared with the Haarmann case in its psychological inexplicability, has caused a panic in Duisburg.

Although Hagedorn was only a naive girl of seventeen at the time, the public compared her twisted actions to the infamous Haarmann, who would bite his victims' necks before having intercourse with their lifeless corpses.[18]

Let us provide our first vampiric *femme fatale* with some biographical details. Käthe Hagedorn was a young petit bourgeois girl, who lived with her parents in a small apartment and helped out in their local store. According to those reporting on the case, she was immature for her years, although she

---

17 The original documents pertaining to the case are no longer available. This essay therefore relies on historical documents (medical reports, newspaper articles, etc.) of the time in order to understand the trial. Magnus Hirschfeld, who was himself involved in Hagedorn's assessment, provides an excellent summary of the case ("Tötung zweier Kinder während der Menstruation"). For an overview, see Stefan Wünsch's article on the Hagedorn murders, which relies on documents found at the Geheimes Staatsarchiv Preußischer Kulturbesitz (Berlin) and the Landesarchiv Berlin.

18 See Pozsár and Farin for a 1924 psychiatric interview with Haarmann (121–478).

was nevertheless prone to masturbation and to touching other girls sexually (Hirschfeld, "Tötung zweier Kinder während der Menstruation" 846). Additionally, she was obsessed with the lives of movie stars, even writing to a Hollywood "Wunderdoctor" to tell him of her woes (Wünsch 243). On the day of the crime in question (June 24, 1926), Hagedorn was on her way to the local swimming pool when she met two children from her apartment block, Käthe, a 6-year-old and Friedel, a 9-year-old, who were happy to follow her. The three set off on foot and decided to pick flowers in the local deer-park. In the process of gathering flowers, Hagedorn went to help Käthe go to the bathroom, when she began groping and attacking the child. When Käthe screamed, Hagedorn stuffed sand and leaves in her mouth, further severing her carotid artery with nail scissors. Friedel was alerted to the turmoil, but, upon his arrival, Hagedorn hit him with a branch, then using the same weapon in severing his neck, too. As both children bled profusely, the assailant ran between the two in order to watch the blood spurt from their bodies; she moreover slashed the girl's wrists in order to draw more blood (Wulffen, *Woman as a Sexual Criminal* 383). She then covered the bodies with leaves, attempting to blame the crime on a man from her apartment block. Hagedorn had, however, been seen by witnesses, and while she tried to flee the city, she was captured and returned to Duisburg.

The Hagedorn case was yet-more shocking for those concerned owing to her never having committed a criminal act before. She was a quiet girl who eschewed male company in favor of idling around; daydreaming about movie stars and crime fiction. According to those reporting on the case, she had had a lesbian affair with an actress whom she met at the local circus (Lessing 221). An important addition consisted in her having just had her first onanistic orgasm a day before the murders, those reporting on the case claiming that she was sexually aroused before attacking the children (Wulffen, *Woman as a Sexual Criminal* 382–83; Lessing 222–23).[19] She was, moreover, menstruating when she committed the crimes, which, according

---

19   Hagedorn apparently read about the murder of children committed in Breslau shortly before committing her crime (Wulffen, *Woman as a Sexual Criminal* 383). She also supposedly read – with lust in her heart – about the case of serial murderer Haarmann (Lessing 222).

to criminologists, indicated that she would have been more predisposed than normal to lascivious and violent comportment (Hirschfeld, "Tötung zweier Kinder während der Menstruation" 846).

Those medical experts who were assigned to the Hagedorn case proffered various hypotheses as to her condition. Two doctors in particular felt that her act was committed in a state of sexual mania, brought on by menses, owing to which she was not criminally liable. Another maintained that she committed the crimes with a degree of *sang froid*: she did not black out from the murders, either figuratively or literally. Ultimately, the court decreed that Hagedorn was not wholly culpable for her crimes, claiming that she acted from a mentally compromised, manic state. Thus, for her misdeeds, she was sentenced to only eight years' imprisonment (Wulffen, *Woman as a Sexual Criminal* 385; Hirschfeld, "Tötung zweier Kinder während der Menstruation" 846–47).

The debate regarding premeditation in this case – that is, whether Käthe Hagedorn *intended* to commit the crimes for sexual gratification – is important in her classification as a female sexual murderer, under the definition put forth by Hirschfeld. Indeed, Hagedorn proffered various exculpatory excuses in court, including that she saw blood and surmised that something had happened in the park (Wünsch 241). While several psychologists proclaimed that she was in a state of insanity and was therefore not responsible for her actions, one medical expert assigned to the case (a certain Dr. Raecke from Frankfurt) believed that the only reason the crimes were committed was Hagedorn's very literal bloodlust (Wünsch 254). Further, Wulffen believed that Hagedorn's actions aligned with her personality, and that her desire for blood and sexual lust provoked her to seek out the crime (*Irrwege des Eros* 141–42). In fact, Hagedorn's premeditation was manifest in her ploy to send Friedel to pick flowers in a different part of the field as she prepared her assault on Käthe (Wulffen, *Woman as a Sexual Criminal* 383).

In this case, the assessments of Raecke and Wulffen paint a picture of a young woman seeking sexual gratification through bloodshed, thereby corroborating Bergh and Kelly's conception of vampirism as an act committed *in order to see blood*. To this end, Lessing mentions the assailant's added desire to achieve sexual arousal by sticking scissors in her victims' bodies

(Lessing 224). Wulffen likewise comments that Hagedorn ran back and forth to observe the spurting of blood, using the scissors to prompt further bleeding by inserting them into the girl's neck (*Irrwege des Eros* 140–41). This repulsive crime partially mirrors psychiatrist Karpman's case study of a frenzied vampiric fantasy, while also underscoring Brittnacher's idea that the vampire is not only involved in tearing the flesh, but of drawing blood in an act of febrile lust (168).

This obsession with blood, as evidenced in Hagedorn's case, brings to the fore the further issue of menses, as foregrounded in Hagedorn's medical assessment, as well as to her sentencing. Hirschfeld, Lessing, and Wulffen all make mention of Hagedorn's period during the act of the crime (Hirschfeld, *Geschlecht und Verbrechen* 388; Lessing 222; Wulffen, *Woman as a Sexual Criminal* 382). In fact, Hirschfeld (one of the case's medical experts), argued that menstruation constitutes a quasi-pathological state, which represents a threat to justice when a woman comes under its sway (*Geschlecht und Verbrechen* 370–71). For Hirschfeld, menses is a poisonous occurrence for the body, leading women to commit criminal acts that threaten the community at large (*Geschlecht und Verbrechen* 374–75). As Creed points out, the womb is a site of terror as it bleeds, with menstrual blood already a liminal source, signaling danger to the community (66–72).

In sum, blood – menstrual or otherwise – is definitive of the sexual murderess, Käthe Hagedorn; her vampiric acts are particularly fearsome to a community that has already been rocked by serial murderers of the likes of Haarmann. Hagedorn appears at once a childlike woman – a naïf or urchin – sheltered by her parents and neighbors (Wünsch 261), who is nonetheless capable of committing heinous sexual crimes. This young woman, who had been deemed incapable of hurting a fly by those around her (Wulffen, *Irrwege des Eros* 141–42), plays out her sexual, blood-lustful desires. Hagedorn also reminds us of the charges of ambiguity leveled against the modern woman of Weimar: a woman enjoying all the privileges and affordances accruing to her sex, while at the same time being associated with sexual predation. We find that descriptions of Hagedorn evidence an expression of the stereotypical interests of the modern woman, including a vulgar obsession with Hollywood, the media, and cosmetics. Her attempt to flee the scene in a taxi – coupled with her shrewd escape from her driver – all evince a transfixion with fantasy and mass media (Hirschfeld, "Tötung zweier Kinder während der Menstruation" 846).[20] What's more, Hagedorn's iconic statement at her trial, "Ich bin die jüngste Mörderin der Welt […] die berühmtesten Leute kommen um mich" (I am the youngest murderer in the world […] the most famous people hang around me. Qtd. in Wünsch 263), reveals a vie for notoriety. Hagedorn's disregard for men, in tandem with her disinterest in marriage and motherhood, further consign her to a liminal space, which, for many, presages her ghastly deeds.

Female Vampires in Weimar Fiction

Just as criminal "vampires" like Hagedorn surprised society with their sexual ferocity and immoral actions, so too do the vampires of Weimar fiction and film. These figures furthermore flaunt their sexuality, having sloughed the shibboleths of customary morality or religious mores (Brittnacher 166). Brittnacher in particular notes a move in fiction around the turn of the century from the *femme fragile* (who concedes to the bite of the male vampire) to the *femme fatale* (who claims vengeance upon man in her quest for blood) (Ibid. 168). Further characteristics of this female vampire include her hypnotic power and more pestilent fears,

20 When Hagedorn's parents began to suspect her involvement, she slipped out in the middle of the night, taking a taxi toward the Belgian border, mimicking a film scenario she had seen. After giving the slip to the first driver (she disappears out of the restaurant, paying neither the driver nor the waiter), she takes a second taxi to complete the journey. This driver suspects foul play and is not deceived when Hagedorn tries to restage the restaurant scene a second time. What is interesting is that she plays an impromptu piano piece at the second restaurant, leaving the driver to believe that she is deranged. Her heightened gaiety is strange in light of the recent murders. For a description of her flight, see Wünsch 244. What is moreover odd is her continued desire to achieve orgasm, even in jail. Wünsch describes an incident where Hagedorn bloodies herself with a cigar cutter, while trying to achieve sexual climax (229). This combination of blood and sex also defines an occurrence that took place shortly before the murders, with Hagedorn biting her lips in order to achieve orgasm (featuring her bloody pillow and lips) (Ibid. 222).

as befitting the organic nature of her transgressions (Ibid.). The duplicity surrounding the Hagedorn case – the good girl turned erotic monster – is also evident in the fiction of the period, whereby the female vampire, who inhabits a waif-like body, also evinces a certain machismo and unbridled sexual depravity.

Hermann Löns's short story "Der Vampir" (1920) features a medical student who is haunted by a "half-blurred, chalk-white, rigid face" while studying for an exam (261).[21] This beautiful shadow with delicate features is a virginal young woman, whom the student admired in the past and had suddenly drowned. She then comes to claim her lover with the determination of the undead. Her erotic protestations – "Kiss my eyes, my mouth, my forehead! Swallow me!" – lead the young scientist to first unpack the reasons and motives behind her quest, finally succumbing to her siren call (Ibid. 264).[22] As he undresses, he feels her ice-cold heavy thump on his heart (Ibid. 265); he is then driven to relive the same sensations until he approaches death, back broken, eyes burning, and head pounding (Ibid. 266).[23] The vampire aims to draw blood from the heart, enervating its source while enlivening herself. Her actions beget a fear of death, a key feature of the *Zeitgeist*'s vampiric literature, a corollary of which is the protagonist's emasculation. In Lön's story, the male scientist leads the first-person narrative, thereby relaying the story of his demise. He is, however, impotent regarding his own fate: a master of science and logical thinking, he is no match for the vampire's erotic desire.

Like Löns's narrative, Leonhard Stein's short story "Der Vampyr" (1918) features another astute male protagonist, Hermann Samassa, who is overcome by the female vampire's insatiability. Samassa is engaged to Klara and employed at the court office of Doctor Herzfeld. Things are going well until a new typist is hired. Small with flowing blouse, waif-like

---

21   "halbverwischtes, kreideweißes, starres Gesicht" (261).

22   "Küsse meine Augen, meinen Mund, meine Stirn! Nimm mich hin!"

23   The student's experience is typical of the vampire story, encompassing extremes of feeling and deadly fear: "Da wieder die eiskalte Bleifaust auf meiner Brust, würgendes Herzklopfen, wilder Funkenwirbel vor den Augen, beklemmende Atemnot in den Lungenflügeln. Noch einmal Todesangst, noch einmal Digitalis, noch einmal Müdigkeit und so weiter" (Löns 265).

face, red hair, and green eyes, this petite woman is the picture of delicacy, while at the same time fomenting sexual unrest: she sends Samassa a note, arriving that night at his rental. Like the medic, Samassa feels a piercing in his chest and blood burst from his wound, thirstily siphoned off by the redhead (10–11).[24] As with the medic, Samassa is unable to extirpate the vampire, whose sexual voracity enfeebles the clerk, imperiling his future marriage and livelihood. In an attempt to save his life, Samassa offers a slew of surrogates to the vampire in order that she may suck their blood and spare his life; these victims include Klara, his fellow clerk, as well as various local prostitutes. In the end, Samassa attempts to kill the vampire, and, in so doing, kills himself; he inherits her poisonous blood, which commences his body's atrophy. Brittnacher reads the ending as a *Liebestod*, whereby Samassa now feels devoted to the vampire, bound by their common blood (178). This love, however, is straightforward sadomasochism: the vampire is the mortal mistress of her male counterpart. To this end, she constitutes a fictive analogue of the deplorable Hagedorn.

In Stein's narrative, we are privy to detailed descriptions of how the blood is drained from Samassa, which becomes a fount of the vampire's life-giving force. Sex and blood signal the loss of everything Samassa holds dear. Even the attractive and accomplished clerk is procured by the vampire, eventually getting overwhelmed by her poison. By contrast, the female vampire experiences no such constraints, whose flourishing is proportional to her victim's suffering. In a kind of corporeal self-actualization, her body blooms, according the approbation of Herzfeld, who is willing to keep his typist and fire his clerk if forced to choose. The female typist's indispensability and skill recalls Weimar's New Woman; she outclasses her male counterpart in the once-macho world of work, while also retaining her prowess in the bedroom. This vampire, delicate as well as debauched, extracts blood at night, without missing a day of work. Her kiss/bite bespeaks

---

24 "Sie hatte sein Hemd zurückgezogen und bog nun den Mund zu seiner Brust herab […] dann spürte er hörbar sein Blut der Bißstelle zuströmen, von den Lippen der Rothaarigen gierig schmatzend aufgesaugt" (10–11).

the demise of the male protagonist, who is drained of his vital powers; his masculinity hydraulically depleted as the vampire grows ever stronger.

Lest one should think these tales were the mainstay of male writers alone, Toni Schwabe's short story "Der Vampir" (1920) shares similar features to the portrayals previously discussed. The duplicitous but innocent lover, dead before her time, bonds with her male counterpart and drinks his blood. The unsuspecting male here inquires as to why she is always so cold. Like the others, he slowly loses interest in life, succumbing to nightly romps with the vampire. Again, her life force grows as his depletes. Schwabe's vampire also draws blood from the heart, bringing the male protagonist into the world of the undead (294).[25] Again, sleights of verisimilitude – in particular the childlike proportions and hallmarks of the vampire's body, which help to conceal its sexual potential – enable the vampire to hypnotize her prey and pierce his heart. Although the male protagonist initially invites his dead lover to come to him, she continues to enter his bedchamber uninvited, so strong is her power over him. This work may seem like an example of *Liebestod* were it not for the strong hold the vampire has over her victim. His blood siphoned off, he is left powerless (both physically and mentally) to act on his own volition. It is in this hypnotized state that the man leaves the world, but a shadow of his former self.

Woman's apparent desire to extract blood is further illustrated in 1920s psychological work. Psychiatrist Carl Jung's dream analysis, which involves a female "vampire," is documented in lecture notes given in November, 1928: Jung mentions a Swiss woman who came to him for treatment, relating a means that she used to fall asleep. Uncannily, she would repeat to herself that she was drinking the blood of Jesus, chanting "I am drinking the blood, drinking the blood of Jesus, the blood, the blood" (Jung 36). This same woman reported that when she fell down in her cellar, she repeated this chant so as to avoid injury (Ibid.). Thus, according to Jung, as

---

25   "Dann fühlte ich deine kühlen Lippen an meinem Herzen. Ein kleiner roter Springquell sprühte deinem Mund entgegen. So fand endlich mein Blut seinen Weg" (294).

well as Ellis and Krafft-Ebing, women believed blood to be the tonic of self-fortification.

By contrast with the foregoing depictions of the *female* bloodsucker, Hanns Heinz Ewers's *Vampyr* (1921) presents a vampiric *male*. He is not, however, empowered by this vampirism. On the contrary, through this he becomes the unlikely object of female bloodsucking.[26] The consummate explorer, Frank Braun, suspects his mistress, Lotte Levi, of cutting him with small surgical knives, which she keeps at her bedside. Additionally, wealthy and influential women of the moon society, as well as an Abbess, a Spanish dancer, an opera singer, and finally his young fiancée, want to have sexual relations with Frank, imbibing his vital powers. Indeed, while the last few pages of the narrative intimate to the reader that none of these women are themselves vampires (for it is Frank who has sucked their blood), the bulk of the story leads the reader to suspect the woman as vampire. The duplicity of the female characters is based on an appearance of monstrous sexuality, which cloaks an underlying innocence.

It is worth examining the power of the female characters in Ewers' novel. His mistress, Lotte, is characterized as dubious in her obsession with Frank. Not only does she appear to flourish when he is weak, her "Jewishness," and leanings toward the mystical, further frame her as suspect. Frank remembers a long rhyme of a Jewess, who hypnotizes a young man, takes his blood, and murders him: "She laid him on a dressing table/And stickit him like a swine" (335). The moon women – members of a secret cult – create similar

---

26 Ewers' novel *Vampyr* is the third in a trilogy, the second being another vampire narrative entitled *Alraune* (1911). Here, the beautiful boy-like Alraune, born from the semen of a hanged man incubated in the body of a prostitute, is death's daughter. Alternatively called "witch" and "creature," she is the child of the man-drake root, an old plant that gives both wealth and destruction to its possessors. Alraune brings wealth to her evil stepfather, while also causing his death, as well as the deaths of others who try to court her. Even her cousin Frank Braun cannot fight her hypnotic sexuality, drawing blood from his heart. It is only through the Christian servant's actions at the end (making the sign of the cross, praying to the saint, etc.) that she is destroyed. *Alraune* was made into two films during the Weimar period: Henrik Galeen's film of 1928, and Richard Oswald's 1930 version.

scenarios of entrapment, using hidden rooms in which to seduce their men. Frank's fiancée even produces the vampire's kiss on the consummation of their lovemaking, throwing herself on him and plunging her teeth into his neck: "Pain – pain. He screamed" (294). Frank mentions that women have always manipulated him like a puppet. For example, Lotte, an accomplished businesswoman, controls every aspect of Frank's public speaking career; his fiancée, through family connections, further influences the fate of his career and general livelihood.[27] These wealthy and talented women – whether vamps or female vampires – control the male figure wherever he goes: "He seemed to have no life of his own […] His reaction to her was feminine – she was the man not he" (327).

The novel's end is particularly disturbing, with Frank slicing Lotte up so gravely that she is unable to leave her bed ever again. However, it is still uncertain whether Frank is in control of the situation, for he continues to receive death threats of unknown origin, and though these may be politically motivated (recall that Frank is a German nationalist living in the U.S. during World War One), the only tangible threats in the novel originate from the women around him. For Frank, the blood he sees everywhere may be his own life force being drawn from his body. He is the stalking "man tiger" who, in turn, is torn up by the bull described in the narrative.[28] Ewers' bloody descriptions of animal abuse mirror Frank's own persecution at the hands of women. Finally, Frank's hallucinations and blackouts render him of unsound mind, and while he is in good health at the end, his strength will once again diminish thanks to his dealings with women.

27   The fiancée has U.S. and international connections, which protect Frank from legal repercussions (he is involved in treasonous actions against the U.S. on behalf of Germany, fomenting revolt in Mexico, and enabling Villa to invade Texas).
28   Ewers illustrates the gruesome death of animals in his novels: animals fight to the death against one another, and are speared, boiled, blinded, etc., by humans. These scenes are so sadistic that the reader has a difficult time persevering with the narrative.

The Female Vampire in Weimar Cinema

The female vampire, as found in the aforementioned literary works, also appears in several notable films of the period. For example, early Expressionist cinema lays bare the inner workings of the psyche to create a creative space for this monster to flourish. Dramatic elements of the *mise en scène* – including dramatic chiaroscuro, menacing stage sets, and claustrophobic domestic settings – evoke the character's inner turmoil, thereby creating a sense that the male character is trapped by his situation (Eisner, *The Haunted Screen* 177–206). This is particularly evident in Robert Wiene's *Genuine* (1920), an Expressionist work that creates a feeling of inner mayhem by utilizing surreal settings that evoke other-worldly sentiments.[29] The eponymous vampire, Genuine (Fern Andra), evokes death in the carnivalesque house of horrors, complete with a madness-evoking blue tint. Wiene spins a tale of a North African priestess who feasts on blood and finds herself transported to Ireland by Milo the explorer. Genuine's underground lair is a hothouse of exotic plants; the two-dimensional stage sets, which are persuasive purveyors of an uncanny and febrile atmosphere, are expressionistic in their nightmarish depiction of tropical flora and fauna. The priestess is hemmed in by the jungle atmosphere, complete with birds on which she feeds. Her costume consists of huge feather plumes, exotic jackets, and harem pants, which bespeak a seductive "Eastern" vibe. Unlike the vampires of fiction with their initially girlish appearances, this female vampire immediately presents herself as a lustful woman (see Figure 11). Carl Mayer's screenplay for *Genuine* provides a description of this supernatural woman: "She is the spirit of this thing, without home, without destiny, without meaning and her dark eyes suck out the secrets of the young man's soul, the will melts, only the whiff of this skin, the smell of these hands and the sweetness of this mouth" (qtd. in Kurtz 72).

---

29 I here invoke the Rohauer version of *Genuine*. Little has been published about this short film. For more information, see Jung and Schatzberg 78–85.

Figure 11. Hans Heinrich von Twardowski and Fern Andra in *Genuine*. Producer Erich Pommer; director Wiene, 1920. Source: DFF-Deutsches Filminstitut & Filmmuseum.

Genuine has furthermore brought harm to the community. We may infer that she has drawn blood from the barber's nephew, the explorer himself, as well as his grandson. The urn of blood that we see at the beginning of the film cannot be far away, as we observe Genuine giving commands to her black servant, "Kill him and bring me the proof." Her biting and kissing in the film are tantamount to an attack. Her actions have dire consequences for those around her, including the nephew, who, after being kissed by the vampire, lies prostrated and stupefied in the village. It is only when the community gets wind of strange happenings that they form a mob and attack the house. All of the occult symbols surrounding Genuine – the sun, moon, planets, strange monstrous creatures, and skeletons (as evident in the stage sets), as well as the magic ring that controls the servant – are designed to protect her power. Ultimately, however, they are of little help against the raging community. Her bird-like structure is invaded by the townspeople; her manservant is beaten to death. Finally, the nephew spills her blood in the hallway, an act of retribution for the blood she has extracted from others.

Like *Genuine*, Carl Theodor Dreyer's *Vampyr: Der Traum des Allan Gray* (1932) likewise features a duplicitous female vampire. A French-German production, this early sound film portrays a male protagonist, Allan Gray (Baron Nicolas de Gunzburg), who stumbles upon the village of Courtempierre, and is drawn into a web of intrigue.[30] According to David Bordwell and Mark Nash, this intrigue is sustained by a kind of cinematic vertigo, in which the viewer experiences the outcome of events and is only given signs of an overriding mood while remaining in the dark regarding the underlying causes of the plot's trajectory (Bordwell 93–109; Nash 41–42, 62–64). For example, the angel at the top of the inn and the man with the scythe are ominous symbols of death, functioning to dissociate elements without additional development. The director moreover uses a wandering camera, as in the opening sequence, that includes shots focusing on a rooftop, absent any obvious significance. As the film progresses, Gray's point of view constitutes the sole, stabilizing force; he is featured in nearly every frame, unifying the otherwise dissociated style (Nash 43). Indeed, it is Gray who moves the viewer through the various scenes: from inn, to factory, to manor house, and ultimately to the graveyard. Although Gray appears to lack agency, he is nonetheless both the fulcrum and impetus of the narrative. He functions to bring the viewer into the realm of the dead as he himself peers into an otherworldly realm, wherein he bears witness to his own impending burial as the vampire's ultimate victim.

Gray's sacrifice is, in fact, attributable to the actions of *two* vampires. His burial is meted out by the old vampiric crone, Marguerite Chopin (Henriette Gerard), who is assisted by her partner in crime, Léone (Sybille Schmitz). Gray must give blood to Léone, the young daughter of the

---

30   I refer here to the Criterion Collection 2008 release of the film. *Vampyr* had its premiere in Berlin in 1932, being poorly received by audiences and critics alike. Peirse notes that the film may be situated in the tradition of European art cinema, borrowing elements from German Expressionism, as well as the films of Eisenstein, Bauhaus, and Surrealism (162).

chatelain, in order to save her life. In a sequence taking place in a doctor's office, Gray achieves "undead" status as he finds a coffin with himself inside, creating three versions of Allan Gray: one is Gray's sleeping body; the second is Gray the adventurer; and the third is the dead man in the coffin. Léone, who has been bitten by Marguerite and acts in tandem with the old vampire to form an occult force, goes against Gray, as well as other members of the household, who find themselves caught up in her drama. The doubled vampire is in fact both "a beautiful, ageless woman and [...] an ancient, crumbling figure" (Creed 72). Her doubling provides assurance that the lineage of the undead remains unbroken, with members tied by "blood [...] cannibalism, death and desire" (Ibid. 72).[31] A general theme of the film is that the village's male members fare very poorly. The vampire's evil helpers, the doctor (Jan Hieronimko) and the corporal, meet with appalling deaths. Furthermore, the chatelain (Maurice Schutz) and the coachman die at the hands of the vampire. Indeed, while the evil Marguerite is herself staked at the end of the film, upon her death the men of the small village, excluding Gray and the houseman, are themselves apparently decimated.

It is helpful to consider Bordwell's division of this narrative into three parts. Part one is marked by the motif of *"giving an object in exchange for loyalty"*; part two by *"bleeding"*; and part three by *"burial"* (110–11). In part two, the character of Léone expresses vampiric lust. After Gray witnesses the murder of chatelain, he enters the house to find the young and beautiful Léone sick in bed. One can see her face above the bed covering – her round head and expressive eyes offer a sensual come-hither glance even in her infirmity. Gray must subsequently hunt Léone down on the grounds outside, as she liaises with Marguerite. In their embrace, which resembles the Pietà, the older female vampire Marguerite joins with the younger Léone, strengthening the latter's relation to her undead status, as well evincing lesbian desire. Léone, with the help of the doctor, facilitates a blood transfusion, draining Gray of his life force. Additionally, she disables Gray

---

31   Nash notes that Gray's role as hero has been usurped by the houseman, who reads the book of the vampires, thereafter staking Marguerite through the heart. Here, Gray is relegated to an "auxiliary role" (53). His inability to influence events throughout the film – especially after Léone gazes at him as he gives blood – evidences his character's emasculation.

by gazing at him (Peirse 165).[32] Following the procedure, Gray waits outside the sickroom, imagining his blood escaping profusely. Gray further witnesses Marguerite enter as a skeleton, bringing Léone the poison for suicide, which would assure the younger's status as a fully fledged vampire. Dreyer and Christen Jul's screenplay expands this dream-like sequence, revealing how Marguerite feeds on Gray, while at the same time Léone is fortified by Gray's blood:

> Now the shape leans over him. The skull comes closer and closer. He thinks it's searching for his mouth, but it leans even lower and seems to want to stop at his throat [...] He feels the soft touch of the skull's mouth brushing against the sensitive skin of his throat. During everything that has just happened, the look of horror has slowly disappeared [...] He now closes his eyes in ecstasy. (67)

Here, the mention of the soft touch as a source of ecstasy would more likely be linked to the soft *femme fatale* Léone, who receives his blood, than the bony skeleton attending him.[33] The symbiotic relationship between the vampire double – the pairing of Léone and Marguerite – here work in tandem to strip Gray of his blood, which he can feel gushing out of him. Again, the screenplay describes this sensation: "The sound of dripping comes from somewhere [...] blood running from his wound down onto his fingers and thence to the floor, where a regular pool has already formed" (64). Gray has both given blood and is yet still *losing* blood. The diabolical doctor in charge of the medical procedure expedites Gray's enervation, feeding both the young and old vampire. It is in this weakened state that Gray escapes the house to witness his own burial.

To shed light on the situation at Courtempierre, Gray consults the *Strange Tale of the Vampires*. Therein he learns that the female vampire transmits her undead status by endowing her victim with her own bloodlust. The vampires have temporarily drained Gray of his life force, essentially trifurcating him into living, dead, and undead, thereby ushering in the third section of Bordwell's thesis. When Gray collapses in the field outside, his translucent double departs his body, traveling toward the doctor's office.

32   Peirse believes that the doctor intends to give the blood transfusion to Chopin (165).

33   The film, draped in a "blanket of whiteness" (Peirce 169) owing to lighting techniques, may also signify the taking of blood.

Gray's undead status gives him the power to look into his own death and burial as an occult vision, while at the same time being unable to halt or intervene in the nightmarish proceedings. The doctor and corporal prepare Gray's coffin for burial, screwing nails into the wood to secure the cover. The camera takes the audience into the enclosed box to observe Gray's face (see Figure 12), whereby we are offered a glimpse of his corpse. More horrifying than this vision, however, is the view from the coffin's small window: as Gray – along with the audience – look through the window, we are confronted with Marguerite, the vampire, who steals a final glimpse of her victim. Gray has not only had his blood leached from him: the vampire has moreover entombed him. The subsequent POV shots – framed from below, looking upwards, as the coffin is carried away – feature a vertiginous vision of the ceiling of the factory, then of the cathedral en route to the cemetery. The sky is framed by the stone building, foreshadowing the steely gray of the gravestones. What enables Gray to escape the vision and become whole again is the houseman's intention of staking Marguerite in her grave.

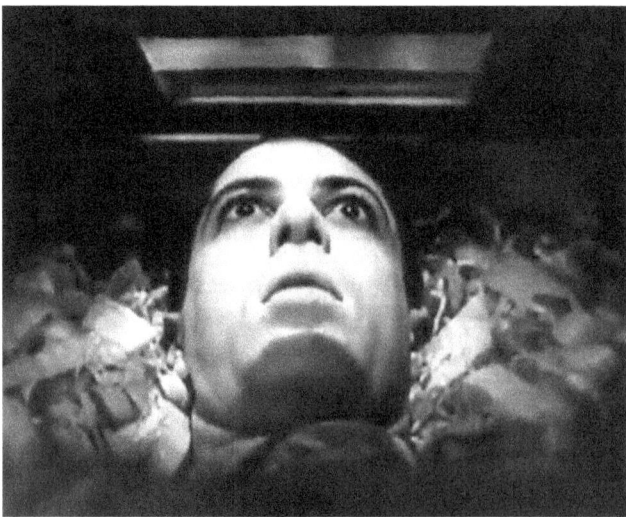

Figure 12. *Vampyr.* Scene from *Vampyr.* Producer Carl Theodor Dreyer; director Dreyer, 1932.

Following the violence of the mock burial, Gray is able to free Léone's sister, Gisèle (Rena Mandel), from her captivity in the doctor's office, thereby enabling their retreat. Gray and Gisèle, the good sister, have escaped in a rowing boat, while the older vampire and her younger counterpart have been violently stripped of their undead status. Ultimately, Léone is brought back to life, unlike her counterpart Marguerite. She is said to be pure again. Still, her tainted blood has rendered her an unfit partner for Gray. Léone's extreme sexuality compares unfavorably to Gisèle's innocence. Ultimately bedridden, Léone remains unchanged from her position at the beginning of the film; in her sheer nightgown, donning unkempt hair, she persists in a state of lovelorn longing.

As in other tales of this genre, the vampire is duplicitous in nature, presenting as an innocent while at the same time posing a threat. In the case of *Vampyr*, Léone has supposedly been freed from her undead status thanks to the death of her mistress. However, we have reason to suspect that she is not fully cured. In fact, the narrative discontinuities in Dreyer's film – the wandering camera, the unmotivated character development, and the effect without cause – all point to a film with an uncertain outcome. Bordwell states that the end of the film is problematic: "The enigma of the absent cause is reiterated, not dispelled, at the very end" (116).[34] We are left with the final shot of the mill machinery grinding to a halt, absent an operator.[35] We are therefore led to believe that occult forces are still at play in the village; it must not be discounted that Léone, the female vampire, has the power to act. She has not been staked, and may have enough of the undead left in her to begin where her mentor Marguerite left off. Léone's persistent demands for blood may yet ring out in the village. Gray himself

---

34 Nash, by contrast, thinks that the ending provides closure, remarking upon its "smoothness" and "spatio-temporal continuity" (43).

35 Bordwell suggests that the machinery is stopped by the chatelain, who has supposedly returned from the dead in the latter part of the film – his large head has appeared in the doctor's office, causing the doctor to flee and the corporal to fall on the stairs: "the father becomes the new 'living dead' of the film" (116). There is, however, no evidence to suggest that the chatelain is responsible for the doctor's death, for the houseman is the one who starts the mill's machinery and is then seen walking away at the end.

has been divested of his blood by this young, sensual vampire. In the end, he should be wary of Gisèle, who has been exposed to her sister Léone and potentially to the vampire's plague.

Woman as Monster: Weimar Fantastic Films

The female vampire constitutes a form of the "monstrous feminine," especially reflecting men's fears about women's sexuality (Creed 5, 7). The dual-aspect enchantress found in *Vampyr* (i.e., the pairing of Léone and Marguerite), creates a monstrous double, who are set on robbing Gray of his blood. Patrice Petro and Linda Williams have posited that the monster figure in early fantastic films is a version of the vampire, standing as a proxy for the minacity of female sexuality.[36] Being a symbol of displaced female sexuality, the monster has the power to disclose suppressed male fantasies, while also brandishing the ability to both annihilate and castrate; like the female vampire, the dual-aspect monster-woman has the power to kill. Petro suggests that, during the Weimar years, the trope of "male subjectivity in crisis" was symptomatic of the period's "apocalyptic vision" of female sexuality (Petro 207). Williams equates the freakishness of the monster with the notion of woman's sexual difference.[37] Stephen Neale moreover understands the concept of monstrousness as revolving around the construction of masculinity and femininity:

> [the monster's] otherness can therefore be conceived [...] as mixing [masculinity and femininity] dangerously together [...] it functions so as to disturb the boundaries of sexual identity and difference [...] it could well be maintained that it is women's sexuality [...] which constitutes the real problem that the horror cinema exists to explore, and which constitutes also and ultimately that which is really monstrous. (Neale 60–61)

36   See Petro 205–17; Williams 83–99; and Eisner 109–13 for an examination of "the double" in Weimar film.

37   Williams states: "There is not much difference between an object of desire and an object of horror as far as the male look is concerned" (88).

In the above set of critiques, the monster figure stands in for woman, representing thereby an extreme form of female sexuality. An interesting twist on this formulation can be seen in Neale's claim that the monster is both a symbol of female sexuality while also constituting a dangerous mix of masculinity and femininity. Attesting to fears about woman's "double morality," as well as her double identity as *Mannesweib*, include those Weimar notions of the masculine woman, the essential duplicity of modern woman in the male world of work, woman's alleged object-ification within the heterosexual romantic relationship, and woman as slave to the coat-dress. Depictions of the masculinized woman by the press ranged from favorably cynical to downright enraged. Indeed, one scoffing fashion editor for the women's magazine *Die Dame* maintains that the masculinization of women's fashion constitutes an inherently *parodic* strategy on the part of women:

> The woman is once again proving her royal capriciousness […] She is obsessed with the outward signs of masculinity – she wants the man's stiff collar, his coat, his cane, his waistcoat. Yes, even his holiest possession, the cylinder hat […] In epochs when the man is very masculine […] he wears his clothing broadly […] Today, however, the man is neither strong nor weak but too realistic, too neuter; he has "no time" for his soul and for his wife. For this reason, the suffering woman responds ironically to this neutered being by parodying his masculinity; she makes fun of these men whenever she is among those who are like her. (Daniel 997–98)

In this passage, woman's masculinization is deconstructed into a kind of masquerade performed and staged by women.[38] This masculinized woman, who wears her unequivocal androgyny as a façade, is further underscored by Joan Riviere, a Weimar psychoanalyst. Riviere turns the tables in claiming that femininity is a masquerade deployed to defuse male anxiety surrounding the masculine woman. Weimar images of androgyny could also be seen as a reflection of burgeoning lesbian communities, which flourished in urban areas throughout Germany. Images of androgyny, which lend to both lesbian and bisexual interpretations,

---

38 See Riviere 35–44. Daniel, Riviere, and the masculinization of woman are discussed in detail in Petro 1989 (79–140).

could therefore signal the lesbian sub-culture's acceptance, thereby providing an underclass with a sense of identity and belonging.[39]

Weimar discussions about the masculinization of women included
debates regarding the roles of actors, such as the film star Asta Nielsen.
Nielsen's widespread popularity – as reflected in the Weimar illustrated
press and especially in women's magazines such as *Die Dame* – reveals an
admiration for her androgynous film roles. For example, in the 1921 film
version of *Hamlet*, her playing of the titular character exploited her androgyny to help portray a prince defending the honor of his father. While
Nielsen's Hamlet must commit acts of bravery and disclose treachery,
Hamlet's strength and wit is ultimately rewarded with his death. Nielsen, in
a highly unconventional trouser role, blurs gender categories and unmasks
a potentially liberating reading of sexual difference as a socially constructed
artifice.[40] The underlying meaning of this portrayal to the Weimar public
(both male and female) is that the blurring of masculinity and femininity must end with the destruction of the androgynous woman. Many of
Nielsen's other roles as the "masculine" woman attest to the above notion,
namely the fate of the prostitute Auguste in *Dirnentragödie* (*Tragedy of
the Street*, 1927). The death of the Lulu figure (played by Louise Brooks) in
Die Büchse der Pandora (*Pandora's Box*, 1929) further illustrates the fate
of the androgynous character.[41] For, her veiled bisexuality, as implied by

---

39   See Lavin 1990 (63–86). Lavin states that the androgynous image could also
      signal cooptation and/or dismissal: "by obeying the injunction to speak about
      sexuality, to represent and explore it constantly, the speaker participates in the
      promotion of sexuality; this, in turn, contributes to the self-image of the bour-
      geoisie as all-powerful, life-enhancing, body-intensified, expanding, and eternal"
      (75). For an excellent discussion on gay and lesbian life in Weimar Germany, see
      *Eldorado: Homosexuelle Frauen und Männer in Berlin 1850–1950 – Geschichte,
      Alltag und Kultur*, ed. Berlin Museum (Berlin: Fröhlich & Kaufmann, 1984).

40   For more information on Weimar's female stars and divas, note Paul Werner, 1990
      and Hanna Vollmer-Heitmann, *Wir sind von Kopf bis Fuß auf Liebe eingestellt: Die
      Zwanziger Jahre* (Hamburg: Ernst Kabel Verlag, 1993), 103–42. For an in-depth
      discussion of cross-dressing films, see Annette Kuhn (1985) 48–74.

41   In an analysis of Weimar films such as Robert Wiene's *Das Cabinet des Dr. Caligari*
      (1920) and F. W. Murnau's *Nosferatu* (1922), the affinity between the monster and
      the woman presents a female sexuality that is out-of-control. The monster figure

Lulu's relation to Dr. Schön and Alwa, while also bespoken by the sexual tension between Lulu and Countess Geschwitz, wins her a fateful date with Jack-the-Ripper.[42]

Das Cabinet des Dr. Caligari, co-written by Hans Janowitz and Carl Mayer, was, from the outset, a revolutionary film. Mayer and Janowitz, both embittered by their wartime experiences wrote an unusual story about a strange doctor and his somnambulist. The story, accepted by Erich Pommer, was eventually made into the film directed by Robert Wiene. In Wiene's film, the "mad" Dr. Caligari (Werner Krauß) and his somnambulist, Cesare (Conrad Veidt), open a booth at a town fair. After meeting with Caligari, a town official and a young student are both murdered by Cesare at the order of Caligari. As Cesare dies in pursuit of his third victim, Jane (Lil Dagover), Caligari, who is being hounded by the police, takes refuge at the local mental asylum. Finally, the framing of the film reveals that Caligari is actually a benign doctor at the institute, caring for the deluded narrator Francis who has invented the whole story.

This odd scenario comes alive on-screen with settings designed by three German Expressionist artists: Hermann Warm; Walter Röhrig; and Walter Reimann. Their canvases, which become settings for the film, are "jagged, sharp-pointed forms strongly reminiscent of gothic patterns" (Kracauer, *From Caligari to Hitler* 69).[43] With slanted chimneys and roofs, and zigzagging streets, the city of *Caligari* represents a transformation of material objects in "emotional ornaments" (Ibid.).[44] Wiene's use of distorted colors,

---

in these two films also betrays a certain androgyny, recalling the Weimar debate on the masculinization of woman and the notion of bisexuality.

42   Note that Louise Brooks's character of Marie in *Das Tagebuch einer Verlorenen* (Diary of a Lost Girl, 1929) does meet a happy ending, however artificial it may seem.

43   For a discussion of Caligari as authoritarian figure, see Kracauer, *From Caligari to Hitler* 61–76.

44   While pre-1918 German Expressionism stressed the metaphysical and aesthetic needs of the individual, prescinding from specific political issues, Expressionist ideas after the War concentrated on political change. The death of German Expression was facilitated by the failure of the German revolution, and a turn from optimism to pessimism took place. With the demise of Expressionism proper came a wave of popularity surrounding broadly "expressionist" tendencies.

lighting, and camera angles, together with the Expressionist sets, creates a sufficiently disharmonious viewpoint of reality, a mood that Thomas Elsaesser relates as a space of excess and intensity (19).[45]

The incipit of *Caligari* bears witness to a scene of entropic excess, replete with two-dimensional, Expressionist clutter. The traveling fair that arrives in town prompts a carnivalesque atmosphere in which all previously accepted social norms are inverted, with chaos ensuing. The fairground heaves with throngs of people: the organ grinder, the merry-go-round, and myriad side-shows all connote a turn toward transgression and a diabolical *détente*. It is in this setting that the mountebank Caligari comes to town with his own peculiar spectacle: the somnambulist Cesare. The monstrous figure of Cesare sleeps by day and kills by night. As advertised in the side-show's rhetoric, Cesare has slept for twenty-five years. His waking moments project doom and destruction for those who dare exchange gazes with him. Moreover, it is to Cesare's relationship with Jane – the film's lone female protagonist – that the town's eventual downfall can be adduced.

It is first and foremost the connection between Jane and Cesare that begets the hypnotic hold over the male protagonist, Alan (Hans Heinrich von Twardowski). Alan's brush with Cesare during a sideshow performance – in particular the seductive gazes exchanged between himself and Cesare – locks him into a terrible doom of prophesy.[46] His hypnotic link with Cesare represents an exchange of desire, whereby Cesare as prophet (or bearer of "forbidden knowledge") is portrayed as a tempting seductress.

As seen in *Caligari*, the representation of inner reality was a concept embraced by publishing houses and film production companies alike. For an analysis of *Caligari* as an Expressionist film, see Eisner, *The Haunted Screen* 17–27.

45   Elsaesser (19) believes that an analysis of Weimar fantastic film must explore points of contact "where there is evidence that the text has seized, worked over, displaced or objectified elements of the historical or the social sphere in order to bring them to representation within the text's own formal or generic constraints." This certainly suits a reading designed to uncover elements of a "fearful" female sexuality. For a collection of excellent essays on *Caligari*, including the aforementioned Elsaesser piece (as well as Petro's article on the monster and the woman), see Budd (ed.) 1990.

46   Cesare states: "The time is short – you die at dawn." Alan is then found murdered in his home the following morning.

Taking account of Linda Williams's idea that the monster's power over the male consists in its sexual difference, the monster as a *reflection* of female sexuality awakens the male's repressed desire.

The figure of Jane – the chaste daughter of the town doctor – marks the conspicuous object of Alan's desires. Both Alan and his friend Francis (Friedrich Fehér) declare their love for Jane, each hoping to win Jane's heart with an attempt at honorable courtship. It is Alan, however, who transgresses these upright intentions, replacing Jane as the object of the gaze with Cesare. Cesare, acting as Jane's surrogate, provides the opportunity for Alan to vent his repressed sexuality. Together, Jane and Cesare release a dangerous female sexuality into the community, which claims several victims (among them, Alan), before its containment through the death of the monster.

While the sexual allure of the Cesare-Jane double is responsible for young Alan's death, the visual exchange between Cesare and Jane in the carnival tent underscores the relationship between the monster and the woman.[47] When Jane goes to the fair in search of her father, she encounters Caligari's tent where she too gazes upon the image of Cesare. As Jane meets Cesare's eyes in his box, there is a moment of horrified *anagnorisis* before Jane flees the scene. Their shared likeness is underscored by the juxtaposition of Jane to a life-size poster of Cesare moments before Jane enters Caligari's tent. Similarities in appearance also link the two characters: both Jane and Cesare have heavily made-up faces, bearing pronounced facial features, with an emphasis on the eyes, eyebrows, and lips (see Figure 13). Presented here is a monster with strikingly androgynous features.[48] Cesare shares much of Jane's feminine physiognomy, as well as feminine gestures and slight stature, which cannot be attributed to a traditionally masculine look. In

---

47 For a discussion of this scene, see Petro, "The Woman" 210–25.

48 Catherine Clément in her article, "Charlatans and Hysterics" looks at the allegory of seduction and hysteria (father and daughter) in *Caligari*. There, she notes the androgynous features of Cesare, reading the somnambulist as a double for the female hysteric: "The male somnambulist, almost androgynous in Caligari's manipulations, is the equivalent of the female hysteric: they exchange the same look, a pure stare, detached from its object, the space where desire passes, an obscure desire" 197–98. See Clément (1990) 197–98.

turn, Cesare possesses masculine characteristics, namely by being called Cesare, and for clearly bearing male sex organs, which, albeit clothed, are evident in silhouette.[49]

Figure 13. *Das Cabinet des Dr. Caligari*. From left to right: Werner Krauss, Conrad Veidt, and Lil Dagover. Producer Erich Pommer; director Wiene, 1920. Source: DFF-Deutsches Filminstitut & Filmmuseum.

The relationship between the monster and woman in their exchange of the gaze is an important one. The monster as a distorted reflection of the woman's own image is "a particularly insidious form of the many mirrors patriarchal structures of seeing hold up to the woman" (Williams 88). Through the relationship of Jane and Cesare, two kinds of Weimar femininity are contraposed and conflated: the typically feminine image of woman (asexual and motherly) in Jane, and the androgyny of Cesare, recalling the greatly defiled repute of the masculine woman.[50] Bearing

49   Cesare wears tight leggings that unequivocally reveal his male sex.
50   Jane (played by Lil Dagover) is the visual epitome of pre-Raphaelite woman, complete with long, flowing hair. She plays the concerned mother figure to Francis

attributes of both masculinity and femininity, Cesare's character stands as a catch-all for dangerous female sexuality; one that is capable of death and destruction when unleashed onto the community. While bearing both masculine and feminine traits – deemed so dangerous in Stephen Neale's assessment of the monster – it is the feminine element that betrays mortal capabilities, tempting out clandestine male sexual desire and using this weakness to catch the male in a Medusa's gaze.[51]

The symbiotic relationship between Jane and Cesare is further determined by Cesare's contact with Jane after Alan's death. Instead of killing Jane (per Caligari's orders), Cesare and Jane form a complementary union: the monster dressed in black; the woman in white. As Cesare lifts Jane out of her bed, carrying her off, both monster and woman seem bound together in a flight from destruction. On the run for reasons of seduction and murder, it is predictable that this union has no real prospect of survival. In the end, Cesare is hunted down by the townspeople, and Jane is returned to the care of her father. While Francis continues to seek out Alan's murderer, it is apparent that the real danger has already been extinguished. The dummy in the cabinet ensures that Cesare enjoys no second awakening.

Ultimately, the mysterious Other who is capable of returning the gaze (Cesare) must be contained in order to ensure the stability of the patriarchal system. What makes *Caligari* a particularly interesting attempt at controlling female sexuality is the framing device found at the beginning and end of the film. In *Caligari*, this is designed to give the impression that a threatening female identity never was. The frame insinuates that the narrator, Francis, is a member of a mental institution. Francis' story, enumerating a series of murders committed in a small town, is determined in the end to be a hysterical delusion. Symbolizing the authority of medicine and the law, a benign Dr. Caligari provides the reassurance that the

---

when Alan is killed. Cesare (Conrad Veidt) is extremely slight in stature, moving on-screen with expressive, "feminine" movements. In the night scene, in which Cesare goes to Jane's bedroom, he glides along the walls with nigh-on balletic elegance. When Cesare enters Jane's bedroom, the viewer almost believes she is capturing a glimpse of actor Asta Nielsen. Indeed, Cesare's "page-boy" hairstyle and chiseled cheek bones recall Nielsen in her role as Hamlet.

51 See Linda Williams (93–94) for a discussion of woman as both victim and monster in *Psycho*, *Peeping Tom*, and *Dressed to Kill*.

evil presence of the somnambulist and his master never really existed. The combination of Cesare and Jane as a dangerous, castrating force is reduced to two harmless mental patients walking around the grounds of Caligari's institute. The only indication in the film that contradicts this reading is the presence of the disturbing Expressionist set within the frame. While the frame's narrative speaks of law, order, and the containment of deviant mental patients, the Expressionist mise en scène reveals continued confusion and excess, marking the continuation of a dangerous female sexuality that lurks just below the surface. On the final analysis, the monster Cesare is not dead, for there is still "something frightful in our midst."[52]

The threat of a female sexuality represented by the woman-monster combo is a common trope of many Expressionist films from early Weimar cinema. F. W. Murnau's *Nosferatu* (1922) is an important example of the link between woman and monster as the sinister Other. This rendition of Bram Stoker's *Dracula* begins in Bremen, where real-estate agent Jonathan (Gustav von Wangenheim) is sent away from his wife Nina (Greta Schröder) to attend to business in the Carpathian Mountains. Upon his arrival, Jonathan is forced to travel through a terrain "macabre with mists, shying horses, wolves and eerie birds" (Kracauer, *From Caligari to Hitler* 77). At his host's castle, Jonathan discovers that his client, Count Orlok (Max Schreck), is the vampire Nosferatu. Jonathan only escapes the monster with the telepathic intervention of his loving wife, Nina. Intrigued by Nina, Nosferatu leaves his castle and sails to Bremen on his ship of horrors, bringing with him a plague of rats and pestilence to the unsuspecting community. Ultimately, Nosferatu finds Nina, although it is Nina's self-sacrifice that signals Nosferatu's demise.

Elements of excess in Murnau's film are consistent with the Expressionist idea of the dominance of an inner reality.[53] The feeling of a trance or dream-like state permeates *Nosferatu*, a film in which "a tangible person might suddenly impress the audience as a mere apparition" (Kracauer, *From Caligari*

---

52   The aforementioned quotation occurs in *Caligari* before Alan is attacked by Cesare.

53   See Eisner, *Haunted Screen* 97–106 for a discussion of *Nosferatu* as an Expressionist film. Note also Kracauer's *From Caligari to Hitler* for a discussion of *Nosferatu* 77–79. For more information on Murnau (*qua* director and about the technical aspects of his films), see Eisner 1973.

to Hitler 78).[54] While Murnau used negative film to create the Wooded Carpathians (viz. through a black sky foregrounded by white trees), special filmic techniques were also developed to allow Jonathan's coach to move through the woods with ghoulish swiftness.[55] Just as the settings in *Caligari* take on an unreal Gothic quality, Nosferatu's castle constitutes the ultimate piece of Gothic architecture, its winding hallways and dark rooms being similar to the vampire's labyrinthian sailing ship.

The vampiric Nosferatu, characterized by Expressionist surfeit and entropy, is the very embodiment of desire. Indeed, like *Caligari*'s Cesare, the monster bespeaks a foreboding female sexuality. The wholesome and chaste beginnings of desire, depicted in Jonathan and Nina's affection for one another at the film's outset, are manifested in the vampire figure. As Jonathan arrives at Nosferatu's castle, the vampire locks him in a dangerous gaze, inviting him to pass the remaining hours of the evening in his company. When Jonathan awakens the next morning, the mark of the vampire eerily adorns his neck. The vampire's need for blood, viz. the monster's enactment of sexual desire (what Linda Williams reads as "milking sperm during intercourse"), is unleashed not merely by Jonathan's presence on the second evening, but by the locket's picture of Nina (Williams 89). As Nosferatu catches his first glimpse of the chaste and lovely Nina, the symbolic exchange between the two brings Jonathan into eminent danger. Jonathan's affection for his wife Nina, as disclosed at the film's incipit, is embodied in Jonathan's visual exchange with Nosferatu. As Jonathan tries to escape the vampire in his bedroom, the monster follows. Framed ominously in the bedroom doorway, moving in a stream of light, Nosferatu overcomes Jonathan, substantiating the dangers involved in desiring the Other.

Nosferatu and Nina together form the object of Jonathan's desire. However, it is only through Nosferatu that this desire can be expressed – and at a dangerous price. While Nina, acting in a somnambulist dream, manages to force the vampire to retreat from Jonathan's bedroom, their mental contact has forged a symbiotic link that enables Nosferatu to leave his contained environment and travel to the bourgeois haven of Bremen.

54   The complete title of Murnau's film reads *Nosferatu, a Symphony of Horror*. This underscores the film's supernatural element.

55   Further note the stop-motion technique used to render the fearful rapidity of the coffins being piled on top of one another at Nosferatu's castle.

He brings the plague with him – the "undeadness of desire" – that thereafter imperils the community (Elsaesser 25).

In tandem with Nina, who waits for the vampire to arrive in his ship, Nosferatu *qua* scourge must be wiped out if the city of Bremen is to live in peace. Like *Caligari*, the monster must be annihilated, and the woman freed from her relationship thereto, in order to reestablish order in the community. In Murnau's film, it is Nina herself who carries this action out. Nina facilitates the monster's gaze by opening her window and inviting Nosferatu to enter her bedroom. While the "Book of the Vampires" notes that a woman pure of heart can break the vampire's spell by giving herself freely until the "cock crows," Nina's embrace and visual exchange with Nosferatu enjoins them, foregrounding an insatiable desire – the chaste Nina is no more. At dawn, the vampire disappears in a puff of smoke, but Nina is also to die (see Figure 14). There is no chance to reinsert Nina back into the bourgeois family atmosphere, for she has crossed the bounds of what is good and proper. All the same, she has also spared the community further contact with the scourge.

Figure 14. Max Schreck in *Nosferatu*. Producer Albin Grau; director F. W. Murnau, 1921.

In *Nosferatu*, the monster and the woman form a symbiotic relationship marked by their interlocking bodies, the vampire performing the bite of the undead. Nosferatu's body melds with Nina's, the ensuing union presenting an act of sameness and difference. While Nina has many of same characteristics and dress as Jane in *Caligari* (traditionally feminine and motherly), she is also related to the androgynous Nosferatu in their common connection to the feminine.[56] Slim with overdrawn facial features and long frock coat, the vampire has traditional feminine features, underscoring this creature's relation to the feminine in Nina.

According to Weimar social constructivism, the "perverse" female sexuality of the masculine woman (as evidenced in the androgynous monster figure) was not deemed to be a disease of a few, but the malady of an age. All working women and modern women alike had the capacity to unleash unnatural female sexual desire that would threaten German society. Weimar novelist, and leading figure in the German women's movement, Gertrud Bäumer, saw this threat to be a crisis for civilization. In her work *Die Frau in der Krisis der Kultur* (*The Woman in the Crisis of Culture*, 1926), Bäumer maintains that the new tempo of modern society forced women to live out their sexual urges at the price of motherhood, thereby at *society*'s expense:

> Aus diesem verhangnisvollen Irrtum droht gerade den Frauen grobe Gefahr. Der Man kann-vielleicht – ohne dauernde Zerstörung seiner Persönlichkeit in den Fluten seines allzumenschlichen Leben zeitweise versinken […] das kann die Frau seltener […] Gewiß, es gibt heute Frauen genug, die das ungebundene Liebesleben des Mannes führen […] es mag glückgefüllte Stunden, es mag lebendige Wochen und vielleicht sogar Monate schenken. Aber das alles ist nur um den Preis einer Verflachung und Vergröberung zu gewinnen […] aus dem heiligen Kreislauf der Natur gelöst, wird unfruchtbar und gewöhlich. (Bäumer 13)[57]

56 Both Nina and Nosferatu are dressed in black. The monster and woman in *Nosferatu* are furthermore related to nature: Nina, in the film's opening scenes, is framed by nature (e.g., the window-box full of flowers), scolding Jonathan for cutting the flowers from the garden. Nosferatu's relationship with nature is evidenced in his power over animals.

57 Bäumer also sees danger in the workplace: "Die sexuelle Krisis ist für die Mädchen in gewissem Maße zugleich Konsequenz und Auswirkung der Berufskrisis. In dem Maße als der Beruf ihnen unergiebig erscheint, richtet sich der Lebensdurst auf die andere Seite ihres Frauenlebens" 25.

> This fatal mistake threatens women in particular. The man can perhaps sink temporarily into an all too human life without destroying his personality […] a woman can do that less often […] Certainly there are enough women today who live the unbounded love life of a man […] it may bring happy hours, lively weeks or even months. But all this is only at the price of flattening and coarsening […] released from the sacred cycle of nature, woman becomes sterile.

Gertrud Bäumer, as well as other Weimar critics commenting on woman's move into the male sphere, bemoans the risk of society's growing banality, as a result of woman's relation to "free love" (Ibid. 22, 25). Not only does the New Woman fail to find "true form" for herself – trapped between masculine and feminine realms – by refusing to assume a traditionally feminine position (mother, wife), she supposedly robs society of the "deeper meaning of life" (Ibid. 28, 33). Thus, the *Neue Frau*'s much-maligned, androgynous image is extremely telling about the ways in which Weimar Germany perceived and interpreted woman's alleged duplicity, bespeaking aspects of both the masculine and feminine.

Conclusion

Depictions of female vampires in psychological, criminal, and fictional works of the Weimar period exhibit an insatiable desire resulting in suffering and death. The occult themes depicted in *Genuine* and *Vampyr* are in keeping with early Weimar fiction, including renderings of death and the Apocalypse. Indeed, just as we are challenged to question the outcome in Weimar films such as *Caligari* (we may ask, "is the respected scientist *himself* a madman?"), we must also believe that the filmic female vampires, Genuine and Léone, have the ability to rise again and terrorize the men around them. Reflecting the threat posed by Weimar's New Woman to traditionally masculine roles, the monster-woman double also acts as a predator of men. To this end, the monster is a cipher for female sexuality that is unleashed onto the community. Thus, *Caligari* and *Nosferatu* illustrate how the monster and woman work in tandem to commit murder and mayhem.

These occult beings – vampire and monster-double – are not infrequent in Weimar culture. For instance, in the Messalina story, "Die Männerfresserin," appearing in the journal *Berliner Leben* (1924), a "ghost of the dead" seduces an unsuspecting man in her grotto, disappearing completely the following day (Figdor 26–27). It is a commonplace of mythology that one must stake the female vampire and behead her in order to expunge the community of her undead status. As the poem suggests, however, this monster is often elusive; withdrawing without notice. The Weimar woman is likewise duplicitous in her presentation, for she exhibits both feminine and masculine traits. Her proper burial is only assured through the emergence of right-wing political factions, which secured the demise of the bifurcated woman, leaving only the wife and mother alive to see the light of day.

CHAPTER 3

The Witch and the Gypsy

The woman who is capable of devastating man with her sexual wiles –
otherwise known as the *femme fatale* and as emblematized in the foregoing exposition of the female vampire and monster – symptomizes
male fears regarding the power of women in a moment of historical
crisis (Doane 2–3). As the Weimar physician Ernst Simmel notes, the
World War One not only made cannon fodder out of its conscripts, it
became the root of a "difficult conflict in which the personality finds
itself confronted with a world changed by the war" (Ibid. 7). In response
to the crisis, Weimar constructions of sexually liberated, occult women
served as convenient mirrors for the fears and anxieties engendered by
disturbing historical developments.

This chapter will analyze the respective figures of the witch and the
gypsy across various Weimar cultural works. Through these guises we
find exemplified yet another intimidating and reviled female character,
who poses a threat to male subjectivity and the social order more broadly.
Numerous depictions present the witch as a sexual temptress: one who
not only exerts her will by concocting various potions, but wields powers
of metamorphosis and transmogrification, deftly taking the form of a
multiplicity of beasts in order to expedite her evil intentions. Barbara
Becker-Cantarino provides a valuable account of the malevolent activities
commonly attributed to witches throughout history: "causing an illness,
causing a person or animal to die; causing a bad harvest or some other (natural) disaster by casting evil charms or spells; acquiring magical powers
through potion [...] and always: having sexual relations with the devil" (2).
In what follows, I shall analyze depictions of witches drawn from various
cultural works of the period. These include Mary Wigman's dance performances, several literary works including *Die Hexe Lil* (*The Witch Lil*, 1921),

Bilda, die Hexe (*Bilda, the Witch*, 1921), and "Meine Mutter, die Hex" (*My Mother, the Witch*, 1922), and finally Leni Riefenstahl's *Das Blaue Licht* (*The Blue Light*, 1932). Additionally, I will analyze certain criminal trials from the period, specifically the poisoning cases involving Klein/Nebbe and Vukobrankovic.

The female "gypsy" was likewise perceived in Weimar culture as capable of tapping into both the forces of nature and necromancy in order to overwhelm her sexual subjects.[1] In particular, I analyze literary depictions of the gypsy woman as sexual temptress, including Wilhelm Lehmann's *Die Schmetterlingspuppe* (*The Butterfly Pupa*, 1918) and Agnes Miegel's *Der Gaukler* (*The Juggler*, 1920). The preternatural powers ascribed to these gypsy women are further reflected in works that will be examined. These include Werner Bergengruen's *Die Zigeuner und das Wiesel* (*The Gypsies and the Weasel*, 1927) and A. Rosalie's *Rache einer Zigeunerin* (*The Female Gypsy's Revenge*, 1928). Finally, I discuss notable filmic depictions of gypsies from the Weimar period, not least Ernst Lubitsch's *Carmen* (*Gypsy Blood*, 1918) and *Sumurun* (1920).

The Witch in History

Throughout history, the witch has met with utter contumely, her figure cutting one of folklore's most dastardly silhouettes. Silvia Bovenschen has followed various historical leads in her attempt to pin down the lore that has begotten our contemporary image of this dark figure. Bovenschen notes that medieval conceptions of the witch, such as in the *Malleus Maleficarum* (*Witches' Hammer*, 1486), share characteristics with the

---

[1]   It should be noted that the word "gypsy" is considered a derogatory term to refer to the Sinti and Romani people of Germany, while not being used self-descriptively by these groups. Although I personally denounce the prejudicial manner in which this term has been historically invoked, I nevertheless employ it here for its peculiar historical significance in the Weimar period.

modern notion of the *femme fatale*, in particular depictions of woman "as sphinx, as demon, as unbridled sensual creature" (Ibid. 90).[2] Since the witch's powers are supposed to spring from her sexuality, no woman is ultimately safe from accusations of witchery (Ibid. 94). What these powers consisted in, according to medieval lore, were seemingly limitless circumventions of nature, including "levitation, psychokinesis, influencing the weather and other natural phenomena; the hexing of illness, accident or death; metamorphosis into animals; exerting magical influence over the processes of sex, birth, etc." (Ibid. 97). The witch's purlieux include various liminal spaces, in particular thresholds and doorways, whereby she is well positioned to take on various guises, thereby undergoing ghoulish acts of transfiguration, in particular adopting a bestial guise to assail her prey (Purkiss 250). Although she is capable of participating in normal social behaviors, the witch is believed to possess a peculiarly *non-human* nature, which distinguishes her from the regular run of humanity (Horsley and Horsley 14). Descriptions of her appearance almost always mention characteristic dusky dress, bespeaking her bent for drawing upon necromantic forces. Regardless of her vestments, her special brand of sorcery was typically performed in silence and behind closed doors (Purkiss 276–77).[3] Moreover, while the witch may initially appear congenial, this constituted yet another ingenious ploy for concealing her true, diabolical intent (Ibid. 278; 281).

The witch of the Middle Ages was often depicted as having a disturbing appearance, signifying a proclivity for deviancy. One illustration in particular emblematizes this common construction, showing her dancing with

---

2　The most famous quote from the *Malleus Maleficarum* concerns witches collecting men's penises: "And what, then, is to be thought of those witches who in this way sometimes collect male organs in great numbers, as many as twenty or thirty members together, and put them in a bird's nest, or shut them up in a box" (Kramer and Sprenger 121).

3　Witchcraft is attributed to a natural power possessed by the witch, *not* with a technique that can be learned (Horsley and Horsley 3). Such powers could be meted out in various ways, whether through "a curse, a weird glance or suspicious appearance" (Ibid.).

abandon and "hair disheveled" (Horsley and Horsley 4). These women would call upon the spirits of forests to assist in their rainmaking and fertility rituals. Embodied in green, blue, or yellow, spirits were poised to aid the witch in locating lost items, curing the sick, and in the concoction of love potions (Horsley 86). The image of the witch in the fifteenth century also included the night-flying specter, who was either busy blessing houses (the good witch) or practicing cannibalism (the bad witch) (Horsley and Horsley 14). She was both maieutic and infanticidal; both a loyal member of society and someone with machinations of harming her own; both a committed wife and a whore of Satan.

According to historical accounts, persecution on counts of witchcraft grew particularly acute in times of cultural crisis. Recall the witch trials of early modern Europe and America (made especially famous in Miller's *The Crucible*), which undoubtedly constituted society's vie to curtail female sexual and social expression, arising (by no coincidence) contemporaneously with large-scale political and economic upheaval (Ibid. 18). These restrictions were based on the perception of the witch's lasciviousness, and her apparent relish in wielding this power in her control of men. Women also posed a threat insofar as they were perceived as being capable of controlling nature, given carnal expression in their ability to menstruate and give birth. Women moreover appeared to jeopardize male identity through their "sexuality, disorder and unpredictable powers" (Ibid. 20). This threat is especially evident as characteristics traditionally associated with men, such as "independence and aggression," which were key attributes of the witch (Ibid. 15).

Mary Douglas observes that the witch is able to transgress boundaries and navigate interstices, which others are hindered from occupying (102). Like the witch, Weimar's Neue Frau similarly transgressed prohibited bounds in her seizure of typically masculine spaces, thereby realizing the habit of social and sexual independence. Weimar's Neue Frau therefore symbolized a transitional state between her former wifely role and a formerly *off-limits* emancipated identity. Notwithstanding the liminality of her newfound status, Weimar's New Woman was still culturally ensconced within an unbroken, and apparently unabating, patriarchy.[4] Newspaper reports often echo the sentiment that women must not try to join the male intellectual world. She must instead find contentment in being a true woman and mother (Thiess 138).[5] Hostility to New Woman's liberated attitude would then be transferred onto the stock image of the witch, who was epitomic in her transgressions and mal-intent.

The Witch in Weimar Dance and Literature

The *Zeitgeist*'s expressive dance moreover evidences a cultural penchant for the occult. Mary Wigman – one of the founders of modern dance in Germany – notes that dance takes hold of one's consciousness without intellectual thought, thereby constituting "internal experiences [...] the mutation or change of our spiritual and emotional conditions as they are alive in our own body" ("The Modern Dance" 150). Wigman incorporates demonic themes in a number of her dances. For instance, her expressive dance performance *Hexentanz* (Witch Dance, 1914) transfixes the spectator through gyrating movements that approach nigh-on necromantic rituals (see Figure 15). Rudolf Lämmel thus captures the spellbinding effect of the performance: "Without music, full of a wild passion for movement, Wigman in a fluttering gray cloak, hair flying. Wildly pounding jumps" (qtd. in Manning, "Feminism" 107).

4   For more information on the perception of woman in this historical context, see Grossmann, "The New Woman" 153–71.

5   Thiess notes: "Denn so wie absolute Freiheit sinnlos ist, kann auch absolute Gleichheit nicht gefordert werden, weil die Welt nun einmal von Bestimmung her ungleich ist und aus dieser Ungleichheit allein die schöpferische Kraft des Menschen erwuchs" (145).

Figure 15. Mary Wigman performing *Hexentanz* (Witch Dance, 1926). Photo by
Hugo Erfurth.

Wigman's other solo dance, *Hexentanz II* (Witch Dance II, 1926), like-
wise entranced the spectator with an ecstatic surfeit of emotional effusion.[6]
In the dance journal *Schrifttanz* 1929, Armin Knab writes of Wigman's
Witch Dance: "Horror becomes rational form [...]. Strange hissing sounds

6   Wigman also performed in the *Sun Festival* in Monte Verita (1917) with Laban's
     dancers. This festival was sponsored by the Ordo Templi Orientis (OTO), a free-
     mason group that was notorious for its occult practices. There is also evidence that
     Wigman was interested in occult questions. For more information on Wigman's
     life and dance, see Manning, *Ecstasy and the Demon*.

are mirrored by convulsive movements, arms are transformed into snakes, a satanic, non-human instinct seems to inspire the gestures" (qtd. in Dunlop and Lahusen 97).[7] In this dance, Wigman wears a mask that covers part of her face, with only small almond-shaped eyeholes. She is draped in a red and gold brocade shift dress, which covers her entire body, except for her hands and feet (see Figure 16). She begins the dance in a seated position, her arms up high, while her clawed hands violently tug at the air. She lunges forward from a crouching to a standing position with a single, animalistic movement. Hedwig Müller describes the end of Wigman's witch perform-ance as asserting spatial dominance: "Lustful greedy chasing throughout the room, a body that gets lost in the intoxication of the conquered, arms that sharply cut the room like swords. Then a final powerful start, and a crashing fall back to earth" ("Lustvoll gieriges Jagen durch den Raum, ein Körper, der sich im Rausch des Eroberten verliert, Arme, die wie Schwerter scharf den Raum zerschneiden. Dann ein letztes, machtvolles Aufrecken und der zerschmetterne Sturz vornüber zur Erde zurück." 199).

Figure 16. Mary Wigman performing *Hexentanz II* (Witch Dance II, 1926).

7   Wigman's 1934 group dance entitled, *Witch Dance* from her *Women's Dances*, again features the witch figure. The women's group shakes, darts, and dissolves in jumps and somersaults (Michel 13). Here, the mass "gallops into all directions,

Although Wigman's costume is not necessarily sexualized, her long hair and intricate brocade dress clearly identify her as feminine. Wigman's red and gold costume further symbolizes the witch's curse of blood.[8] Moreover, her mask functions to rebuff the male gaze, which would otherwise inevitably objectify her. As Manning notes, Wigman literally undermines the spectator's power by throwing the gaze back at the audience (Manning 129). We are fortunate enough to have Wigman's own account of her preparations for this performance. She remarks: "I looked into the mirror by chance. What it reflected was the image of one possessed, wild and dissolute, repelling and fascinating [...] there she was – the witch – the earth-bound creature with her unrestrained, naked instincts [...] beast and woman at one and the same time" (qtd. in Sorrell 40–41).

The ability of the witch to not only transfix but to *trounce* men is brought out in Thea Malten's novel *Die Hexe Lil* (*The Witch Lil*, 1921). There, the main character, Lil Andersen, evokes the mythological figure of Lilith, in both action and name.[9] In the novel, a young, working-class woman interposes herself in the male-dominated world of the theater by bewitching both the theater elder, Richard Wingering, and his aristocratic student, Reimar von Laßwitz. Their first encounters with Lil send them down a path of destruction. However, while Reimar narrowly escapes death by evoking memories of his family and hometown sweetheart, Richard Wingering is not so lucky, being compelled to commit suicide in confrontation with her preternatural prowess. As she meets both men at Wingering's house, there is something in the way Lil expresses herself that forces both men to take note. She possesses the grace and beauty of an Angora cat: "She had fine lovely features and skin so transparent and delicate [...]. In each of her movements lay a heedless soft graceful body"

---

joins for a wantoning circle dance and rushes off disappearing from view" (13–14). Wigman as mistress of the witches encourages the throng to return by performing her own whirling dance.

8   Barbara Creed notes that menstruation is linked with the witch's curse (74). Woman is thus closer to nature than man thanks to her proximity to, and ability to control, natural forces. Witches are further associated with the abject in the form of "filth, decay, spiders, bats, cobwebs, brews, potions and even cannibalism" (76).

9   Another Weimar novel, which foregrounds a "witch" figure and has a typical *femme fatale* plotline, is Rudolf Presber's *Die Hexe von Endor* (1932).

("Sie hatte feine, reizende Züge, und eine so durchsichtig zarte Haut [...]. In jeder ihrer Bewegungen lag eine achtlose weiche Grazie." Malten 40). Her delightfully small feet and subtly young body leave Wingering speechless, convinced that she must play Lulu or another Strindberg character at the theater. Later in the café, as Lil takes down her long brown hair, Reimar is likewise overcome. Without his knowledge, she discovers everything she wished to know about him (46). In his pursuit of Lil at the beer hall, Reimar is drawn to this "kleine Hexe" (small witch) with her glowing checks and eyes; he soon forgets his childhood sweetheart, Hedwig, in his desire to dominate Lil.

Wingering is similarly captivated by Lil's sexual presence. As Lil and Wingering smoke and drink in his apartment, he objectifies her as a lady of the night, asking about her love life and offering her money so that she can maintain her lifestyle. Wingering is literally transfixed by Lil's forthrightness and smile, which leave him staring at the door after she leaves. It is obvious that the attraction of men to Lil is completely unlike that of other women. As Reimar considers distancing himself from Lil, he is unable to accomplish his retreat: he wants to turn away, but her eyes and smile lock him in place (95).[10]

Lil's behavior evokes the archetype of the witch, who initially appears good-natured, in spite of her true intentions to mete out harm to those whom she attracts. Lil comes and goes as she pleases, drinks with other men, and unabashedly informs Reimar first, and then Wingering, that she will not be faithful. Not only does Lil apparently metamorphize from feminine to masculine, she is moreover capable of crossing the bounds of class and culture as she navigates between her humble apartment in the city slums and the loftier footholds of high society, the purlieux of Reimar and Wingering (131). Indeed, despite her sensuality, Lil is dispassionate, declaring that she hates everything that is nice (151). She is unstoppable in her desire for a career in the theater, which she eventually achieves in the city of Vienna. Her childhood mentor, Mellanius, issues a curt summary of Lil's goals, remarking that she gains her advantages by manipulating the

---

10   "Er wollte sich wegwenden – doch ihre Augen, ihr Lächeln schienen ihn festzubannen" (95).

men she ensnares through her feminine wiles (137).[11] Having bewitched
Mellanius in her youth, she will, in turn, cast a spell on all of the men she
meets so that she can achieve her ultimate objective, placing a curse upon
all of mankind in her pursuit of fame (120).

Lil seamlessly navigates two worlds: coquettish femininity and masculine power. She practices this shape-shifting through moving from the
world of her bourgeois suitors back to the Stammtisch of her youth. Lil's
peculiar ability to captivate men initially leads to a sexual relationship with
Reimar while she secretly cajoles Wingering into giving her monetary assistance. Despite her impoverished background, she quickly ascends the social
ladder and seamlessly adopts the accouterments of the upper class. Her silk
strapless dress beguiles Reimar, who is thereby also *bewitched*. He endures
Lil's sadistic treatment, proclaiming that he cannot live without her (192).
And, although Wingering reprimands Lil that she should be burned in the
marketplace, it is *she* who has subjugated *him* as her slave (107).

Lil's final destructive deeds include conjuring Reimar's near-fatal
illness, while driving a wedge that marks the demise of Reimar and
Wingering's friendship, ultimately resulting in Wingering's death. Lil's
unflagging desire to be drinking and dancing – along with her romantic
absenteeism and infidelity – causes Reimar's health to abruptly deteriorate.
He loses his appetite, becoming a nervous, enervated wreck. After finally
collapsing as a result of exhaustion and sickness, Lil – utterly unmoved –
discards him, making him his family's problem (220). Reimar is also compelled to confront Lil's infidelity. Wingering knows that when he takes Lil
from Reimar, he will lose both his friend and his life. He is, however, forced
to pursue Lil owing to some uncanny, insuperable power on her part. His
words of abject vanquishment, delivered in Lil's presence, give voice to this
strange, deleterious desire: "I love you, although I know that cutting one's
throat is less dangerous than loving you. Because you can only lose your
life, but there are, however, more valuable things to lose" (195).[12] In the end,

---

11   "Alle, die dich lieben [...] spucke auf sie, verderbe sie – all die Männer – und laß
      eine Stufe für dich sein – eine Stufe nach oben!" (137).
12   "Ich liebe dich – obgleich ich weiß, daß es weniger gefährlich ist, sich den Hals
      abzuschneiden, als dich zu lieben. Denn dabei kann man nur das Leben verlieren –
      aber bei dir verliert man wertvollere Dinge" (195).

Reimar is spared Lil's power by returning to his hometown. Wingering, after marrying Lil, succumbs to her depravity, the newspaper article citing his death intimating that Lil masterminded his suicide. Ultimately, Lil's power of bewitchment besmirches both men.

Lil capably crosses the boundary from the dark, dirty streets of her youth to the glitz and glamor of high-society Munich. She enacts a deft mutation from guileless student, at the novel's incipit, to that of an arrant temptress. She initially appears caring but reveals her true self to be cold and calculating. Since her ultimate aim is succeeding in the theater, she uses Wingering and Reimar to help make her mark. Her traditionally masculine characteristics – her solipsistic pursuit of career, her egoism, and her characteristically unshakeable strong-mindedness – enable her to make great strides in the male-dominated theater world. Her libidinousness is particularly expressed in her manipulation of myriad sexual partners (Reimar; the Expressionist painter; Wingering, etc.). In sum, Lil's unique sexual allure – along with overt allusions to her mythological namesake, Lilith – marks her out as an archetypal witch. As the *Malleus Maleficarum* states: "What else is woman but a […] natural temptation, a desirable calamity, a domestic danger, a delectable detriment, an evil of nature, painted with fair colours!" (Kramer and Sprenger 43). With but a glance and a gesture, she works her magic on her male counterparts, thereby wreaking havoc and despair. Indeed, at the novel's conclusion, far from being burned at the stake, she seizes her rightful place as the theater's lead actress.

The witch Lil is illustrated above as a modern *agent provocateur*. There are, however, yet more traditional depictions of witches in Weimar literature. In turning now to Isabelle Kaiser's novel *Bilda, die Hexe* (*Bilda, the Witch*, 1921), we need to delineate the medieval understanding of witchcraft, which the author draws upon.[13] Although Kaiser's witch evinces all of the qualities of the contemporary *femme fatale*, the novel is set in the historical period of the medieval witch burnings. For, not only does the novel feature evil witches (who deploy their characteristic powers with mal-intent), the novel also foregrounds the kindly witch, Bilda, who uses

---

13 Another Weimar novel about the historical witch burnings is *Der Sohn der Hexe* by Fritz Goens (1929).

her powers for good – healing the sick and nurturing her community. In this way, Kaiser's novel centralizes the standoff between good and evil.

This conflict reaches a crescendo in the clash between Bilda – the young, virginal, blond niece of farm-owner, Oswald Maienberg – and the house servant, Krischona – the mistress of Maienberg's son, Lienhard. Having endured her adolescence in a convent, Bilda's arrival on the farm is marked with the ominous release of a black dove from her carriage. Bilda's striking beauty immediately catches the eye of Lienhard, who nicknames her "the slender rose bush" (30). Krischa, meanwhile, feels immediately threatened by her, and seeks to thwart her. While Krischa is described as a sensual, dark-haired young maid ("a wild beauty" with "a cat-like grace" 36, 39), the servant, Hudi, bears many of the "unattractive" characteristics typically attributed to witches, including hooked nose, pointed chin, and wide mouth (24). Nevertheless, they are both Satan's brides, the young Krischa having taken Satan as her master in a blood pact, and Hudi following her partner's death in war.

In spite of their counterposed intentions, both Krischa and Bilda are able to wield their dark magic to maneuver and manipulate those around them. Lienhard is enchanted by the wild charm of Krischa, who gladly and passionately requites his love (77).[14] Lienhard is moreover attracted to the good deeds of Bilda. Owing to this, she possesses a power that both captivates and ensnares him. Along with the older farmer, and the servants who are also influenced by "the small witch," Lienhard is convinced of Bilda's preternatural powers. It is this turmoil in Lienhard that drives Krischa to swear a hex on Bilda: she concocts a plan to frame Bilda as a witch, remarking that if she herself burns at the stake, then they both will burn, side by side (75). Availing herself of a combination of spells and potions, Krischa seeks to keep Lienhard close to her.

Having captured the hearts of both the young and old Maienberg, Bilda also wins the love of the political prisoner, Loki, who is enchained on the farm. Bilda cures Loki of his deadly fever using special herbs from the mountain; she likewise heals a number of the villagers without requiring

---

14   "Leidenschaftlich hatte er sie geliebt, bezaubert von dem urwüchsigen, wilden Reiz dieses einfachen Mädchens, das sein Land bebaute und seine Liebe so heiß erwiderte" (77).

assistance from the male apothecary. She confidently instructs the towns-people about the use of herbs, forbidding Maienberg and the other male workers to touch Loki in case the disease spreads further. She rebuffs Lienhard's advances, castigating him for his flawed character, stating that she quite simply isn't attracted to him.

Like Bilda, Hudi gathers herbs on the mountainside, which, along with Krischa, she peppers into her death-dealing potions (93). In order to frame Bilda, Krischa kills livestock, drugs Lienhard, and summons a hailstorm ("Hexenhagel") in order to destroy the village's crops.[15] Krischa's malevolent actions pique uncertainty regarding Bilda's intentions. Krischa blames the community's bad fortune on the triumvirate of witches – herself, Bilda, and Hudi:

> What have we done? Listen! Last night was St. Bartholomäusnacht [...] All the devil's brides had wreathed their heads and shoulders with verbena and cemetery ivy. [...] They appeared in the form of dogs, cats and black pigeons [...] Last night Bilda Wyß was queen. (210–11; 213)[16]

In Kaiser's novel, then, the good witch, Bilda, and bad witch, Krischa, constitute counterposed forces, albeit emerging from the same spiritual energy. Indeed, in spite of their feminine mystique, they capably tap into masculine forces to realize their respective goals. The inquisition against the witches that follows does not distinguish between the two accused: they are both subject to imprisonment; their hair is shorn and they are subjected to torture in an effort to extract a confession. Bilda, however, is not maimed like the others. Eventually, seven accused women are brought forward, Krischa ultimately owning up to her plot against Bilda, thereafter burning at the stake and receiving a sensual kiss from Lienhard. Bilda is saved and lives in peace with the aristocrat Johann

---

15 Witches are linked "with drugs, with altered states, with madness and hysteria, with the disruption of language, with forbidden words, with excitingly unsayable desires" (Purkiss 78).

16 "Was wir getan haben? Hört zu! Gestern abend war St. Bartholomäusnacht [...] Alle die Bräute des Teufels hatten sich Kopf und Schultern mit Eisenkraut und Friedhofsefeu bekränzt. Sie erschienen in Gestalt von Hunden, Katzen und schwarzen Tauben [...] Gestern abend war Bilda Wyß Königin."

Georg Landtwig (formerly known as Loki). Bilda remains a witch despite her marriage to Landtwig, while Krischa's spirit lives on through her haunting influence on Bilda.

The plot of *Bilda, die Hexe* therefore takes the form of a clash between the virtues of good magic and perils of its dark, necromantic counterpart: one is as pure as nature's lily, the other rides with Satan; one puts to use nature's healing power, the other leverages nature's destructive force (poisonous herbs, bad weather); one acts out of kindness, the other from avarice and aggression. Becker-Cantarino notes that, as with *Faust's* Gretchen, there is always a shadowy, witchlike figure lurking behind the virginal beauty. To this end, Gretchen is a duplicitous figure, both virgin and whore, her sexuality condemning her to the demonic realm of night and flight (7–8). Indeed, while Bilda does not commit the crimes of poisoning and killing like Gretchen (for Bilda is not a double figure), her very presence sets the crimes of the novel in motion, including the jealous, heinous acts of Krischa and Hudi.

The witch's reputation as "Giftmischerin" (poisoner) matches the commonest allegation against the accused during the witch trials of the late Middle Ages (Bever 960). Historically, both good and bad witches were equally suspect. Richard Horsley explains that good witches were called upon to aid the community in their nightly visits (89). These witches were folk healers whose mission consisted in curing the sick, not bringing harm to the community. However, those accused of healing were made to confess a relationship with the devil, like their counterpart practitioners of the so-called "evil eye" (Horsley and Horsley 9).

Hanns Heinz Ewers' short story, "Meine Mutter, die Hex" (*My Mother, the Witch*, 1922) similarly foregrounds the figure of a witch, who again betrays a dual-aspect *qua* healer and destroyer. In Ewers' tale, the son of a witch advises his brother in a letter not to marry for fear that his offspring will also be cursed as witches. Their elderly mother beguiles those who meet with her: strangers talk to her on the roadside; people of all walks of life send her flowers; she compels various creatures from the animal world. Physicians even consult her on the treatment of various ailments, her uncanny penchant for natural remedies proving therapeutic in alleviating corns, warts, and freckles (Ewers 335). The mother is moreover capable of granting the wishes of those around her. For example, a sculptor is granted special riches because "she wish[ed] it" (Ibid. 337). These powers for good can likewise be turned to evil with the aid of poisonous mushrooms, as well as the toxic henbane (*Bilsenkraut* 327). Indeed, the body of a female servant emerges in the Rhein river after she had stolen from the mother. Likewise, a store frequented by the mother is looted as recompense for swindling her (Ibid. 340).

While the mother is beloved by all, thanks to possessing the power to heal and enchant, she also enjoys the power of pestilence, thereby spreading disease and taking lives. In the moonlight, the mother smears a strange salve on her broom and flies out of the window to meet Satan (formerly the ram that she visits at the zoo) (Ibid. 358–59). She shape-shifts into a gray cat, and cavorts with a coven of witches.[17] In Ewer's tale, one can never be quite sure of the mother's true intentions. The supposed hostility evinced by the witch is often designated "covert violence" (Bever 968). Indeed, in spite of her protestations about healing the infirm, one can never be sure whether or not her real desire was in fact to level harm upon her unwitting victims (Ibid. 960).

Thus, just as the witch in the story was accused of murdering a "sleeping foe" with a uncanny concoction (Ibid. 959, 968), so too do we find *actual* cases of women in Weimar who were charged with poisoning their abusive husbands or lovers. Two famous cases of this kind were those of Klein/ Nebbe (1923) and the Vukobrankovic trials (1918 and 1923). Both scandals were similar in portraying their defendants as sadistic murderesses. Purportedly aided by her lesbian lover, Margarete Nebbe, Ella Klein was charged with poisoning her husband, Willi Klein, with arsenic.[18] In her

---

17   It is interesting that the letter of the brother to his sibling – warning against marriage and the fear of passing on witchcraft – has little effect upon the impending marriage: the new couple pledge to have a few girls who will be "nice witches," just like their grandmother (Ewers 361).

18   Ella had left her violent husband several times, each time returning to the marriage with the insistence of her parents. Alfred Döblin in his coverage of the case, which was entitled *Die beiden Freundinnen und ihr Giftmord* (1924), foregrounded the *sociological* context of the case rather than the barbarity of its perpetrators. Joseph Roth in his article for the *Berliner Börsen-Courier* (1923) was not so generous: "Die Frauen Klein und Nebbe wurden Mörderinnen aus Liebe zueinander und erst in

letters to Nebbe, Klein wrote about proving her love by silencing her husband ("zur Ruhe zu bringen") (Siebenpfeiffer 103). During the trial, both women were lambasted as sadistic, hysterical, and unscrupulous: they supposedly had the "moral decay" of the criminal written all over their faces (Ibid. 105).[19] Similarly, the Austrian, Milica Vukobrankovic, was tried once in 1918 and thereafter in 1923 for poisoning her employer. In Ernst Weiß's case study – entitled *The Vukobrankovic Case* (1923) – he describes Vukobrankovic as seductive and cold, evincing tendencies toward homosexuality and other putative forms of sexual deviancy (Herzog 48).[20]

Criminologist Erich Wulffen observes that cases of women using poison in history were typically associated with witchcraft (189). According to Wulffen, the secrecy and deadliness of the act of poisoning brought sadistic satisfaction to the poisoner. This titillation is further heightened by a sense of power akin to the so-called "rape impulse" (190). Wulffen proffers several motives that may potentially explain why women choose poisoning as their mode of injuriousness: "The female disposition readily harbors sexual motives leading to poisoning – jilted or insulted love, jealousy, sexual revenge, disinclination and hate for the marital partner" (Ibid. 191).[21] Not wanting to restrain her sexual desires or economic aspirations, the witch opposes masculine domination, invoking her keen-eyed malevolence to poison and wreak havoc (Ibid. 192). Women who poison are

---

zweiter Linie aus Haß gegen die Ehemänner. Die Beseitigung der Männer war nur ein Mittel – der Zweck war die Erfüllung der Sehnsucht" (953).

19   "Anstelle zweier sadistischer, hysterischer, skrupelloser, berechnender, hinterlistiger und verschlagener Frauen, denen die 'moralische Verkommenheit' ihres Verbrechertypus 'ins Gesicht geschrieben stand'" (Siebenpfeiffer 105).

20   Weiß's work was part of the "Outsider series," *Außenseiter der Gesellschaft: Die Verbrechen der Gegenwart* published by Verlag Die Schmiede 1924–25. Other writers in this series include Alfred Döblin, Iwan Goll, and Theodor Lessing, who offer studies about Weimar criminal cases. For more information about this series, see Herzog 34–56.

21   Wulffen dedicates an entire chapter to "Murder of Husband." While the husband, in many cases, may have been brutal toward the wife, she is ultimately to blame for marrying out of "purely social and material reasons": "she is disappointed in marriage, feels forsaken, suppressed; her sexual needs can find gratification only outside of the marriage bonds; a lover always comes along, who later becomes the accomplice in the murder" (233).

moreover believed to suffer from several psychological maladies, including homosexuality, hysteria, and narcissism (Ibid. 218).

Furthermore, on Wulffen's account, Vukobrankovic is witch-like thanks to her degenerate sexuality and proclivity for sadism. Her spiritual nature, her "cold and mysterious" demeanor, as well as her natural talent for dissembling, erect a barrier behind which she can conceal her malefic deeds (Ibid. 226–27). In her cross-examination, Vukobrankovic testifies that she poisoned the food in the house when it was apparent that [publisher S.] had been unfaithful to her. Vukobrankovic in fact gave expression to her maleficent motives, writing from her jail cell: "The trial judge is the same beast as all the others […] My greatest desire would be to hang his scalp on my Christmas tree […] I should like to tear the prosecutor's face to pieces!" (qtd. in Ibid. 226).

The Witch in Weimar Cinema

The witch figure – the shape-shifting harbinger of destruction – is also given a platform in Leni Riefenstahl's debut movie *Das Blaue Licht* (*The Blue Light*, 1932). Produced by Heinrich Sokal and Leni Riefenstahl (also being directed and scripted by the latter), this "mountain" film was critiqued by its reviewers for focusing on cinematography to the detriment of the plot. In the article "Das Blaue Licht" (1932), the *Film-Kurier* notes: "The epic style is written without comment. Some things remain unclear in terms of action" ("Der epische Stil wird kommentarlos geboten. So bleibt einiges handlungsmäßig undeutlich").[22] Premiering in Berlin at the Ufa-Palast am Zoo in the March of 1932, waterfalls and

---

22   The March 29, 1932 article, "Kunst und Natur sei eines nur" in the *Film-Kurier* notes that various critics in Berlin have panned the film: "Ein Teil der Berliner Tagespresse hat […] 'Das Blaue Licht' so gründlich blamiert, daß man sein blaues Wunder erleben konnte." The article's author feels that these negative reviews, which label the film as "Kitsch," do not do the film justice. Conversely, the work may be considered "Dichtkunst" with a feeling for nature ("Kunst und Natur sei

mountain summits were enumerated as among the film's highlights. Remarking upon the spectacles of natural beauty afforded by the picture, H. Angel from *Das Lichtbild-Bühne* (1932) writes: "What we are shown here in terms of mountains and forests is unique […] the play of sun rays on mountain peaks, mounds and tree tops, with flowers, grottos and clouds, has no peer in the history of cinematography" ("Was uns hier an Berg – und Waldaufnahmen gezeigt wird, ist einzigartig […] mit Sonnestrahlen auf Berggipfeln, Halden und Baumkronen, mit Blumen, Grotten und Wolken spielt, hat ihresgleichen nicht in der Geschichte der Kinematographie").[23]

Spearheading earthly sublimity is the film's arbiter of nature: Junta, the wild mountain witch, enacted by Riefenstahl herself. The depiction of Junta as a witch figure is referenced in the film's 1951 retitling in Austria and Germany as *Die Hexe von Santa Maria* (*The Witch of Santa Maria*). Eric Rentschler describes Junta as an agent of the uncanny: a "witch" and a curse to the village, she assumes the role of martyr only after her death (34). Rentschler understands *Das Blaue Licht* as a horror film insofar as the community must confront the uncanny: Junta represents the dangerous sensuality that must be exorcised from the village (Ibid. 38, 45). It is only when her lifeless body is found by her lover, Vigo – a painter visiting from Vienna (Mathias Wieman) – that the community stands protected. The film's additional, romantic images feature the mystery of nature with settings that evince an "eerie and ethereal aspect" (Ibid. 37).

Siegfried Kracauer likewise takes Junta to be a "witch."[24] For, she possesses a special power to reach the blue light that radiates from Mount

---

eines nur"). For more information about the controversy concerning the film's various participants, see Rentschler 31. Riefenstahl denied authorship to Balász, Sokal (production), and Carl Mayer during the Nazi period (31).

23   The film's fantasy sequences were created with Agfa's new emulsion infrared negative. Coupled with a red filter, this filmic technique would afford a magical effect, redolent of moonlight (Fanck qtd. Wallace 26).

24   Kracauer also notes that Junta is a "sort of gypsy girl" (*From Caligari to Hitler* 258). See "The *Zigeunerdrama* Reloaded: Leni Riefenstahl's Fantasy Gypsies and Sacrificial Others" by Anjeana Hans for a reading of Junta *qua* gypsy.

Cristallo, while also acting as a magnet for men who are "drawn away like somnambulists," plummeting to their deaths from the mountainous peak (*From Caligari to Hitler* 258). For Kracauer, Junta is elemental power incarnate, the glow of the crystals representing her "very soul" (*From Caligari to Hitler* 259). Peggy Wallace further notes that Junta is persecuted in the village for being a "witch" (16), the villagers murderously pursuing her with sticks and rocks, scapegoating her for the deaths of their young men. Her entry into the village to sell her strange mountain herbs corroborates her reputed witchery, owing to which she must be eradicated.

The film's story is framed in the present with the promise of a retelling of the Junta myth. A couple's arrival in the village is accompanied by foreboding clouds. As the modern woman and her dapper husband – both dressed in car coats – check in to the village hotel, they discover the tale of Junta in an ancient book presented to them by the hotel manager. Junta's picture on the book's cover fades to reveal the real person in a nineteenth-century context, who then appears juxtaposed to a raging waterfall. In this flashback, Junta commands natural phenomena (Bovenschen 97). Her prowess in matters of nature is evident in her ability to navigate the rocky landscape and in her deft selection of herbs from the mountain shrubs. Peculiarly beautiful with her slight frame and excitable demeanor, she is known by the villagers as the "devil's witch," moreover deemed "abnormal" by the innkeeper (Max Holzboer) who greets Vigo. The innkeeper tells Vigo the story of the boys who fall from the mountainous rock as they stalk the blue light. This description is quickly followed by a shot of the villager's son Tonio (Beni Führer), who is both agitated and enchanted by Junta's ingress into the village.

The "damned devil's witch," Junta, is synonymous with the blue light and the natural dangers of the mountains. The light of the mountain commands the gaze of the village's young men from their barred windows. While Tonio passes the moonlit night pondering the emanation, it is also suggested that it is not merely the light that draws Tonio to the mountain. The reoccurring waterfall, nestled in this scene, reminds the viewer that the

men are transfixed by the natural force relating to Junta,[25] whose prowess
consists in her natural flair for finding the grotto of blue crystal as others
have similar ambitions dashed.

Tonio and Vigo are both transfixed by the sight of Junta. Her natural sexuality, however, is not to be possessed by the men she seduces.
Tonio's attraction to Junta turns violent as she walks through the village
at night. With a burning lust, Tonio grabs Junta and pulls her into an
alcove, grunting in the darkness, suggesting that Junta has been assaulted.
She reacts by running across the village bridge into the forest, crossing the
boundary to her safe haven in the mountains. This event, however, is not
forgotten. The following night, one of the young villagers tumbles to his
death in pursuit of the blue light, signifying that, notwithstanding their
attempt to pursue and possess Junta, such acts of pleonectic vying incur
grave consequences.

Vigo's pursuit of Junta leads him into the mountains. Although he
constitutes a welcome addition to Junta's family – which already includes
the shepherd boy, Guzzi, and the herd of sheep and goats – she rebuffs
his sexual advances. As he tries to kiss her, she pulls away in shock, Vigo
noting: "Junta, little witch […] you make me behave like a fool." As exemplified in Junta, the witch figure irresistibly charms both people and animals.
Numerous reaction shots of goats, sheep, and even a dog listening to Junta
clarify her wielding the forces of nature. The animals listen attentively to
her as she talks about the injustices committed against her in the village.

Junta is not, at first, perceived as a dastardly character. In fact, she
comes across as a timid, urchin-like woman, whose relationship with
nature renders her a kind of pariah figure in the community (see Figure
17). However, just as the shadow on the mountains signifies an evil that
has befallen the community, so too does the diminutive Junta represent a
veiled threat to those around her: her preternatural control of the mountain grotto, which nobody may penetrate except for herself, coaxes men
to their deaths.

---

25   This waterfall is a proxy for the insuperable, natural force of Junta both at the be-
      ginning of the flashback and in the final frame, reiterating her power and eternal
      presence.

Figure 17. *Das blaue Licht* (The Blue Light). Producers Leni Riefenstahl, Henry
Sokal; director Riefenstahl, 1932.

In particular, Tonio is cursed for his violation of Junta. He too is eventually drawn to the moonlit crystal. Indeed, as he approaches his goal, he
is mysteriously forced down the mountain as a rock crumbles in his hand.
Junta's sensual yearning for the crystal, culminating in her somnambulist
pilgrimage and prayer in the cavernous grotto, evokes the natural power
prompting Tonio's demise. As Rentschler notes, "sexual energy becomes
a spiritual force" (40). The forces of nature represented by the clouds and
moon overshadow the Christian tribute to the fallen boys. Here, nature
and Junta reign supreme over a town that has been forsaken by a Christian
God, even the village priest crossing himself when he encounters her.

The city-dweller, Vigo, uncovers Junta's magic by way of a map that he
makes after following her up the mountain. When the villagers discover
the route to the grotto, they "rape it" of its minerals, signifying the rape
and destruction of Junta on Rentschler's reading (Ibid. 48). She is unable
to withstand the assault on the fount of her magical powers. Upon viewing

the destruction of the crystals, accompanied by items of the villagers strewn throughout the cave (axes, ladders, clothing), she falls to her death, bereft of her previous power. In this instance, the mountain is hazy with clouds, which impede her vision. The eerie premonition of the forest's craggy, dead trees foregrounds the witch's mountain demise. The blood-red wine, drunk by the villagers after pillaging the crystals, is symbolic of the ritualistic murder of the witch. Never again will she cross the bridge into the village and besiege the psyche of the village men.

The story of Junta the witch therefore constitutes a cautionary tale, which reminds us that magic comes at the cost of the witch's blood. The film's final scene features the modern woman looking at the book about Junta, which fades into a vignette of the waterfall. Just as the waterfall is everlastingly powerful, it too may be appropriated by the person who can unveil its secrets. To this end, the modern woman sharing the frame has been warned.

Gypsies in Germany and the New Woman

As we move onto the gypsy figure, we find a woman who mirrors the witch with her sexual-magical exploits. Almut Hille notes similar stereo-types of gypsies and witches regarding their alleged pact with the devil ("Manche Esmeralda" 71). The systematic prejudice against the "gypsies" (otherwise known as "the Romani people" of Germany), has a long his-tory. In 1492, the Romani were banned by the Elector of Brandenburg, followed by Emperor Sigismund's revocation of his 1423 letter ensuring their protection (Strauss 83). After the fifteenth century, Sinti were persecuted, tortured, and murdered as restitution for their supposed crimes, including such preposterous charges as cannibalism (Figueira 81). A seventeenth-century conspiracy moreover charged the Romani with failing to harbor Mary and Joseph on their flight from Egypt, thereby condemning them to wander the land as nomads (Ibid. 82). Their rejec-tion of the Christian God is further supported in the prejudicial belief that they forged the nails used on Christ's cross – a belief that goes so far as holding that gypsies are, in fact, Jews who have disguised themselves by adopting a foreign speech and appearance to escape pogroms (Ibid.).[26] Like the Jews, the Romani were viewed as monsters and vermin who did not belong in Europe.

This contempt continued throughout the eighteenth and nineteenth centuries, as the Romani were commonly accused of a laundry list of crimes, including "thievery, magic, trickery, bloodshame, and racial contamination" (Ibid. 88). From 1761–82, Maria Theresa and Joseph II outlawed gypsy no-madism, self-governance, and their use of the Romani language. Gypsies were not only banned from "begging," but also from gainful employment as horse traders, musicians, and coppersmiths.

Heinrich Moritz Gottlieb Grellmann discusses the purported gypsy relation to trickery and magic in his 1787 work *Historischer Versuch über die Zigeuner betreffend die Lebensart und Verfassung, Sitten und Schicksale dieses Volkes seit seiner Erscheinung in Europa, and dessen Ursprung* (Historical Essay on the Way of Life and Constitution of the Gypsies, Customs and Fates of this People since its Appearance in Europe, and its Origins). In particular, Grellmann observes the supposed powers of the female gypsy, who is capable of infecting livestock with disease using a malodorous salve. Grellmann notes that the "healing" treatment by the "Zigeunerin" (female gypsy) enables the sickened cattle to eat again: "Dadurch ändert sich der Geruch des Thiers, und da es hungert, ist es kein Wunder, wenn es sogleich mit heizer Begierde anbeißt. Von diesem einzelnen Beyspiele schließe man nun auf mehrere" ("Through [the treatment], the smell of the animal changes and it becomes hungry, it is little wonder when it eats then with great appetency. From this example, one can conclude others." Grellmann 98–99). In this example, the local villagers attribute healing powers to the female gypsy in spite of their dubiety. Grellmann hints that the gypsy woman is guilty of similar acts of "magic" involving deception.

Prejudicial treatment of the Romani burgeoned in the Weimar period following the establishment of stringent policies in 1927 that required all gypsies living in Germany to be fingerprinted and registered (Strauss 86). Indeed, a law enacted in 1929 made it a punishable offense for gypsies to

---

26 Throughout German history, representations of gypsies have been interchange-able with those of blacks and Jews, as all were considered "colored"/outsiders (Figueira 88).

travel or live in a "horde," defined prejudicially as a group exceeding the size of a traditional, nuclear family (Trumpener 853).

Social-scientific writings of the period further reflect many of the standard prejudices held against the Romani people. In Erich Wulffen's chapter, "Female Swindlers and Cheats," the noted criminologist links the gypsy to various prophesies involving "love, engagements, marital bliss and the death of a husband" (Wulffen 116). The gypsy woman further employs fortune-telling as a means for defrauding others (Ibid. 117). Wulffen describes the gypsy's necromancy thus: "Being more sensitive than the male she is the great initiated one who governs over mysterious powers. Her strange being fascinates her victims so that they believe themselves hypnotized" (Ibid.). Wulffen moreover notes that the gypsy's "witchery" is located in the motor nerves that enervate her fingers. She furthermore exhibits self-reliance without needing to rely on the support of a male partner if required to take care of herself (Ibid.).

Newspaper articles published in Weimar not only note female gypsies' prophetic abilities: they also charge them with criminal behavior and louche expressions of sexuality. Adele von Finck's 1929 article, "Zigeuner, Magie, Karten" (Gypsies, Magic, Cards) for *Der Querschnitt* notes the association of gypsies with music, but also thievery, lying, and deception (473). In describing this "race" of deceivers, Finck notes that they have most recently appeared in communist female communities; dressing in brightly colored rags, they secretly don expensive, oriental jewelry and coins (Ibid. 474). According to Finck, gypsies found their way to Bavaria in order to pan for gold in the rivers, setting up house in secret parts of the forest.

Finck associates the female gypsy with magic, nature, and the devil. Well-to-do German citizens would consult these women in secret meetings, asking for love potions and amulets: the main activities of women were "quackery, making love potions, and magic" (Ibid. 474).[27] Gypsy fortune-tellers, however, could not live for long in one area. These acrobats,

27 "die Haupttätigkeit der Frauen bestand in Quacksalbereien, Herstellung von Liebestränken und Zauberei aller Art" (474).

dancers, and card readers were quickly perceived as robbers, arsonists, and child-stealers. Considered foreigners in their communities, gypsies supposedly could not be trusted: "Their Christianity was also considered hypocrisy. They were accused of being in league with the devil" ("Auch hielt man ihr Christentum für Heuchelei, man bezichtigte sie, mit dem Teufel im Bunde zu stehen." Finck 474). In her 1929 "Ein Kommentar zur Zigeunerfrage" (A Commentary on the Gypsy Question), Jo Mihaly additionally notes society's distrust of the gypsy, quoting King Friedrich Wilhelm I on their preferred fate: "All gypsies over the age of 18 should hang on the gallows without regard for the person" ("Alle Zigeuner über 18 Jahren ohne Ansehen der Person an den Galgen zu hängen seien." 300). Mihaly notes contemporary German legal practices, citing the 1928 edict from the city of Rummelsburg, which states that all gypsies face on-the-spot eviction (Mihaly 300).

Gypsy women in particular have been portrayed in German cultural representations as thieving, promiscuous, demonic, animalistic, selfish, mystical, and bound to nature (Figueira 83–85). Female gypsies supposedly bewitch their victims using trickery and magic, the "Zigeunerin" evincing a sexuality that is both primitive and animalistic. Her unbridled sexuality and barrenness render her "racially unfit" and "diseased"; virtue cannot be found in the gypsy woman, who is a "virtueless procuress" (Ibid. 84, 86). These gypsy women are supposedly "robbers of children, evil stepmothers, or procuring witches who deceive and dominate their victims" (Ibid. 86).

These stereotypes regarding gypsy women should be considered in the context of the sexual emancipation realized by Weimar's Neue Frau. Instead of limiting her libido to the remit of conjugal relations, the New Woman openly indulged her sexual impulses. According to various historical sources, Weimar's Neue Frau replaced the virtues of modesty and chastity with the willful objectification of sex (Flake 138–39; Hollander 41–43). Otto Flake elaborates that the supposed emancipation of woman has rendered her "unromantic" (135), spiritually eviscerating the notion of the "ideal" woman, leaving behind a woman with only the basest instincts (Ibid. 136).

Female Gypsies in Weimar Literature

Depictions of gypsy women in Weimar literature regularly portray them as entrancing seductresses, who ensnare their male victims with their sexuality. Hille notes that these characters are often described as both literally and spiritually threatening to Germany's "racial purity" (*Identitätskonstruktionen* 30). Wilhelm Lehmann's novel *Die Schmetterlingspuppe* (1918) depicts the gypsy woman as a seductress, who entices the naïve teacher Stanislaus Loeski to the gypsy encampment. Leaving his beautiful girlfriend behind in typhus-ridden Germany, Loeski seeks refuge in the mysterious city of Dubran in Ireland. However, a new type of death awaits him as he falls victim to the "Mongolian looking" *Zigeunermädchen* (gypsy girl) with high cheekbones, swimming eyes, and large mouth. She subdues him merely with the force of her breath (194). As he goes to meet her in the moonlit night, she curiously queries him about the plant possessing the darkest leaves. Loeski quickly responds to her question, informing her that it is "die Haselwurz," or wild ginger (194). It is immediately obvious that he associates her with this plant, escaping her embrace following his recognition of her malintent. Hille remarks that this sort of reference to dark plants connotes the allure of a sexual encounter with a dark woman in spite of her alleged racial impurity (*Identitätskonstruktionen* 91).[28]

In Agnes Miegel's short dramatic piece, *Der Gaukler* (*The Juggler*, 1920), the gypsy Elisabeth – characterized with all of the stereotypical features – is responsible for minting a jealous rivalry between her husband, the juggler, and the Baron. She arrives at the Baron's estate to perform in her husband's juggling and tightrope act along with her dance performance (*Der Gaukler* 62). She expresses the joy of her dance in a heated performance for the Baron and his friends, declaring: "I lived like the white flowers

---

28   Several other literary works depict the female gypsy as sexual temptress. The young
     girl in Helene Christaller's story *Zigeunertaufe* (1922) exploits her sexuality as a
     ruse to pilfer from the townspeople (68–71). Hermann Hesse's novel *Narziß und
     Goldmund* (1930) similarly depicts how the beautiful gypsy, Lise, brings the pro-
     tagonist, Goldmund, to his downfall as a result of their sexual encounter (74, 83).

lived. / The pleasure of light, the sweetness of warmth. / The cool night's dew runs through me. / With boundless joy, / that only moves the silent creature" (Ich lebte wie die weißen Blumen leben. / Die Lust des Lichts, die Süßigkeit der Wärme, / Die Kühle nächt'gen Taus durchrannen mich / Mit einer grenzenlosen bangen Freude / Die nur die stumme Kreatur bewegt. Ibid. 78). The tale ends in disaster when the husband shoots his wife during a novelty act involving seven bullets. The juggler realizes in the end that Elisabeth has always loved the Baron, whom she met as a young girl travelling with her gypsy band. The Baron holds the gypsy woman in his arms as they share a passionate kiss just before she dies (Ibid. 79).

Further Weimar literary works foreground the supposed magical powers of the Zigeunerin.[29] In Werner Bergengruen's novel, *Die Zigeuner und das Wiesel* (1927), the magical "schöne Zigeunerin" (beautiful gypsy woman), Gisterna, who is described as having red lips, high cheek bones, and dark eyes, travels from village to village performing her craft of fortune-telling (46, 54). Having been beaten by her husband, Bischothilo, she travels some distance behind the group, making a living from fortune-telling, stealing chickens, and curing cattle. Just as Grellmann in his 1787 *Historischer Versuch über die Zigeuner* describes the gypsy woman who sickens local cattle with salve, so too does Gisterna partake in this dubious healing practice (51).[30] Her magic is a ruse: she smears the grazing cattle with animal fat so that they cannot eat, only to later "cure" them by wiping away the cunning tallow.

The real power attributed to Gisterna in *Die Zigeuner* is connected to her taming of the so-called "magic weasel." Tramping through the forest, Gisterna finds a mother weasel with a baby in tow.[31] This baby bears the

29   Agnes Miegel's story *Die schöne Malone* (1926) features shaggy gypsy women ("zottlige Zigeunerweiber") as card readers (26). Karl Aloys Schenzinger's novel *Der Hitlerjunge Quex* (1932) presents the gypsy woman as an ominous fortune teller at the Berlin fairground (15, 28). For a list of Weimar works featuring the gypsy woman, see Hille, *Identitätskonstruktionen* 60–74.

30   See Hille, *Identitätskonstruktionen* 68–74 for a comparison of Grellmann's coverage of gypsies and Bergengruens's novel, *Die Zigeuner.*

31   Gisterna pulls out her knife and cuts the throat of the mother weasel. She then roasts and eats the weasel meat, noting the power that washes over her body (Bergengruen 50).

sign of the Stechapfel (thorn apple/jimson weed), otherwise known as "the devil's trumpet" or "devil's weed," in a shape adorning the weasel's fur.[32] According to Gisterna's tale, the human who possesses the weasel with the sign of the thorn apple will have luck in love, and all his wishes will come true (49). Gypsy lore further claims that if one takes three weasel hearts out of living creatures, eating them immediately, then one becomes endowed with the art of prophesy.[33] Weasels, then, are undoubtedly worth procuring, since not only is a trick-performing weasel a means for extorting money from the cheapest Gajo (non-gypsy, 49), the weasel is also a bearer of good luck, owing to which it is capable of protecting the entire "horde" of gypsies from evil spirits:

> Ein Wiesel mit dem Zeichen schützt die ganze Horde vor den Mulos, den knochenlosen Nachtwesen, die aus totgeborenen Kindern entstehen und jedes Jahr an ihrem Geburtstage von ihren Genossen gekocht werden müssen, um neue Lebenssäfte zu gewinnen. Aber das sind Dinge, von denen nur die Zigeuner wissen. (Bergengruen 49)

> A weasel with the sign protects the whole horde against the mulos, the boneless night creatures that arise from stillborn children, that have to be cooked every year by their comrades in order to gain new juices. But these are things only the gypsies know about.

We learn here that the weasel is able to protect the bande of gypsies from the evil spirits of dead children, whose life-sustaining juices are procured by cooking their carcasses. It is also suggested that these rituals are a form of magic whose secrets are only known to the gypsies. In Gisterna's story, the magic weasel can help to win back the love of her husband, Bischothilo, as well as the respect of her gypsy bande, including the female elder, the Puri Daj. Magic is harnessed by not only the young gypsy, Gisterna, but

---

32   A magic plant for the gypsies, the Stechapfel was a weed that supposedly transformed into a human being in the person of the female elder (Bergengruen 49). For the gypsies, the hedgehog, the thorn apple weed, and weasel are supposedly magical instruments that bring good luck to the group (Ibid. 50).

33   The fur of the weasel is further believed to heal wounds, while its blood can cure epilepsy (Bergengruen 49). If a weasel strikes a human, however, the person will either lose his life or, minimally, his sight (49).

by the longhaired, gray elder woman, who uses snake meat and saffron to heal an ailing child (52). The magic of the weasel, however, is not enough to keep Gisterna alive. As Gisterna and her husband walk the tightrope in a performance for the village, the weasel (as the third member of the act) refuses to participate in the finale. He instead chews through the rope, causing the two gypsies to tumble to their deaths. The villagers scream with shock as Gisterna suffers a mortal fall (60).

The villagers' temporary fixation with the alien gypsies is then followed by a restoration of law and order, as symbolized by the deaths of those practicing necromancy. To this end, the community must expel the foreigners. Dorothy Figueira discusses the apparent dangers associated with the nomad who does not share the ideas of the state, nor does she contribute to the economy, living like a pariah at the bounds of civil society (80). The nomadic gypsy Other must therefore be "controlled, ostracized, and/or exterminated" in order to safeguard the community from moral decay (Ibid. 89). Like the weasel with its eerie, Stechapfel emblem, the gypsy is likewise marked out as magical, owing to which she is forcibly cast out.

In A. Rosalie's novel *Rache einer Zigeunerin oder Der Mensch denkt und Gott lenkt!* (1928), Baron Hans von Delmenhorst and his father Dagobert, as well as various other individuals, are caught up with a dangerous female gypsy, Wlaska, who is described at the beginning of the novel as a "dämonische Schönheit" ("demonic beauty" 28).[34] The young trickster, Wlaska, first lures the musician, Hendrik, away from his betrothed, prompting his lover's suicide. The evil Wlaska then cavorts with Baron Dagobert only to be rejected by him as she grows old and "ugly." In her fury at the Delmenhorst family, Wlaska commits a host of ills, including spawning a gypsy son, Franz Rustan, who will scheme and murder in the service of Dagobert's son, Hans, as well as participating in acts of poisoning, extortion, murder, child-stealing, and kidnap. The female gypsy in *Rache einer Zigeunerin* is so depraved that it is only thanks to the intervention of the pure woman, Nelly, that she can be ritually cleansed before her death.

---

34   A. Rosalie is the pseudonym for Anny Huber, a female author from the Weimar period.

Wlaska's curious sexuality incorporates a magical dimension, owing to which she enchants, beguiles, and seduces men into doing her bidding. Hendrik, Nelly's father, tells the story of the beautiful gypsy, whom he met in his younger years. She was the toast of Munich, beguiling the male population with her talent and beauty (Rosalie 27).[35] The youthful Hendrik regales how he had been dared by his drinking partners to solicit Wlaska's affection; in so doing, he is overwhelmed by her gypsy wiles (Ibid. 28). Frederik is forced by this temptress to give up his betrothed, his oaths, and his future. Wlaska's plot to inform Frederik's fiancée of the affair ends in the suicide of his beloved, and Hendrik's eternal guilt. The gypsy woman reacts to her handiwork with an uncanny laugh that still resounds many years thereafter (Ibid. 29).[36] Wlaska's seduction of Frederik, and her delight at his undoing, provides the backdrop for her ensuing dark deeds.

The criminal acts of Wlaska committed in her later years echo her youthful malice. Once her affair with Baron Dagobert ends, she roams the countryside with a gypsy bande, coupling up with a gypsy man, thereby begetting her son, Franz. Furthermore, her ability to concoct poisonous combinations accords her renown for her preternatural prowess (37). Wlaska's contrivances at Castle Ebensee cause her to be connected with murders (37). Castle Ebensee is also the scene of Wlaska's magic: here, she mixes poisonous draughts that lead to the mortal condition of Baron Hans' wife, Isabella, and their son. While Wlaska's herbs are trusted by villagers to heal the sick, they are at the same time used against Isabella and her son to create a deathly trance. As Isabella describes her illness, while thereby losing consciousness, she hears a roaring in her ears; Wlaska's laugh being so dastardly that it could only erupt from a "demon's throat" (41).[37] It is

---

35 "Die Hauptanziehungskraft übte eine junge Künstlerin, Wlaska, aus, die sowohl durch ihre staunenswerten Leistungen in der Arena als auch, und zwar hauptsächlich durch ihre außerordentliche Schönheit, einen förmlichen Aufruhr unter der Männerwelt Münchens erregt hatte" (Rosalie 27).

36 "nur ein gräßliches Lachen schlug an mein Ohr, das ich nach vielen Jahren noch oft in meinen Träume ernahm" (29).

37 "Es wurde schwarz vor meinen Augen; in den Ohren brauste es, […] ein Lachen, wie es nur aus der Kehle eines Dämons hervorkommen kann" (41).

Wlaska who gives to Isabella's uncle the idea of the poisonous draught, imparting to him the means for righting Isabella's secret, transgressive marriage to Hans (43). Upon inspecting the seemingly lifeless bodies of his wife and son, Hans leaves his family for dead.[38]

Wlaska betokens a threat to the Delmenhorst family in her cavorting with the dark arts.[39] Her involvement in the poisoning of Graf Theodor by Baron Hans and Franz in the Ormeul forest is the family's most guarded secret. Theodor's murder, orchestrated by Wlaska's son, Franz, ensures that Hans is able to commandeer the estate of Delmenhorst, thereby wielding power and seizing its fortunes (46–47, 132). Wlaska is involved in the plot insofar as she mixes the poison responsible for the murder; its magic ingredients guarantee that the crime will go undetected (132).[40] Wlaska then extorts money from the two men in order to keep the poisoning in Paris a secret from the authorities.

The gypsy Wlaska knows and sees all that goes on at the Delemenhorst estate. The female gypsy's desire for revenge is absolute. She enacts her revenge on Isabella by stealing her baby from its pram, further causing Isabella's death by revealing the Baron's dealings in Paris. Wlaska plots with her son Franz to kidnap and murder Nelly, so that Nelly's adopted daughter does not realize her heirdom at Delemenhorst. In summary, Wlaska has the power as a member of the gypsy tribe to control the lives of those around her. Wlaska reminds her son of this magic: "We are certainly hated and despised, but we are feared even more, and this fear is a power whose ghostly arm covers all creatures on earth […] with irresistible magic." ("Wohl werden wir gehaßt und verachtet, aber noch viel mehr fürchtet man uns, und diese Furcht ist eine Macht, deren gespenstischer Arm alle Geschöpfe dieser Erde […] mit unwiderstehlichem Zauber umspannt") (47). Wlaska's ability to ensnare and spellbind others is associated with the

---

38 Isabella and her son are later kept isolated in a house for another three years by the uncle; we may assume that their captivity is Wlaska's idea.

39 Furthermore, Wlaska's way with animals shows her devilry. For instance, she is able to tame Franz's horse (Rosalie 45). She also reads the palm of the servant Anna (Ibid. 100).

40 "kein Arzt der Welt findet in dem Körper des Toten davon eine Spur" (132).

properties of hell and the devil (Ibid. 48). Despite her change of heart at the novel's conclusion, she must nonetheless die in recompense for her sins.[41]

Max Horkheimer and Theodor Adorno note that magicians (broadly construed) pose a threat to social order, leading to community expulsion and ostracization (25). With this dynamic in mind, we may note that gypsies are compelled to wander in response to this social pressure. The 1928 edict from the city of Rummelsburg evidences the desire to keep gypsies at a distance: "Immediately notify the responsible land-hunting officer of any arrival of gypsies and gypsy gangs in districts or estates, so that he can break up and deport the gypsy troops" ("[J]edes Eintreffen von Zigeunern und Zigeunerbanden in Amts- bzw. Gutsbezirken sofort dem zuständigen Landjägerei-Beamten mitzuteilen, damit dieser die Zigeunertrupps sprengen und abschieben kann." Mihaly 300). According to this edict, gypsies must be moved on as soon as the appropriate authorities catch wind of their presence.

Female Gypsies in Weimar Cinema

The female gypsy's preternatural prowess – apparently grounded in an otherworldly force – is featured in several Weimar films. The most notable of these are Ernst Lubitsch's *Carmen* (*Gypsy Blood*, 1918),[42] while Lubitsch's costume films, which include *Die Augen der Mumie Ma* (the *Eyes of the Mummy Ma*, 1918), *Madame Dubarry* (*Passion*, 1919), and *Anna Boleyn* (*Deception*, 1920), all foreground fantasy in a post-World War One *Zeitgeist* of revolution and upheaval (McCormick 67–68). These films all betray a beautiful woman who wreaks havoc on the community, owing

---

41   Wlaska dies after being attacked by an advancing German army. She falls from her horse while travelling with Nelly to look for the latter's daughter, Marina.

42   The film version used here is eighty minutes long. *Carmen* was released in the U.S. in 1921 as *Gypsy Blood*. It was edited significantly to remove overtly sexual moments and scenes. See Powrie (et al.) 56–57.

to which she needs exorcising (or at least subduing) to restore order. Far from being "escapist fantasies," these films comment upon gender relations in a period of German cultural chaos. For instance, in *Carmen*, it is the titular *femme fatale* who is scapegoated for the fall of the honest soldier. And, although she is capable of predicting the future through palmistry, her devilish magic results in the downfall of a well-meaning man, as well as several others surrounding her. In his 1920 review of the film, Karl Figdor notes that Carmen lures the male world of Seville and Gibraltar into sexual decline.[43]

Carmen, screened in Berlin in November, 1918, begins with a framing device involving three gypsy men sitting around a campfire.[44] The intertitle foreshadows events to come: "When night winds blow, and campfires burn / From Gypsy lips the Gypsies learn / Gypsy magic and Gypsy lore / Of Gypsy Blood in the days of yore."[45] The story is set to be one of magic and intrigue, including the bewitching of a man named Don José Navarro (Harry Liedtke), Dragoon of the Almanza regiment. The story's incipit evinces great promise for Don José: his betrothed (Greta Diercks) and mother (Sophie Pagay) are awaiting him at his village home, while he has also been promoted to the rank of sergeant. However, he then meets La Carmencita (Pola Negri), the dangerous, eponymous gypsy, whose sexual powers are more than Don José can handle (see Figure 18). He quickly becomes enmeshed with her, accepting her rose as his "first folly," thereafter becoming so spellbound by her that he helps her to escape after a fight breaks out in the tobacco factory (his "second folly"). His final mistake (or "third folly") consists in allowing Carmen's gypsy-smugglers to breach the

43 "Fünf lange, fast richtig bis zum Ende ausgewachsene Akte durch, lockt sie (Carmen) die Mannswelt von Sevilla, Gibraltar usw. […] Vor allem die spanisch dekorierte 'Sünde,' wie man in tugendhaften Kreisen nicht nur in Angelsachsien, sondern auch anderswo seit den seligen Mönchs- und Hexenzeiten die fleischliche Verlockung zu benamsen gewohnt ist" (Figdor).

44 The screening of the film was followed by a shooting outside, associated with the German revolution (Negri, *Memoirs* 142).

45 Powrie et al. suggest the possibility that the original German did not have any bookending (sc. beginning and end sequence), although they note that this was Lubitsch's idea (*Carmen on Film* 57).

wall he is guarding, as well as killing the Colonel who is likewise in love
with her. Himself reduced to a smuggler, he ultimately foregoes Carmen's
love, her interests instead lying with the bullfighter, Escamillo (Leopold
von Ledebur). Sooner preferring to see her dead than with another man,
Don José stabs Carmen.

Figure 18. Pola Negri and Harry Liedtke in *Carmen*. Producer Paul Davidson; director Lubitsch, 1918.

The twin seduction of Don José and the Colonel is reinforced in the
first of many dance scenes, where Carmen is asked to perform for the
Colonel's party. As hundreds of partygoers drink and carouse at long
tables, Carmen enters the hall and jumps on a table to sway and dip, tambourine in-hand. Scenes of Carmen dancing are interspersed with face
shots of an intoxicated man, then of the lustful Colonel, who directs his
gaze toward her. Spurring on the male gaze with come-hither zeal – which
includes the ogle of the lowly Don José, who can scarcely take his eyes off
her – Carmen embarks upon a hypnotizing spectacle of spins and twirls,
until she is finally carried away. Carmen so enchants the Colonel that he
beckons to see her again. Reading his palm, she prophesies his impending
death ("You must beware of black-haired girls, Senor! Else, one will cause

your death").[46] After meeting Don José in the gypsy tavern she secures his undying love. Dressed in a seductive headscarf with large, hooped earrings and plaid skirt, her status as the gypsy Other drives Don José into a state of delirium. He clutches and pulls at Carmen – eyes wide and dark – scarcely able to liberate himself from her as the bugle beckons him back to the military compound.

The seduction of both Don José and the Colonel is evidenced in their visit to Carmen's home in the decrepit gypsy locale of Calle de Candilejo. Behind a door with a white cross – betokening death and martyrdom – Carmen seduces Don José as a reward for granting passage to the gypsy robbers via his unguarded gate. Plying him with wine, she again reads his palm, promising turmoil. Deploying her artful gypsy magic, Carmen melts lead, thereafter tossing it into cold water in order to predict Don José's future; the melted metal takes on the shape of a cross and skull, foretelling Don José's demise ("A cross and skull – no good luck with men Joseito!"). Forgoing his future, yet still motivated by his *amour fou* for Carmen, Don José slays the Colonel, who has entered her house.

Carmen's gyrations seduce Don José: her enchanting palmistry an apparent guarantor of the trouble awaiting him. Her sexuality ultimately trounces Don José, as she transmutes from her former guise as an astonishing seductress – with her wild, energetic hemlines and transfixing accessories – into the figure of an arrant ruffian, escorting her troupe of gypsies into the mountains with utterly masculine nonchalance.[47] Her sexual prowess is especially persuasive over Don José, as she clamors over the rocky cliffs, giving orders to her male counterparts and shooting at the cavalrymen. All the while Carmen authoritatively leads her gypsy bande, Don José is contrastingly prostrated, the juxtaposition of the two

---

46 Anat Zanger reads this dance sequence as "staged ethnography," whereby Carmen dances for the white man. This sequence pairs with the "ethnographic sequence" in which the gypsies dance spontaneously (84).

47 Not only is Carmen both feminine and masculine, she also possesses "animal agility": after escaping capture, she opens Pastia's gate with her chin and shoulder (Powrie et al., *Carmen on Film* 65).

bespeaking an insuperable power differential.[48] Here again we are supplied with a broader cultural vignette, namely of a woman riding roughshod over her enfeebled fellow man. She reigns over him physically; her swamping shawl slung over her shoulder. More a "man" than a woman in this merciless landscape, Carmen defeats Don José, who can do nothing but lie on his side as she tells him that she loves the matador.[49]

Carmen's carnal allure is epitomized through her seductive dress. She wears a beautiful costume for the bullfight, including a velvet dress, ornate headpiece, with gleaming pearls and a pure, white veil. While the bullfighter effortfully grapples to withstand her devastating allure as he escorts her to the fight in his carriage, Don José struggles being without her, stabbing her in the back so that she cannot become any other man's possession.[50] In the end, Carmen falls dead, arms askance, Don José embracing her lifeless body. This final manifestation of sexuality marks Carmen's death and Don José's doom. However, the final part of the film issues a caveat. As the three men once again sit around the fire, the storyteller utters an apparent injunction: "So runs the tale. But some say she did not die [...] for she was in league with the Devil himself!" The flickering light here suggests a transcendental, gypsy intervention, as promised in the opening sequence. Indeed, with her powers of seduction, we are led to believe that Carmen is still effecting her peculiar brand of magic, although perhaps now in conspiracy with the Devil himself.

Carmen possesses the ability to seduce men merely through her dance and can moreover predict the day of their deaths through her perspicacious palmistry. She crosses the borders of the gypsy slums of the city to

48   Zanger notes that Carmen's masculinity is apparent as she initially throws down her flower and takes the initiative in lovemaking (86). When Carmen leaves for Gibraltar on business to Egypt, she even dons a man's coat and hat while bargaining on the waterfront, connoting her masculinity.

49   Carmen tells Don José that "a dog and a wolf cannot live together." He grabs her and lists all of the sacrifices he has made for her, before falling down, trounced, and vanquished.

50   This idea is redolent of Robert Browning's dramatic monologue *Porphyria's Lover* (1836), whereby the possessive and monomaniacal male eternalizes the romantic tie between himself and his darling, Porphyria, through her murder at his hands. He thereby immortalizes their bond while also debarring other potential suitors. Theirs is now a *de facto* everlasting love.

the criminal realm. While well-meaning individuals cannot traverse the craggy rocks of the smugglers (for, this is the gypsies' secret hideaway), Carmen is in her element.[51] Anat Zanger notes that borders and boundaries are guarded by a dominant society, ready to protect themselves against the unstable, nomadic energy of the gypsy (89). When these boundaries are breached, the excesses of the "alien culture" are able to penetrate and co-opt the dominant culture (89).

With her large, engulfing shawl and puissant persona, Carmen emphatically transgresses her gender identity. As she travels to the port city dressed as a man, she seduces officers, secures criminal contacts, and lures her lover, the matador. Carmen's magic exists in her powers of seduction, in her ability to read signs and symbols, as well as in her indisputable efficacy in a man's world. In the end, Carmen *qua* gypsy may escape her fate: her salvation consisting in her association with the Devil.

Gypsy magic was a common trope in Weimar culture. Books such as Margarethe Fahnert's *Die Kunst des Kartenlegens* (*The Art of Card Laying*, 1926) noted the old sources of gypsy magic, while Weimar articles such as Adele von Finck's "Chirologie und Chiromantie" (Chirology and Chiromancy, *Querschnitt* 1928) discuss the gypsy penchant for palmistry. According to Finck, palm-reading in the times of the Egyptians, Persians, and Romans gave way to the chaos of history. It was alleged that travelling gypsies (of the likes of Carmen) drew on this ancient, occult tradition, ultimately to harm others (Ibid.). Given their talent for the Tarot, gypsies were believed to possess a bona fide ability to predict the future (Finck, "Zigeuner, Magie, Karten" 474).

The gypsy as our titular "black magic woman" and sexual *femme fatale*, as depicted in Ernst Lubitsch's *Carmen*, recurs in his fantasy film *Sumurun* (1920). There, a troupe of travelling entertainers enters the city, causing mayhem.[52] The dancer, played by Pola Negri, attempts to seduce both old

---

51　The military manages to find the gypsy hideout in the mountains after Don José saves his fellow soldier from being executed by the gypsies; the soldier returns to the barracks and alerts the troops. The soldiers then attack the gypsies with gusto. Don José is able to escape the onslaught, going into hiding in the gypsy tavern.

52　*Sumurun* is an adaptation of a 1910 pantomime by Friedrich Freska of the same name. For more information on the film, see Kracauer, *From Caligari to Hitler* 50, 52; Eisner, *The Haunted Screen* 85–86; and McCormick.

and young sheiks in this so-called "oriental" fantasy. Commenting on the dancer in 1920, the *Berliner Zeitung am Mittag* had the following to say: "Pola Negri, the dancer: embodied passion, fetterless glowing flame that consumes men, a sparkling cat, crouched forever to jump" ("Pola Negri, die Tänzerin: verkörperte Leidenschaft, fessellos, glühende Flamme, die Männer verzehrt, eine funkelnde Katze, ewig zum Sprung geduckt" (qtd. in *Lichtbild-Bühne*)). A comedy in which women pursue men, the Negri character dances her way into the hearts of those in power only to perish at the film's terminus. Rick McCormick reads this film as a veiled commentary on the "Other" status of the German Jew. He notes that Wilhelmine- and Weimar-era representations of "Orientalism" refer not to Islam, nor to the Middle East, but to Eastern European Jewry (71). Although Lubitsch's oriental fantasy, which includes portrayals of bazaars and harems, can indeed be seen as "[prejudicial] against *Ostjuden*" (McCormick 72), this film can also be read as a commentary on the gypsy Other. To this end, Lubitsch's *Carmen* predefines the female gypsy, a rubric according to which the character of *Sumurun*'s dancer is likewise typecast: this overtly sexualized woman travels in a pack, crossing borders and boasting a near-preternatural mastery over interpersonal affairs.

Sumurun features a gypsy troupe that comes to town to perform. The dancer of the troupe manages to convince the young sheik that the performers must remain in the city by sexually enticing him, thereby securing a spot in the old sheik's harem. The hunchback from the troupe loves the dancer, and, thanks to a series of mishaps (for instance, he takes magic pills and is carried, unconscious, through the city), he is able to follow her to her various destinations. The parallel story involves the love between Sumurun – the old sheik's favorite concubine – and the fabric trader, Nur Al-Din. As the two are separated by the palace walls, they conspire to unite and finally defeat the old sheik, who is slain by the hunchback as retribution for the dancer's murder.

Made two years after *Carmen*, *Sumurun* is indeed similar to Lubitsch's 1918 gypsy tale. The film's incipit features the gypsy caravan, which traverses rugged mountains *en route* to the walled city. The wagon is clearly a gypsy home, bearing a colorful cloth draped on the inner walls and a stringed instrument mounted in the background. Inside are a host of characters, including the beautiful, seductive dancer (Negri) donning large earrings and colorful clothing, who passes her time seducing a young male gypsy. This game, in turn, arouses the jealousy of the hunchback (Ernst Lubitsch). The old woman (Margarete Kupfer) lays cards and drinks in the corner. As the group sits around the campfire in a scene similar to the frame of Lubitsch's *Carmen*, we also witness a black slave following the troupe. He is pictured as a conniving character, convincing the dancer that she must ingratiate herself with the slave trader (Paul Biensfeldt) in order to join the sheik's harem.

The gypsy troupe, comprising the seductive dancer, the hunchback musician, the "old hag," and "the slave," then gain access to the town, promising to entertain the community. With the coming of the "minstrels," the town reverts to pandemonium: people emerge from various doorways and alleys; children dance; dogs take off in packs. The musical entrance features the hunchback on the guitar and the old crone on the flute, and is completed by the dancer, whose arms move wildly with scarf in-hand. The seductive dancer secures the troupe's evening performance by showing the young sheik (Carl Clewing) her seductive dance moves: she sways, twirls, and falls to the ground. For her trouble, she is offered a bag of coins and the guarantee of an evening meeting with the sheik.

Sumurun begins with the promise of a gypsy carnival, including music and dance. In a Weimar context, gypsies were supposedly known for their disruptive presence at festivals. Their association with carnivals and disruption is evident in journals of the time. Christa Hatvany-Winsloe in her 1929 article "Zigeuner" describes the stereotypical gypsy predilection for wild celebration and clamorous brouhaha, where alcohol flows alongside frenetic movement and music, whose tempo increases with gypsies – both young and old – chanting "tanzen, tanzen, tanzen" ("dance, dance, dance" 472). According to the author, the festival is only over when one has spent all of one's money and has hugged and kissed the gypsy women: no festival, no market, no event is conceivable without the gypsies (Ibid.).[53] Hatvany-Winsloe further foregrounds not only the cheer of

---

53 "Kein Fest, kein Markt, kein Ereignis irgendwelcher Bedeutung ist denkbar ohne die Zigeuner" (472).

the gypsy presence but also its menace. The reader is warned that the word "Zigeuner" (gypsy) is a curse word. The author provides an historical incident as warning: "One hundred and fifty gypsies were hanged once. Men, women, and children. Why? Because of cannibalism" ("Einmal wurden hundertundfünfzig Zigeuner gehängt. Männer, Frauen, Kinder. Warum? Wegen Menschenfresserei" 471). Here, the festive nature of carnival is tempered by the act of consuming human flesh, as well as the promise of retribution against the Other, who has supposedly committed the grim deed.

With the film stock tinted red, the carnival sequence in *Sumurun* features an audience who is in a heightened state of anticipation. In close-up shots, we see black individuals and children, who, in their childlike amusement, act as proxies for a breakdown of social norms. The performance begins with both the old crone and the hunchback: the crone performing a snake act, hoisting the animal above her shoulders, her backside to the audience; the hunchback, meanwhile, strums his guitar and dances with a life-size stick puppet. It is the female dancer, however, who moves the audience to ecstasy. Like Carmen's performance at the Colonel's ball, this gypsy dancer elicits reaction shots from the men in the audience. Adorned in an outfit with jeweled headpiece, circular earrings, bracelets, and a v-shaped jeweled belt, the dancer twirls, falls, and dips to the ground, creating a round, flower-like formation captured in an overhead shot. She finally falls down on her knees, pulling the veil over her head and twirling like a matador, exiting the stage in a rapid movement. Reactions to her dance are registered by the men in the audience, specifically the older sheik (Paul Wegener), who is transfixed by her sexuality. She returns the gaze of the sheik, bespeaking her own sexually predatory nature.

As in *Carmen*, the gypsy dancer *qua* sexual predator reinforces her reputation through dance (see Figure 19). Her goal is to impress the old sheik and join the harem. In her departure scene, she rebuffs the desperate hunchback, spending her last moments in the tent looking at herself in the mirror. She is not only forced to juggle the hunchback's and the old sheik's attention: she must also flee the young sheik, who continues to pursue her in the city streets. She literally hangs from a bridge to avoid his affections, choreographing a triangle of men whose desires she is effortfully opposing.

Figure 19. Pola Negri in *Sumurun*. Producer Paul Davidson; director Lubitsch, 1920.

As the gypsy dancer prepares to meet the old sheik, she further manipulates her appearance to create a masculine persona. Her sleeveless blouse and spotted harem pants present a particular virility. Indeed, while she wears jewelry and dons a silk sarong at the end, we are left with the impression of the dancer strutting around in trousers – a not-unfamiliar sight for a Weimar audience. Paul Poiret vilifies the garçon style with its "pointed shoulders, [and] bosoms without breasts" (33). Brazen acts of a woman in pursuit of her own advantage, not to mention sexual satisfaction, are captured in the gypsy's further encounter with the old sheik in his bedroom, where she plays chase with him, as well as in her embrace of the young sheik before his sleeping father.

In *Sumurun*, we find a gypsy woman who crosses borders from the country to the city in search of seduction. Her powers of persuasion, as evidenced in her dance performances, draw in the male suitors, in particular the powerful old sheik and his son. Her seductive quality is so puissant that each suitor is forced to kneel in her service. The hunchback gypsy is forced to rely on "magic" to comfort himself in his rejection: he ingests "magic pills" that will make "all trouble […] vanish" through a death-like sleep. Here, gypsy magic – prompted by the dancer – is enacted on the carnival stage. Seduction, sleep, and death will haunt the various characters, who come into contact with the dancer.

The gypsy dancer seduces multiple men to their ultimate demise in a way not unlike Lubitsch's character of Carmen. The gypsy dancer also has her counterpart in the beloved harem slave Sumurun (Jenny Hasselqvist), who acts as a counterpoint to the dancer with her own gypsyish character-istics: we may assume that Sumurun has come to the city from the outside (likely trafficked through the slave trade), and is proactive is the seduction of her suitor. Under the threat of death, she flirts with the fabric trader Nur Al-Din (Harry Liedtke), tossing him her flower. She manages two secret meetings with him: one in his shop, the other in the palace. Each time she meets with him, they embrace in an act associated with a woman in a harem.[54]

Finally, Sumurun's ultimate act of seduction – like that of Carmen and the gypsy dancer – involves dance. Armed with pillows, fine wine, and foodstuffs, Sumurun seduces Nur Al-Din within the palace walls. She bounds, gallops, and twirls, leaping over her lover in a seductive prance. One should take note of the reaction shot of the fabric trader during the dance: he leers at Sumurun in a manner not unlike that of the old sheik during the gypsy dancer's performance. The following two shots of the gypsy dancer and Sumurun substantiate their relationship. As the old sheik takes a necklace from Sumurun and gives it to the gypsy dancer, we see the women side by side. In costume and appearance, they appear un-cannily similar.

Not only is Sumurun a gypsy stand-in, complete with seductive nature and harem garb, it can also be argued that Nur Al-Din likewise bears the hallmarks of the gypsy stereotype. For he is a fabric trader whose moral

---

54   Sumurun's female attendant (Aud Egede Nissen) is in charge of staging her meet-ings with Nur Al-Din. Sumurun's constant presence during the meetings suggests that she is behind them. McCormick also notes Sumurun's status as subject vis-à-vis her lover Nur Al-Din: "Sumurun swoons, but nonetheless it is she who stands up, pulling *him* up to her so that she can kiss him, her head positioned *above* his, her hands holding *his* face. *She* is the subject, and he the object, of desire" (74).

stature is repeated questioned, while his actions clearly typecast him in a gypsyish role (for example, in his secret meeting with Sumurun in his shop, he puts a bracelet on her leg and kisses her feet). Moreover, the farcical slave double act constitute not only a mirror for their gypsy owner, but an apotheosis of gypsy stereotypes: Mutti and Putti steal jewelry from the gypsy troupe and attempt to hide the supposed dead body of the hunchback. The elaborate comic performances by the slave "twins" further mimic the gypsy performers; wrestling, dancing, and creating comic moments that rival the performing troupe in intensity.

The harem is ultimately unleashed on the community, portending a perpetual state of carnival. The final shot of the lovers, Sumurun and Nur Al-Din, signals a new order in society: one grounded in seduction and trickery. Sumurun's similarities to the gypsy dancer are numerous, thereby marking her out as a gypsy. If Nur Al-Din is also representative of an alien outsider, then the film may be comically suggesting how gypsies are able to infiltrate and dominate the social order. Gypsy presence, like that of the witch, is always tinged with danger, magic, and mystery. According to Hatvany-Winsloe: "One can assume everything from gypsies, but never learn the truth" ("Vermuten kann man von Zigeunern alles, die Wahrheit aber nie erfahren." Hatvany-Winsloe 471).[55]

Conclusion

Ultimately, then, the witch and gypsy, as found in various cultural depictions from the Weimar period, can be understood as proxies for the threat posed by the emancipated Neue Frau to the social order. Although the witch is seemingly innocent in her demeanor, she nonetheless has the ability to cause harm with her use of herbs and magic, as well as through a command of nature. When her sexuality is met with the right

---

55 Danger in the film is encapsulated at the end where the dancer is stabbed by the old sheik; the old sheik kills his son and is then murdered by the hunchback. This violence is committed with either daggers or sabers.

counter-magic, as in the case of *Das Blaue Licht*, then society may be safe for the time being. However, the witch *qua* keeper of secrets is formidable. Her masculine independence and aggression (Horsley and Horsley 15) give her the upper hand. Although she risks burning at the stake, her power is never truly extinguished. Like the witch, the gypsy woman's seductive dance performances are symbolic of the sexual liberation realized by German women following the World War One. She is able to draw on both the forces of the natural world, predominantly through the mixing of herbs, and the supernatural realm, through her use of fortune-telling, palmistry, and necromancy, which work to subdue and dominate men.

The Trance-Dancer and Medium

Following the discovery of such newfangled phenomena as radioactivity in the early twentieth century, strict divisions between the spiritual and the physical realm became irrevocably blurred (Linse 16). Ulrich Linse describes this cross-contamination in the following manner: "Die Geister konnten sich 'materialisieren,' und beim neuen Bild des Todes war der Unterschied zwischen Diesseits und Jenseits [...] 'nur subjektiv getrennte Welten'" ("the spirits could 'materialize,' and the new idea of death held that the difference between this world and the next was 'merely a subjective separation'" Ibid.). The supernatural sphere thereby emerges as fertile ground wherein Weimar's enigmatic Neue Frau can prosper. Shifting between these two worlds in Wilhelmine and Weimar Germany are the figures of the trance-dancer and medium. The trance-dancer in motion would bring out hidden energy and abilities, while providing access to an inner-world, unbreachable by conscious aware-ness and exceeding rational control (Pytlik 68). The medium acted as a direct conduit from this world to the next: the practice of spiritism often depended upon the medium's characteristic craft, communing with the souls of the deceased. Various kinds of mediumism were prac-ticed in the early twentieth century. These included the so-called "in-tellectual medium," who specialized in automatic/mechanical drawing or writing, and the "physical medium," who practiced levitation and/or materialization (sc. causing substances or shapes to appear) (Ibid. 36–38). According to spiritualists like Karl du Prel, the earthly body's death promised the materialization of the astral or immortal body, all facilitated by the medium's art (Du Prel, *Der Spiritismus* 21).

In this chapter, I analyze the female trance-dancer and medium as emblems of the New Woman's marginalization. The hypnotic effects pro-duced by the trance-dancer are respectively exemplified in Anita Berber's expressive dance, Fritz Lang's 1927 cinematic masterwork, *Metropolis*, and Arnold Fanck's 1926 film, *Der Heilige Berg* (*The Holy Mountain*). These works proffer cultural representations of the New Woman, construed as overtly sexual and occultic, owing to which she posed an apparent threat to the social order. I furthermore offer a study of mediumism during this period through various Weimar cultural works, viz. Mary Wigman's expressive dance, which ably demonstrates New Woman's liminality. Dance continued to incorporate occultic themes following the Nazi takeover, as illustrated by Mary Wigman's 1934 series *Frauentänze* (Women's Dances). In particular, Wigman's *Totenklage* (Lament for the Dead), *Tanz der Seherin* (Dance of the Prophetess), and *Hexentanz* (Witch Dance) evinced occult elements of mediumism, prophesy, and magic in relation to woman. In conclusion, I explain how the occultic Neue Frau became a casualty of Hitler's Third Reich: women under Nazi rule losing their ability to participate meaningfully in public life.

Trance-Dancer as Hypnotist

Cultural representations of the occultic trance-dancer are rooted in the tradition of expressive dance (*Ausdruckstanz*), as well as hypnotism. Selma Jeanne Cohen discusses German expressive dance as coming from the inside out, enabling the dancer to bring her ideas to the audience (162). Like the sexually liberated New Woman, the expressive dancer employs freedom of motion to communicate her corresponding freedom of thought. The expressive dancer is hypnotic insofar as she both inveigles her masculine audience while also casting a spell on them.

Although hypnosis (as a therapeutic methodology) was practiced in the medical community – garnering the respect of many doctors during the World War One and beyond – it kept its connections to mysticism. Early proponents such as Albert von Schrenck-Notzing believed that hypnotized individuals could practice telepathy and clairvoyance in their altered states (von Schrenck-Notzing; Gauld 464; Moll 398–99). Schrenck-Notzing's ideas were vindicated by Albert Moll's description of hypnotism as potentially linked to occult phenomena, including "thought-transference, mental suggestion, telepathy or [...] telaesthesia," with telepathy being "the transference of thoughts, feelings, sensations, &c., from a person A. to a person B. by some means other than the recognized sense perceptions of B" (Moll 398–99).

In *Studies on Hysteria* (*Studien über Hysterie*, 1895), Freud and Breuer theorized that a traumatic event etiologically undergirded hysteria, which could be revealed through hypnosis. Although much remained at the level of the unconscious in the hysteric, the condition corresponded with an expressed symptomatology. This "splitting" activity was important in treating the hysteric (Breuer and Freud 221). Using hypnosis, the therapist could create a vacancy within consciousness, freeing the patient from resistance and amnesia (Ibid. 216). Over the next thirty years, the study of hypnosis and suggestion would be linked to the supernatural through telepathy as a potential form of thought transference. The art of supernatural persuasion is critical to understanding the allegedly "occultic" underpinnings of the trance-dance in its emerging twentieth-century form. Exemplifying the early pairing of hypnosis and dance is Madeleine Guipet's 1902–03 visit to the Parisian magnetist Emile Magnin for headache treatment,[1] who not only cured her condition with hypnosis but further utilized music to impart a trance-like state. Madeleine, who had no previous dance training, began to dance as if a professional, occasionally lapsing into a state of catalepsy or statuesque stasis (Schrenck-Notzing, *Die Traumtänzerin* 28). Schrenck-Notzing interpreted this aspect of catalepsy as proof that Madeleine was hysterical, while also noting that hypnosis enabled one's natural instincts and movements to break loose from cultural repression: "What Madeleine reveals is nothing less than her inner nature, her sculptural expressiveness, her musical feelings in easy beautiful form" (Ibid. 76). In Madeleine's first Munich séance, Schrenck-Notzing put her in a trance, requesting that she dance to the music of Mozart.[2] This performance led to Madeleine's début

1   In this chapter, I invoke Albert Moll's definition of hypnotism, which connects the latter to spiritualist phenomena such as "thought-transference, mental suggestion, telepathy or [...] telaesthesia." This definition takes account of hypnotism's relationship with mesmerism insofar as hypnosis did not necessarily require the hypnotist to induce sleep (Moll 398).

2   The trance-dancer, Lina, was a contemporary of Madeleine Guipet, who likewise evinced a proclivity for dancing to music under hypnosis. When photographs

at Munich's Schauspielhaus, whereby male members of the *Psychologische Gesellschaft* – Germany's first occult research group – watched with utter fascination (Treitel 117).[3]

Examining a photograph of Madeleine Guipet dancing at the Schauspielhaus, Corinna Treitel notes that, in her performance, Madeleine assumes a more powerful position than the male researchers: "Guipet's creative unconscious commanded the scene, and in the face of her talent the men of the *Psychologische Gesellschaft* had to be content to sit, literally at her feet, and watch the performance" (Ibid.). In the photograph, Guipet's body strikes a sensual pose, her arms outstretched and head tilted to one side; her form-fitting dress adding to an utterly sexualized posture, while the scientists' heads – visible in the foreground – are dwarfed in size and significance by the dancer's body. Max Dessoir comments on the dream-dancer Madeleine in his 1919 *Vom Jenseits der Seele* (From the Far Side of the Soul), noting that this gentle and charming lady transmogrifies into a demon-like creature with supernatural gifts (68).[4] According to Dessoir, Madeleine's transformation through hypnosis and the séance has led to her assuming occultic clout.

In the role of dream-dancer, then, Madeleine was herself an empowered hypnotist, who captured her audience with her sensual and demonic dance. Contemporary critic, Ernst Schur, underscores this point in his discussion of the dream-dancer: "The female dancer is not in a trance, but we [the audience] are" (Schur 56). Artist and founding member of the *Psychologische Gesellschaft*, Albert von Keller's paintings of Madeleine reveal a fascination with her dance. Works like *Madeleine Guipet als Traumtänzerin* (Madeleine Guipet as Dream Dancer, 1904) and *Madeleine Guipet als*

---

were taken of her dance, light streams were registered. Scientist Albert de Rochas theorized that this light had occultic properties, with projections of thought and feeling supposedly travelling outside of the body in the ether (Witzmann 624). In the cases of Lina and Madeleine G., the movement produced during trance-dancing could allegedly be directed by otherworldly powers.

3   The *Psychologische Gesellschaft* was respectively founded by Adolf Bayersdorfer, Gabriel von Max, and Albert von Keller in the 1880s (Treitel 110).

4   "sie verwandelt sich aus einer liebenswürdigen und anmutigen Dame in ein dämonisches Wesen von übernatürlichen Gaben."

Kassandra (Madeleine Guipet as Cassandra, 1904) render the sublime subject with her occultic contours (see Figure 20). Keller's depiction of Madeleine as Cassandra cajoles the spectator to come under her spell.[5] In the painting, Madeleine's ecstatic look and outstretched arms envelop the viewer. Although her head and body are turning leftwards, the movement of her costume suggests forward motion, hinting that we are within reach of her sensual grasp. In each and every one of Keller's paintings, Madeleine controls her inquisitors with intense intrigue and mesmeric moves; she virtually steps off of the canvas in vanquishment of her viewer.

Figure 20. Albert von Keller. *Madeleine Guipet als Traumtänzerin* (Madeleine Guipet as Dream Dancer), 1904.

5   For Keller's paintings of Madeleine, see Müller.

The powers attributed to the trance-dancer, Madeleine, were born from a combination of eroticism and a connection to the occult. Weimar publisher and dance author Ernst Schertel believed that trance-dance was brought about by a deep, erotic trance, which, in turn, became an occult expression ("Erotik, Tanz Okkultismus" 309). In his 1926 article, "Gibt es hypnotischen Tanz?" ("Is there Hypnotic Dance?"), Schertel proclaims the trance-dance an otherworldly force: "Der Ekstatisierte bewegt sich in einer visionären, also scheinhaften Umwelt, und er handelt nicht mehr nach dem Willen seines Wach-Ichs, sondern unter dem Antrieb einer 'höheren Macht'" ("The ecstatic individual moves in a visionary or pseudo environment and acts not with respect to the waking-ego, but under a higher power's urging" 33). He remarks that the ecstasy brought about through dance could endow one with the occultic powers of clairvoyance, telekinesis, levitation, and materialization, along with other phenomena ("Erotik, Tanz Okkultismus" 308). Trance-dance resembles ancient-religious dances, consummated with frenzied music, masks, as well as costumes or artistic nudity, featuring the individual dancer who is transposed into another realm ("Gibt es hypnotischen Tanz?" 34).[6] In these instances, the trance-dancer becomes a sensual somnambulist who effortlessly moves to the music.

Schertel's "Gibt es hypnotischen Tanz?" reveals eight separate images featuring close-up shots of a sensual face (with eyes closed), as well as medium shots of bare breasts, with the 15-year-old actress, Inge Frank, assuming postures that resemble Charcot's erotic hysterics.[7] Full-body shots capture the actress striking a dance pose: her back arched, hands pointing downwards, and arms raised in jubilation. Here, we bear witness to the

6   Schertel employed photography to trigger the state of ecstasy supposedly required for the trance-dancer. He also got nude dancers to move between one another with shut eyes (Toepfer 65–66). Schertel led an experimental troupe of dancers known as Traumbühne Schertel.

7   It was not uncommon to find photographs in the popular press revealing women in trance-like positions, with eyes closed and heads thrown back as if orgasmic. The most disturbing of these images show women with white masses of teleplasma streaming from their mouths and noses. This teleplasma could bear the face of a loved one, which is either visible in the slime or simply represents the spirit of a dead individual. See *Der Querschnitt* 12.12 (December 1932) for several images of women and teleplasma.

so-called "ecstatic" essence of dance transforming into a spectacle of desire, drawing the viewer in to ogle Frank's auto-erotic display. Schertel's photographs of nude dancing were in keeping with a time that saw well-known figures like Celly de Rheydt and Anita Berber performing dance routines in the nude. Based on Schertel's depiction of dance, we can designate various expressive performers of the Weimar period *trance-dancers*.

It is Anita Berber who perhaps represents one of the best examples of this period's erotic dance, which may be characterized as *trance-dancing*. Berber studied under Emile Jacques-Dalcroze, master of rhythmic gymnastics, then becoming a professional dancer in 1917. Berber went on to perform such ecstatic dances as "Selbstmord" (Suicide), "Morphium" (Morphine), and "Haus der Irren" (Mad House), creating a stir when she published – along with Sebastian Droste – a book of poetry and images entitled *Die Tänze des Lasters, des Grauens und der Ekstase (Dances of Vice, Horror and Ecstasy*, 1923). Although Berber was a pioneer of expressive dance – not least being the first performer to dance nude onstage – she achieved renown for her notorious lifestyle; her hypnotic, public persona exemplifying the powers of the trance-dancer.[8]

Berber and Droste's book *Die Tänze des Lasters* defines the ecstasy of dance as movement designed to commune with a higher power.[9] According to the text, dance is an expression of inner experience, whereby the dancer plays no other role than embodying emotions like ecstasy and horror. In these dances, the body – with all of its parts – is set into motion through instructions from the soul, thereby acting upon "[d]as Aufhorchen fremder Urkräfte die aufschreiend uns erschrecken und zerreißen" ("the crying out of primal powers, which frighten and tear at us" 15). Dance evokes primitive powers that are then translated into occult themes, encompassing a connection between this world and the next. In Berber's dance "Astarte,"

---

8 For more information on Anita Berber as a Weimar artist, see Funkenstein. Berber also appeared in two dozen films from 1917–25. See Fischer 31–49.

9 *Die Tänze des Lasters* featured dances that Berber and Droste performed in Berlin. It is not known whether the poems were read alongside the dance, although they describe the *purpose* of the dances. As Karl Toepfer notes: "Berber and Droste understood dance as an art that emerges out of writing and completes itself through publication in the form of a book" (92).

she enacts the goddess of fertility, sexuality, and war, depicted as the feminine moon ("Weiches heiliges tropfendes Silber") (*Die Tänze des Lasters* 8). The silver goddess ultimately possesses the power to wreak havoc on earth-dwellers, as evidenced in her ability to punish while extracting sadomasochistic delight (8–9).

Berber and Droste's book also presents a combination of ecstasy and otherworldly imagery in a description of the dance, "Mord, Weib und Gehenkter" (Murder, Woman and the Hanged Man), which was to be performed by both authors.[10] In this dance, woman murders boy, while an innocent man must pay for the crime through the hangman's noose. In an extended scene, which takes place in the woman's room, her reaction to the crime bespeaks a combination of fear and desire. As the living dead suddenly enter the room and surround the woman, she in turn places her neck in the noose.

One can well imagine the reaction to Berber's captivating dance images, which were enhanced through architect Harry Täuber's stage design. In particular, the design that was to be utilized for "Mord, Weib und Gehenkter" featured wooden scaffolding (representing the gallows) that included a red ladder among other elements (*Die Tänze des Lasters* illustrations). The dancers were then able to move around, as well as cling to, this structure. Täuber designed similar platforms for dances, such as "Moderne Tänze" (Modern Dances) and "Kokain" (Cocaine), creating pedestal-like structures upon which Berber could either crouch or dangle her legs.

In addition to dramatic staging, Berber's costumes and dance moves warrant close scrutiny for their eroticism. From her frayed skirt and halter-neck top, as worn in "Moderne Tänze," to her corset dress with its lace-up bustier, many of her costumes were merely decorative, designed to expose her body. According to Czech choreographer, Joe Jenčík, writing in 1930, Berber's "Salome" showcased the lower half of her body, bending over through her legs to her stomach: "This perspective allowed [Berber] to see

10   Toepfer believes that "Murder, Woman and the Hanged Man" was never performed live, although it might have been staged in the now-lost 1923 film *Tänze des Grauens, des Lasters und der Extase*, which starred Berber and Droste. See Fischer 94.

somebody in love boundlessly obsessed by sex, without a head and breasts
[...] love concentrated only in the lower part" (qtd. in Toepfer 84–85).
In this dance, Berber, almost naked, rises from a large, blood-filled urn,
writhing with blood dripping from between her legs. To the music of
Richard Strauss, Berber here simulates both menstruation and masturbation (Ibid. 85).

Considering Berber's dance performances, it is little wonder that her
audiences were often left mesmerized. Expressionist poet Leopold Wolfgang
Rochowanski, writing in *Die Tänze des Lasters*, describes the audience's
physical reaction to Berber's dance as "Spannung. Gestörte Atmung.
Bewaffnete Augen. Erwartung [...] Pause der Wünsche. Lösen der Knoten.
Keine Atmung. Erhöhte Atmung" ("[t]ension. Unsettled breathing. Eyes
like daggers. Anticipation [...] A pause of desire. Loosening of ties. No
breathing. Increased breathing" 67–68). In Max Herrmann-Neiße's 1924
portrayal of the cabaret scene in Berlin, he notes that Berber's dance carried
a certain portent, namely that those who are greedy will receive an elec-
tric shock, a lesson exemplified by an unbelievably self-important dancer
(148).[11] Finally, Paul Niklaus, in 1919, sees Berber's dance as a slow pro-
gression into a state of ecstasy capable of moving the viewer. Her dance is
not yearning that comes from experience, rather one that is born out of a
dream (Fischer 19).[12]

In addition to Anita Berber's onstage, theatric trance-dances, Richard
Oswald's *Unheimliche Geschichten* (*Weird Tales*, 1919) features Berber *qua*
filmic trance-dancer. This time, however, Berber is director of the spirit
world, a power she wields through expressive dance and the art of séance.
Unheimliche Geschichten is a film that foregrounds overt female sexuality;
Berber's character awakening the dead with eroticized gestures. The film
begins with a framing device, featuring three ghostly characters who haunt
an antiquarian bookshop: the prostitute (Anita Berber); Death (Conrad

---

11   "Anita Berber's Tänze sind erlebte Inbrunst [...] für alle plumpe Begehrlichkeit,
      die gleich mit ihren schmutzigen Pfoten mitten hineintappen möchte und von
      der unheimlichen Selbstherrlichkeit dieser Tänzerin einen elekrischen Schlag als
      Denkzettel bekommt."
12   "Ihr Tanz ist nicht die Sehnsucht, die aus dem Erleben erwachst, sondern eine, die
      der Traum gebar."

Veidt); and the devil (Reinhold Schünzel). As customers leave the bookstore for the evening, the characters leap from their portraits, terrorizing the bookseller and plundering the shop's wares. This initial frame leads the viewer into five separate horror stories, authored by such notables as Edgar Allan Poe ("The Black Cat") and Robert Louis Stevenson ("The Suicide Club").

The female mesmerist is the protagonist of the second installment, based on a short story entitled "The Hand" by Robert Liebmann. Here, two men enter a dice game to court favor with their *inamorata* (Anita Berber). As the two men throw dice to decide a winner, the game of chance leaves the assassin (Veidt) ahead, only to be strangled by the murderer (Schünzel), the eerie scene promising a premonition of the supernatural. The assassin's dying hand cramps into a claw, which clings tightly to the murderer and remains visible when the girlfriend (Berber) finds his dying body. Jagged silhouettes, framed on the wall, as well as chiaroscuro lighting, imbue the scene with unmissably macabre undertones. The claw-like hand of the murdered man is brought back to life when the murderer joins Berber's character at her dance début several years thereafter. In a montage featuring the murderer glancing – and Berber dancing – the dead man's hand and body then appear onstage. The reappearance and disappearance of the murdered man are invoked by Berber's trance-dance, costume, and gaze. Donning a black cape and tights, Berber twirls around the stage, the dance ending with Berber *qua* toreador, her arms extended as though casting a spell on the audience.

In *Unheimliche Geschichten*, then, the Berber character summons the dead through dance. She begins in a crouched position, shifting in a series of turns. She raises and lowers her arms, finally kicking out to demark the end of her performance. Berber's rapidly changing contortions – interspersed with her slow, caressing arm movements – are followed by a series of gestures that beckon Veidt's spirit to appear offstage. While Berber twirls like a dervish, the Veidt figure appears, first as a claw-like hand gripping the curtain, then as a ghostly figure offstage. To emphasize the dancer's connection to the spirit, Berber consummates her own dance with claw-like hand gestures. She then crumples to the floor in a manner redolent of physical exhaustion.

After Berber's captivating performance at the club, she invites the murderer and two other men back to her home for a séance. As it commences, the murdered man's ghostly apparition is superimposed onto a window, appearing later as a huge, ghostly head. Berber leaves her hands on the table, calling forth the footprints of the deceased. She again clenches her hands in a claw-like gesture and scratches the table, preempting the ghost's return. The final moments involve a sequence in which Berber inhabits the foreground of the frame as Veidt's ghoulish specter strangles Schünzel in the background. The positioning leads the viewer to infer that Berber is primarily an accomplice in the murder. Furthermore, Berber uses dance movements to inspect the body, pacing cat-like while extending her clenched hands as if to detect her prey. At this point she smiles, expressing apparent satisfaction at the sight of the macabre scene.

Berber, whose real-life exploits are exemplified in this scene of sexual liberation, captures in her character the social stigma placed upon promiscuous women. Frequenting seedy nightclubs, Berber is a seductress who preys upon innocent men that fall victim to her spell. She is equivalent to "beetles and spiders who live in the cracks of the walls," waiting to prey on those unsuspecting individuals who are spellbound by her unbridled sexuality (Douglas 102). Berber courts danger and coquettishly cajoles those involved in the séance, controlling the Schünzel character through the seductive snare of the dance.[13]

In *Unheimliche Geschichten*, then, Berber's *femme fatale* character represents the threat that Weimar's Neue Frau posed to the more traditional roles of wife and mother. Through her seductive dance, Berber casts her spell, thereby incurring the death of some and the resuscitation of others. In a Weimar context, critics such as Arnolt Bronnen regarded Anita Berber's dance and unbecoming sensuality as a marker of increasing sexual division. Women such as Berber jettisoned their traditional feminine

---

13   At the beginning of the story, which is based on "The Hand," the characters of Veidt and Schünzel vie for the affection of Berber. As they celebrate with champagne in a night club, it is Berber's wild, twirling dance with a third man that convinces Veidt and Schünzel that they must go head-to-head for her affection. In this state of jealousy, one kills the other, which results in a second murder of the returning spirit.

status: "sie verzichteten auf ihre göttlichen Rechte, sie warfen ihr Leben hin" ("they waived their God-given rights and threw away their life" 71). Portrayals of selfish women – who fulfill their own desires at the cost of men's – became a critical *leitmotif* leveled at the New Woman. The Neue Frau's trivialization of love – thereby annihilating the traditional family unit – is clearly emphasized by Ostwald, her unreasonable sexual demands constituting not only a threat to the nuclear family but society writ large.

Trance-Dance in Weimar Cinema

One can detect similarly ecstatic powers as those attributed to the figure of the Neue Frau in Weimar cinema. Perhaps the clearest illustration of this can be found in Fritz Lang's *Metropolis* (1927). There, the robot Maria (Brigitte Helm) hypnotizes the audience at the upper-crust men's club with her sexual dance of doom (see Figure 21). In Freder's (Gustav Fröhlich) "Whore of Babylon" dream, the evil Maria mystically emerges onstage from a large, smoking cauldron. Dressed in a half-moon head-dress with a lace cape and belly costume, Maria gyrates and twirls her body, calling to mind Berber's inimitable expressive dance (Toepfer 83–86). Lang follows this by thematizing the audience's gaze in a series of camera shots that cut from images of male faces to a montage of disembodied eyes. Hereafter, the film crosscuts from images of Maria looking at an audience of men to images of the audience in a trance-like state, suggesting that she may be disseminating a telepathic message. Although she is decidedly the object of the male gaze, Maria's ability to spellbind these menfolk is cinematographically reinforced through Lang's low-angle shots, and huge "eyeball" stage props (Lungstrum 131–32).[14] Under Maria's control, the men have lost the ability to determine their destiny, their faces melting into a collection of disembodied eyeballs. Her dance

14   Lungstrum comments on the hanging globes that resemble eyeballs, noting that
      Maria both receives and returns the gaze in this scene: "the reproduction of the
      eyeball is shown not only as a male activity looking at her but as part of her own
      dance act on stage, staring back at and dominating the men" (131–32).

culminates with a cut to a montage of eyes and then to one single eye. She is finally seen riding atop a large cauldron on stage, supported by a platform of serpents and the seven deadly sins. As the men of the club run to surround her, the message of the scene is clarified through the appearance of the grim reaper – Maria's hypnotic hold over the men will cause them to commit sins for which they will pay with their lives.

The theme of hypnotism resurfaces at the end of *Metropolis* with the

Figure 21. Brigitte Helm in *Metropolis*. Producer Erich Pommer; director Lang, 1927.

pairing of female movement and hypnotic suggestion. Following Maria's rabble-rousing in the catacombs, her animal-like lunging sends the male workers into a frenzy. The series of shot reverse shots, in which Maria incites rebellion as the men listen with trance-like wonderment, is only broken by a high-angle shot of the helpless men ("your time has come"). It is, however, the collage preceding this sequence that foregrounds the phenomenon of hypnotism. A collection of disembodied heads features small visages at the top of the frame, underscored by larger heads at the bottom. The bottom of this moving superimposition displays one large eye, as well as the robot Maria's face, who is shouting. The men in the audience appear transfixed by Maria's command. As if bringing us under Maria's spell, they break the fourth wall as their gaze turns to the filmic audience. The montage of the film – in which all shapes and sizes of heads and eyes are left altered – underscores a narrative whereby both high-society and working-class men succumb to Maria. Although the "Whore of Babylon" is ultimately burned at the stake, the damage has been done to the city of Metropolis: Maria's dance of sin imploring a sea of men to do her diabolical bidding.

Andreas Huyssen observes that *Metropolis* places woman at the center of the male gaze, which becomes a proxy for the camera itself ("Vamp and the Machine" 75). Scenes from the Yoshiwara club, as well as the catacombs, prove that the *femme fatale* robot is not only an object of the male gaze: she returns this gaze from whence it came, and with disastrous results, thereby underscoring the hypnotic potential in woman's concentrated glance. We may additionally note that, historically, film *itself* boasted the same abilities to unleash emotional turmoil and destructive force upon its unsuspecting spectators. As Michael Cowan claims, there was an early twentieth-century assumption that cinema's erotic depictions could arouse in the audience so-called "atavistic regression" (242).

The ability of women to hypnotize men through dance is a theme that prevails in Weimar cinema. For example, Henrik Galeen's *Alraune* (1928) presents yet another example whereby a vamp played by Brigitte Helm hypnotizes and seduces her "father," Professor Jakob ten Brinken (Paul Wegener), with her sultry moves.[15] Galeen's erotic woman is conceived from the semen of a hanged man implanted into the body of a prostitute. The invocation of the mandrake root in Alraune's birth further signals the realm of the occult. Moreover, in Robert Wiene's *Genuine* (1920), we find a female vampire (Fern Andra) from Africa, who is brought to a small town where she terrorizes the male community. Moving about in her exotic, caged environment, she transfixes every male she meets, blossoming on a diet of blood while commanding her male servants to do her bidding.

These cultural examples of the hypnotic *femme fatale* showcase her ability to force men to run amok, committing crimes in her name. Indeed, Weimar criminologist Hans Schneickert notes that crime is often committed in the name of woman (30). Wulffen further posits that woman's

15   Hypnosis captivated the popular and scientific imagination following World War One and was regarded as a potential treatment for shell-shocked veterans. Forel and Moll's respective publications of the same name (*Der Hypnotismus*) were important scientific works to this end. Andriopoulos furthermore provides an interesting analysis of Weimar cinema and the cultural context of hypnosis (91–127).

participation in crime constitutes a kind of "sexual discharge" (69). Themes of crime and sexuality are closely associated with the occult woman, who, according to Wulffen, "may be found in hundreds in the metropolises and in the medium-sized towns" (115). These women are the equivalent of "medieval witches," who work their magic through eros (116). Not unlike the New Woman, they imperil mankind with insatiable desire.

Another film that features the hypnotizing *femme fatale qua trance-dancer* is Arnold Fanck's naturalist masterpiece *The Holy Mountain*. Here, the dancer Diotima possesses powers of controlling not only men (like the robot Maria) but the forces of Nature Herself through ecstatic dance (see Figure 22). As Eric Rentschler remarks, the entire film revolves around Diotima's gaze: "Her image alone [giving] rise to powerful reactions; her gaze likewise transmits a remarkably arresting force" (155). The film foregrounds themes of obsession and revenge as the characters of Diotima (Leni Riefenstahl), Robert (Louis Trenker), and Vigo (Ernst Petersen) are caught up in a tragic love triangle. It is Diotima's hypnotic dance, which mints the men's enchantment, that later secures their destruction. As the men bear witness to her dance, thereby coming under the spell of her gaze, Robert turns against Vigo in a jealous rage with reference to Diotima.

Figure 22. Leni Riefenstahl in *Der heilige Berg* (The Holy Mountain). Production UFA; director Fanck, 1925–26.

Following the opening credits, the film incipit kicks off with a close-up of Diotima's face in a trance-like pose: her eyes closed; her face tense with concentration. We are then privy to a montage of sea and dance, in which the dancer's silhouette, perched on a rock, morphs into waves and then a cliff. She is "wild and boundless" like the sea; mortally powerful. In addition to jutting rocks and waves, the sky grows stormy, the intertitle informing us that, like nature, Diotima's world is movement: "the dance." In her "dance to the sea," Diotima is shown casting her hypnotic spell: arms sweeping upwards, her face fills the screen with an ecstatic gaze. Her trance-like visage – mimicking her initial close-up – prompts nature to produce huge tidal waves, which crash against the rocks. The remaining montage moves from Diotima's hypnotic close-ups and full-body silhouettes to turbulent waves. Finally, she is shown striking a ritual pose in praise of nature, crouching in exhaustion on the rocks as the sun breaks through.

Diotima's dance is designed to call forth her lover through telepathic suggestion, producing his shadow atop a mountain peak. The film's intertitle states that Diotima dances to satisfy her longing for him. The problem with Diotima's desire is that she induces two men to lust after her. The male protagonists, "two friends from the mountains," then appear directly after the dance. Robert and Vigo are juxtaposed to blue-toned scenes of rock and sea. It is this tension between the sea of the dancer, Diotima, and the mountain heights of her male admirers, that sets the stage for disaster.

Leni Riefenstahl's performance of the film's first dance segment is clearly situated in the expressive style of the time, seemingly owing much to Mary Wigman. Riefenstahl was in fact a professional dancer who had a brief solo career in the early 1920s before turning to film. Riefenstahl attended Wigman's dance masterclass in 1923 and thereafter continued to study with the Wigman group for several years. Commenting upon her complicated relationship with Wigman, Riefenstahl explains: "I had a very hard time integrating into the group dancing of the Wigman School. I found the style too abstract, too rigorous, and too ascetic, where my own urge was to surrender completely to the rhythms of the music" (Riefenstahl 33–34). Despite her claims, Riefenstahl's dance can certainly be categorized as expressive. One may even note the resemblance between her costumes for *The Holy Mountain* and Wigman's costumes, Diotima's dreamy cloak of blossom resembling the full cape of Wigman's witch costume ("Witch Dance," 1914), while her "wedding dress" ("Devotion") looks like Wigman's early costuming. The opening sequence of the film follows the pattern of Wigman's solo dances, capturing the occult overtones of the unconscious and the supernatural found in her dance.[16]

In the initial hotel sequence, we see in a series of shot reverse shots, the effects of Diotima's gaze on the hypnotized faces of the male protagonists. It is clear that young Vigo is smitten with Diotima, offering her a mountain flower. Vigo's older mentor, Robert, is similarly overcome, the sequence closing with Robert encircled by rarified mountain scenery. The clouds, recalling the film's incipit, symbolize Diotima and envelop Robert on his upward climb. The dancer has captured him, her gaze delimiting his impending actions. The result of the dancer's hypnotic power is death for both men.

Diotima invokes a trance-like state, which, in addition to moving the characters on screen, cannot but mesmerize the film's viewer. Hellwig claims that the hypnotic power of cinema can cause members of the audience to become anxious, as well as leading to bodily harm ("Hypnotismus und Kinematograph" 313). In extreme cases, cinema was taken as a medium for hypnotic suggestion, causing the viewer to repeat an action seen on-screen, often to his or her detriment (Ibid.). Stefan Andriopoulos notes that hypnotic suggestion was defined as a key characteristic of cinema in early twentieth-century cultural discourse, "giving rise to the fear that the spellbound audience might succumb to the irresistible influence emanating from the cinematic apparatus" (123). Furthermore, the pairing of sound and the visual in cinema of the late 1920s led to the idea that aural stimulation produced in film could also bring about a trance-like state (Ibid. 119).

Rentschler additionally notes that the irrational and irrepressible forces of nature are suggestive of female sexual energy (Rentschler 152). We see this especially in *The Holy Mountain* through Diotima's trance-dance (first performed in nature), as well as in her ability to seduce the young men in their mountain milieu.[17] Rentschler states that "[woman] possesses

16 For more information about Wigman, see Manning.
17 Diotima/Riefenstahl is an expert skier and mountain climber.

for modern men an irresistible primal fascination, bearing powers that impassion onscreen beholders and lead them to self-surrender and perdition" (Ibid. 159). Schrenck-Notzing notes that dance creates a type of fascination in its tension between life and death: it is the "battle between the childish joy of life and the terrible power of destruction, [which] moves us" (*Traumtänzerin* 175). Through her practice of expressive and ecstatic dance, Diotima hypnotizes the men under her sway, moving them to acts of passion and thereby their destruction.

The Medium

The hypnotic capabilities of the trance-dancer seemingly vindicated fears regarding Weimar's New Woman, who boasted a similarly stupefactive influence over the post-War male psyche. Just as the trance-dancer *qua* hypnotist is portrayed as an erotic menace, the female medium was likewise considered a threat to society. Practitioners of mediumism believed that they could awaken the dead and commune with them by means of the séance. W. von Gulat-Wellenburg defines the medium as an "experimental subject," endowing her with "psycho-physical energy" and "exterior power" (1). Contributing to fears regarding her influence was the female medium's sheer outnumbering of her psychic male counterparts, as noted by Corinna Treitel (61, 64–65).[18]

Mediumism, of course, enjoyed a long history before Weimar and we ought to consider some of the practices immediately preceding the interwar period.[19] Munich parapsychologist Albert von Schrenck-Notzing's pre-war work, *Phenomena of Materialization* (*Materialisations-Phenomene*),[20] offers

---

18   Sharp notes that the qualities associated with the "feminine" were also those attributed to the best mediums, viz. the ability to be "volatile, emotional, [and] sensitive" (162).

19   Both Treitel and Wolffram cover the continuing interest in the occult from the period of Imperial Germany through Weimar.

20   The text was first published in 1913 and then updated in 1920.

us a sense of how the medium operated (see Figure 23).[21] One of his most famous investigations involved Eva C. (Eva Carrière), formerly known as Marthe B., who delivered séances assisted by her friend Juliette Bisson. Eva C. produced emanations known as "ectoplasm" from parts of her body, thereby generating what bystanders reported to be visible apparitions. Eva was moreover able to bring body parts – including feet and faces – to life. Commenting upon these apparitions, Schrenck-Notzing notes: "The expression of the face is more clearly brought out. It seems pleasanter, and the lines of the profile are strikingly soft […] The composition and arrangement of this head appear to be a remarkably artistic performance, quite apart from the question as to how it was done" (*Phenomena* 143). These apparitions were further documented and captured in the popular press. Photos of women leading séances often included women in rigid or trance-like poses. The most disturbing of these photos depicted women with white masses of teleplasma streaming from their mouths and noses.[22] This teleplasma could bear the face of a loved one, palpable in the slime, or it might simply represent the spirit of a dead individual. While Eva C. was given the initial plaudits for generating ectoplasm, her capacities were soon debunked (the medium's phantom "Dorsmica" resembled images in the paper *Le Miroir*) (Brandon 156).[23] According to Schrenck-Notzing:

> Immediately after the disappearance of the substance I examined her face […] without finding anything by means of which this phenomenon [spirit] might have been produced. The face was indeed quite moist as if with mucus […] During the phenomena she groaned and trembled, and when she was awakened, she was very exhausted. The conditions of the experiment during the phenomena described constitute a great step in advance. (*Phenomena* 52)[24]

---

21   Schrenck-Notzing's 1920 edition of this work was significantly revised, adding a more "scientific" rhetoric to the description of the potential spirit world. In this chapter, I cite the 1920 edition.

22   See *Der Querschnitt* 12.12 (December 1932) for several images of women and teleplasma. The theme of woman and the occult was also evident in popular journals such as *Berliner Illustrirte Zeitung*, *Berliner Leben*, and *Die Dame*.

23   For a thorough discussion of Martha B./Eva C., see Brandon (127–63).

24   Ectoplasm and teleplasma are the same substance: a sticky material that supposedly represented the physical manifestation of a deceased individual.

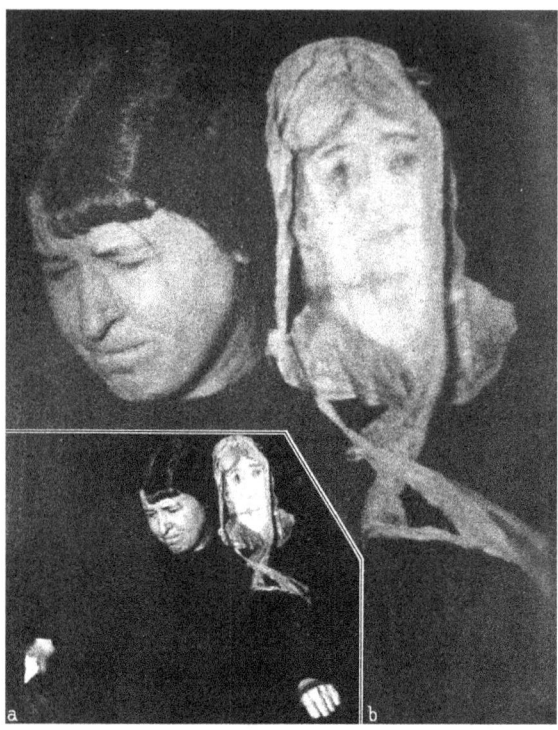

Figure 23. Ghost rendering. Albert von Schrenck-Notzing. *Phenomena of Materialisation: A Contribution to the Investigation of Mediumistic Teleplastics*. Trans. E. E. Fournier d'Albe. London: Kegan Paul, Trench, Trubner & Co., 1923.

Thus, on Schrenck-Notzing's account, Eva C. literally gives birth to the spirit; her physical effort, which would involve groaning and trembling, implying that her performance incorporated a sexual dimension. Indeed, Eva C.'s manifestation of spirits through plasma and apparitions of body parts led Schrenck-Notzing to notify the scientific community about these unexplained phenomena. He was even prepared to collect empirical evidence to provide positivist proof of spirits (Ibid. 12). In keeping with Schrenck-Notzing's account of the spirit world, various examples of Weimar mediumism are recorded in the journal *Psychische Studien* (edited by Professor Friedrich Maier and Hans Freimark). One such example appears in Fritz Tretzel-Groschlattengrün's article "Mediumistische

Erscheinungen" (Occurrences of Mediumism, 1921). Here, he notes that belief in ghosts is so common in the contemporary period that this popularity provides an indirect proof of a spirit world (43). The author's narrative involves an acquaintance, whose sister is a working medium, and is able to obtain information through the practice of mechanical writing; the mother of the family asking questions as the sister directs the pen (Ibid.). The mother is then able to strengthen the medial bond by placing her hand on the writing hand of the sister. She spells out words, which are not preplanned; the longer the process, the more precisely the words can provide answers to the questions asked (Ibid.).

Tretzel-Groschlattengrün goes on to tell a story about a female medium who was able to describe her brother's ordeals as a soldier in Kolmar without prior knowledge of his actions. The medium reveals the name of her brother's new airplane, as well as news that he was involved in a skirmish (Ibid. 44). This information was obtained neither through telepathy nor unconscious knowledge on the medium's part. The author recognizes the medium's supposed ability to tap into a spirit identity, declaring that she was in touch with a god-like presence (Ibid. 45).

Another Weimar work entitled *Maria, Eine Stimme aus dem Jenseits?* (*Maria, a Voice from Beyond?* 1928) by Willy Jaschke further exemplifies the female medium's relation to the spirit world. Albeit fictional, *Maria* was based on Jaschke's extensive experience as a parapsychologist.[25] The work's introduction notes that there are many laypeople who would like to participate in a séance in order to commune with the dead. The story is one of a young Frank Werner who seeks out a medium in order to commune with his late fiancé, Maria, who perished in a Munich train crash. Finding an advertisement in a newspaper, Frank meets parapsychologist Erich Loertzen and several other affiliated mediums, including a physical medium who can make contact with entities that move objects and leave handprints (20), as well as the trance medium, who works in a dream-like state to call upon spirits.[26]

---

25   See Treitel 243–48 for coverage of Jaschke's *Maria. Eine Stimme aus dem Jenseits?*
26   Loertzen makes it clear that the success of the séance depends upon the calm, committed condition of its participants as much as it relies upon the medium (23).

In Loertzen's home, which doubles as a controlled laboratory, Werner is put in contact with a trance medium, Luise Weber, whose ability to call up the male intelligence "Salvian" and the young female entity "Gretchen" enables Werner to make contact with his lost love.[27] Frau Weber had realized her medial powers three years previously through a family séance, which had been brought to the attention of Loertzen. Frau Weber is able, through a dream-like state, to extract exacting details about those who have passed and are endeavoring to make contact with the living through a séance. For example, the female medium is able, through the entities of Salvian and Gretchen, to acknowledge the male spirit Lulu, the deceased son of séance participant Frau Würdig (79). Lulu's precise description is given by the medium, thanks to which the medium is forced to awaken from her trance, having been shaken by the emotional response of Frau Würdig.

The precise circumstances of the séance constitute a prelude to the final session, whereby Frau Weber is able to make contact with Werner's fiancé, Maria. Maria's description is provided by the medium through Salvian: she is young with curly blond hair, blue eyes, and a narrow face (89). In order to confirm further details, the spirit of Maria speaks through the medium, asking séance member, Major G., to go into the next room to write down the details. Not only does the medium give Maria's particulars – " 'Verlobungsfeier – zerbrochene Vase' und 'Wendelstein-Geburtstag' […] 'Werner hätte eine gepresste Rose von ihr' " (Engagement celebration – broken vase and Wendelstein-birthday […] Werner has a pressed rose from her) – Major G. also records the same information while writing "mechanically" in the adjacent room (89–90). Through these details, Werner is reassured that his fiancé is prospering on the other side. He, as well as the other séance participants, have indeed made contact with the spirit of the deceased Maria. Thus, like Tretzel-Groschlattengrün's mediumism through mechanical writing, the example of Frau Weber *qua* medium

---

27   The entity "Salvian" is suggested to be "Gretchen's" father in this work. The medium Frau Weber as "Gretchen" recites the poem supposedly taught to her by her father. The last stanza reads: "Im Sterben Hoffnung geben / Mag Erdenweisheit nicht, / Jedoch bei Dir ist Leben, / Ist Liebeskraft und Licht. / So mag die Schöpfung enden, / Und was Dich Vater heisst, / Das ruht in Deinen Händen. / Empfange meinen Geist!" (Jaschke 77).

affirms the connection between the spirit world and trance-like states, as well as through the practice of mechanical writing.

By the 1920s, mediumism was a popular arena for debate in Germany. While certain experts (including Schrenck-Notzing, Tretzel-Groschlattengrün, and Jaschke) vouched for the validity of this occult "science," scholars such as the psychologist Alfred Lehmann were skeptical of its legitimacy. Lehmann, whose book *Aberglaube und Zauberei* (Superstition and Magic) was in its third edition by 1925, commented upon the workings of the medium:

> the wish, to serve as a spirit's mouthpiece, will soon cause autohypnosis and trance, while the self-suggesting personality expresses itself in speech and writing. If the person present does not make do with these manifestations, the medium can develop into a materialization medium; it is certainly the case that a medium has gradually developed in various directions. (656)[28]

Weimar popular journals likewise fluctuated between legitimating and debunking the credibility of occult practices such as mediumism, the Tarot, palmistry, and astrology. Indeed, medical doctor Friedrich Schwab argued in an article sympathetic to the medium[29] that we are not privy to all of the mysteries of Nature, owing to which we ought to withhold our disbelief and embrace a variety of occult phenomena with scientific rigor (859). It is not so much the fact that we *support* the world of ghosts through the discovery of teleplasma but that we "build a bridge [...] so that we could possibly penetrate the puzzle of the source of life itself" (Ibid. 861). Schwab thereby vehemently argues that those who are skeptical of such phenomena should confront their own prejudices in order to embrace the scientific evidence.

Mediumism met with equally forceful attempts to expose its ostensive claims. Carl Graf von Klinckowstroem was notable for publishing several essays on the deceitfulness of mediums. In works such as "Der Unfug des Mediumismus" (The Nonsense of Mediumism) and "Taschenspieler und Medien" (Conjurers and Mediums), he disputes parapsychology as a valid

---

28 See also Moll's *Der Spiritismus* and *Psychologie und Charakterologie der Okkultisten* for further negative renderings of the occult medium.

29 "Teleplasma, eine mysteriöse Substanz" (Teleplasma, a mysterious Substance).

area of scientific enquiry, stating that mediumism is a playground for credulous fantasies, whereby so-called "experts" are duped by stipulations placed on the conditions of séances. In order for researchers to take part in the séance, they must conform to the medium's wishes, making the deception's unmasking virtually impossible (Klinckowstroem, "Der Unfug" 473). Klinckowstroem further notes that the medium determines the tricks of her trade, including "darkness, noise through music, song or other increasing entertainment, the chain of hands, the forbiddance of unexpected light sources or access" ("Taschenspieler" 862). Scientists who experimented in the field of the occult encouraged the medium's swindling by precluding true accountability. This preclusive attitude to transparency is corroborated by the behavior of parapsychologists such as Schrenck-Notzing, who prohibited magicians from attending séances, thereby screening out one method of control. Trick experts such as Harry Houdini, who worked in the U.S. in an effort to uncover the swindling of mediums, were unwelcome in Europe (Ibid. 863–64). Indeed, it was normally a medium's friend (e.g., Juliette Bisson in Schrenck-Notzing's work with Eva C.) that enabled the medium to ring bells, tilt tables, and produce teleplasma.

Writing with regard to psychic swindles, in his work *Woman as a Sexual Criminal* (*Das Weib als Sexualverbrecherin*, 1923) Erich Wulffen likewise criticized the woman practitioner of the occult arts, condemning the female spiritualist for exploiting her victims by playing on their superstitions (115). In his chapter "Female Swindlers and Cheats," Wulffen notes that the deception practiced by the woman spiritualist is not a far cry from the profession of procurement, for, in both cases, there exists a veiled erotic motive (Ibid. 116). Thanks to their possessing a natural talent for acting, women are able to make the fraud of prophesy more believable.

As suggested earlier, the obsession in the Weimar press with women's involvement in the occult may be taken to signify woman's apparently ambiguous position in society. New Women were at once described as careerists, mothers, sexual predators, and/or homosexuals. This confusion begot attempts to define such perceptions of women in order to make sense of her liminality. In Wulffen's description, the spiritualist woman's profession is akin to procurement, whereby her sexual avarice comes to the fore. Klinckowstroem likewise detects swindling and deceit in the actions of the medium, who uses darkness, music, and the help of her assistant to trick séance participants. Concerning the issue of fraud, the legal status of occult activities became a hot topic during the Weimar era, with Bavarian law forbidding anyone from accepting payment or gaining advantage from magic or necromancy, whether through "fortune telling, tarot, treasure hunting, symbol and dream interpretation or other similar jugglery" (Hellwig, "Hellsehen als strafbare Gaukelei" 124–25). Laws forbidding the occult were also on the books in Hessen and Baden.

Mary Douglas notes that a community will often seek to restrain the spiritual powers of persons bearing an interstitial status, as confirmed in the confrontations of Klinckowstroem, Wulffen, and contemporary legal rulings regarding spiritualism (Douglas 102). Bernhard Bauer further underlines the suspect nature of the supernatural woman, documenting her supposed power as mysterious and demonic (339), thereby reinforcing the notion that the supernatural woman was someway positioned to undermine the social order.

Mary Wigman's Weimar Dance

The powers attributed to the medium are also exhibited in the period's modern dance. The expressive dance of Mary Wigman drew extensively on Wilhelmine and Weimar discourses of the occult. Although expressive dance (*Ausdruckstanz*) may appear as wholly improvised to the audience, it is, in reality, rigorously choreographed. Trained in the school of rhythmic dance, Wigman's dance is meticulously orchestrated and executed. This underlying structure is made explicit as Wigman thematizes the mathematical basis of her work:

> Aus der Vermählung von Körper und Raum entsteht: die gerade Linie, der Kreis, die Acht, das Drei-, Vier- und Fünfeck übereinandergelagert, sich kreuzend, einander durchdringend, als Kugel, Pyramide, Kubus dreidimensional erlebt.

> out of the union between body and space there develops: the straight line, the circle, the octagon, the triangle, the square and the pentagon arranged one on top of the

other, crossing and penetrating each other, experienced three-dimensionally as spheres, pyramids and cubes. (Wigman qtd. in Witzmann 617).

The mathematical precision of Wigman's dance mirrors the language of scientific rationality and technological advancement that inhered in the Weimar era of so-called *New Objectivity* (Neue Sachlichkeit).[30] The New Woman's participation in this apparently objective discourse signaled her rite of passage into the masculine realm. Writing for *Uhu* magazine in 1931, Stephanie Kaul notes that history gave birth to the masculine woman, for, between 1914 and 1921, poor living conditions prompted women to pursue life's pleasures (Ibid.). The obliteration of social distinctions furthermore caused the collapse of boundaries between men and women, with women beginning to style themselves in the image of male objectivity: "Above all women [...] wanted to conquer and demolish the whole world in objective speech" (Ibid.).

Wigman, on the one hand the protégé of Rudolf von Laban, while, on the other, an artist and businesswoman in her own right, opened her influential Dresden dance school in 1920. Wigman's dances were ecstatic spectacles whose movements were capable of tapping into a fount of other-worldly energy, which could be transmitted from the stage through the gaze of the viewer. In her own words from 1925, Wigman describes the motivation behind her elemental dance:

> [Elemental dances] are the medium and symbol of those forces born of the soil. Their purest form is the demoniacal grotesque in all its variations. Everything apparitional, spectral, whether confined to earthly or released to transcendental experiences is fashioned out of the grotesque. All sensations of anxiety, all chaotic conditions of despair arising from torment, hatred, or fury, grow in this medium of expression up to and beyond the boundaries of the purely human and blend themselves with inhuman, demoniacal violence. (qtd. in Sorell 93)

Wigman's expressivity is perhaps best represented in the demonic movements of her solo masterwork *Hexentanz* (Witch Dance, 1914), which was either performed with full orchestration or (yet more hauntingly) with the accompaniment of percussive beats. Wigman's other solo dances,

30   See McCormick for a discussion of woman and "New Objectivity."

including *Ekstatische Tänze* (Ecstatic Dances, 1917) and *Der Spuk* (The Haunted, 1920), similarly convey feelings of unbounded reverie.

Wigman's dance was generally solo, with her typically assuming the position of an intermediary between this world and the next. For example, her *Tanzmärchen* (Dance Stories, 1925) is set in the underworld and includes guardians, magicians, and a demon in its cast of characters, which she assumes in sequence to evince her supremacy. Moreover, her 1926 *Totentanz* (Dance of Death) sketches the boundary between life and death. There, the community of female dancers represents the dead who have come back to life, with Wigman resisting Death's call by battling the beast. In the end, all of the female dancers succumb, Wigman stating: "[*Dance of Death*] never lost touch with the threatening unknown powers hovering over it all the time" (qtd. in Sorell 101).

Mary Wigman's obsession with death in her dances can be considered alongside attempts to commune with the dead in various occultic practices. Wigman's masterwork *Totenmal* (The Call of the Dead, 1930) has her actually performing the role of the medium in an attempt to commune with the war dead, represented by a male choir and actual soldiers' letters, which are read offstage during breaks in the dance performance (see Figure 24).

Figure 24. *Totenmal* (Call of the Dead, Wigman, 1930). Unknown photographer.

The central theme of the performance is played out in the confrontation between the male and female choruses.[31] The female chorus is made up of grieving women who have come to make contact with the spirits of the dead, represented by the male chorus. When all the women are assembled, Wigman's character instructs them to form a "hill of suffering" in order to conjure up the male spirits, who then appear on a platform (Wigman 95). The spirits of the fallen soldiers stand still – clothed in solemn robes – each with an arm raised in protest to the violation that has been committed against their spirituality. The women are incapable of withstanding the presence of the dead and flee the stage, leaving Wigman with the task of yet again evoking, and single-handedly confronting, the spirits. Wigman's character is thereby forced to confront the Demon, who angrily appears onstage in response to her attempt to intervene in the world of the dead. Wigman's character ultimately cannot withstand the demon, owing to which she must lose her life.

Let us now consider the elements of mediumism as presented in *Call of the Dead*. Although not *formally* identified as a medium, Wigman's character calls forth the dead through strenuous physical gestures. In a composition entitled "The Hall of Conjuration," Wigman overcomes the bounds of space and light to move into another dimension. She achieves this state of transcendence by tracing geometric figures such as the triangle, the arch, and the circle in the air. She moreover manages to evoke movement among the dead spirits until she is thwarted by the imposition of the demon. Conserving her vital forces, she unleashes her strength in a final act to conjure the spirits. In addition to investing all of her physical energy into the act of conjuring, Wigman's character draws upon all of her emotional resources. The Speech Choir describes her character's emotional display: "Selbst ein Bildnis ihres Traums / kommt sie andächtig / geschlossnen Augs den Weg herauf / das Schweigen über ihrem Angesicht /

---

31   I am reconstructing the performance using Talhoff's published script, *Totenmal* and M. A. Moralt's 1930 English translation *Call of the Dead*. I also rely on Mary Wigman's memoir *The Language of Dance*. For photographs of the performance, see Manning's *Ecstasy and the Demon* 150–52, 156, and Müller and Stockemann's "… *jeder Mensch ist ein Tänzer*" 91–92. Also consult Manning's "Ideology" for additional details and interpretation of *Totenmal*.

ist wie ein heilend Licht / verdammt sei wer dies Schreiten stört / Hinweg-
!" (Talhoff, *Totenmal* 43) ("See now the Woman. / On the wings of her
dreams / Comes she in devotion, / Eyes closed, up the path. / From the
peace of her face / Shall the world draw healing. / A curse be on him who
stays her footsteps. / Away!" (Talhoff, *Call of the Dead*)). In a renewed act
of movement, Wigman finally allows the Spirit Chorus to move forward. In
her last call, she travels like a "night-hunting animal," moving in circles and
then backwards and forwards (Ibid.). In turns, Wigman "rises and sinks,
sways and wavers" until, in the final phase of the call, she moves beyond
her body into a superhuman existence marked by a rotating dance, which
enables the dead to make contact with the living (Ibid.).

The death of Wigman's character underscores Douglas's idea that
the spiritual power of the interstitial Other must be reined in so as not to
threaten the broader community. Douglas notes that "unconscious powers
[…] provoke others to demand that ambiguity be reduced" (102). The need
for the character's death mimics legal restrictions placed upon women who
practiced the occult in Weimar. District Court judge, Albert Hellwig, discusses the prosecution of three women who practiced spiritualism – Frau
Günther-Geffers, Frau Hessel, and Frau Diederich – insinuating that occult
practices should not be tolerated by the legal community (Hellwig, "Gibt
es nachweisbar echte Fälle").

Furthermore, Wigman's performative uses of the triangle, the arch,
and the circle – not to mention her nigh-on mathematical choreography –
place her in the same arena as scientific discourse, traditionally off-limits
to women. The New Woman, brandishing her education and new public
persona, participated in the once traditionally male realms of art, literature,
and politics. Russian émigré, Alexandra Kollontai, describes Germany's
emancipated women as female heroes, who assert their personality and
fight for their rights as representatives of their sex (Kollontai 6).

In Wigman's *Totenmal*, the lights finally go down on the female
medium, jointly promising the extinguishing of her spiritual prowess and
brute existence. Commenting upon the scene, Wigman remarks: "Only
then when the back of the head touched the floor, the almost superhuman
tension was able to loosen. The back gave in, the arms fell limp. With a
deep breath I could release myself from the self-imposed spell. The lights

went out. *Totenmal* had come to an end" (Wigman 98). The physical toll of communing with the dead leads to her demise; her power has literally been enervated from her by the community, whose insistence on her actions (through the chanting of the chorus) propelled her forward. As the male spirits rejuvenate and dominate the last scene, Wigman's character dies on the periphery: the community has both used up woman's powers, while also dispensing with her completely.

Mary Wigman therefore represents a different aspect of the New Woman, posing a serious threat to the masculine order. As self-possessed choreographer and businesswoman, Wigman embodies an objective aspect of the New Woman both in her professional work as a teacher and in her mathematically precise – yet eerily destabilizing – dance movements, as invoked in *Totenmal*. Still, it is Wigman herself who self-censures in that work, designing her own character's downfall for having trespassed in the forbidden spirit world, evincing a prescience and humility that reveals women's self-effacement in an ever-patriarchal society.

The National Socialist Context of Dance and the Occult

One can also find continuity in occultic themes in Wigman's work before and after the Nazi takeover. The early Nazi period (1933–36) saw both a continuation and a rejection of occult trends that characterized woman as a spiritual force. Dance especially exhibited the progress of occultic themes following the Nazi takeover. To this end, Mary Wigman's 1934 *Frauentänze* (Women's Dances) – in particular *Totenklage* (Lament for the Dead), *Tanz der Seherin* (Dance of the Prophetess), and *Hexentanz* (Witch Dance) – evinced the occult themes of mediumism and prophesy. Hitler's distaste for expressive dance, as practiced by female dancers like Wigman and Gret Palucca (Kant 120–21), was only realized by Goebbels and other cultural officials several years into the Reich.

Joseph Goebbels's 1934 German Dance Festival in Berlin – the premiere venue for Wigman's *Frauentänze* – sought to define the nature of female powers, including "passion, prophecy, and finally the abyss, which we recognize from Goethe's Walpurgisnacht" (qtd. in Manning, *Ecstasy and the Demon* 177). Wigman's early Nazi work embraced woman *qua* spiritualist, setting up the occultic elements that would continue throughout the Nazi period. As with National Socialism, great emphasis was placed on emotion, intuition, and the apocalypse in modern dance (Ibid. 173). Wigman's support for these ideas is revealed in her 1935 work, *Deutsche Tanzkunst*:

> The new German dance does not result from a fixed program. It received its stamp through the few creative personalities who, by incessant striving, gave it unity of content and form. This struggle centered around essentials – dealing with man and fate, the eternal and the transient. The path toward sources, toward the primeval of being, was laid open again [...] That this dance possessed the courage of confession to life as the eternally mysterious weaving and affecting, that it was searching for God and fought with the demon, that it realized the ancient Faustian desire for redemption [...] this determines its German-ness. (Wigman 15–16 (qtd. in Koegler 41–42))

In this passage, the otherworldly notions of the eternal, primeval, and the mysterious, as exhibited in Wigman's Weimar work, become pillars of her post-1933 rhetoric. As in *Totenmal*, the dancer (*qua* medium) must here contend with the demonic in order to achieve redemption. It is interesting to note that a fight with the "other" world results in a kind of redemption that forms the cornerstone of "German-ness," an issue that Wigman concerns herself with post-1933. Indeed, the Nazis awarded "Aryan" dancers like Wigman stipends from 1933–36 to continue their careers, with occult themes – so prevalent in early *Ausdruckstanz* – finding continued expression in the modern dance of the Nazi era.

Exemplifying Wigman's occult work from this time includes her participation in the German Dance Festival in Berlin 1934, organized by Joseph Goebbels and his Cultural Ministry. Susan Manning explains that the images from the festival's program, including "Greek sculpture and Romantic Ballet," reveal that experimental dance was no longer relevant in a National Socialist context (*Ecstasy and the Demon* 175, 177). The festival's nod to classicism did not, however, thwart Wigman's fervor for occult themes through modern dance. Indeed, Wigman had been commissioned by the Ministry to develop new material, on the proviso, however, that the dance group did not incorporate any Jews. Her premiere of *Frauentänze* features five dances: *Hochzeitlicher Reigen* (Wedding Dance); *Mütterlicher Tanz* (Maternal Dance); *Totenklage* (Lament for the Dead); *Tanz der Seherin* (Dance of the Prophetess); and *Hexentanz* (Witch Dance). In these dances, occult themes are notable through various thematic devices, styling, as well as their execution (see Figure 25). The first dance (*Hochzeitlicher Reigen*) features a woman (Ruth Boin) moving toward marriage and maturity as her mother (Mary Wigman) looks on with devotion. Wigman, dressed in a dark floor-length gown for the first number, replicates this dark demeanor in her second *solo* number, *Mütterlicher Tanz*. Dancing in a cloak-like garment that also covers her head, the fabric's color and style are reminiscent of Wigman's costume for her original witch dance (1914).

Figure 25. *Schicksalslied* (Song of Fate, Wigman, 1935). Photo by Charlotte Rudolph.

The underlying, ominous tone of the first two dances is echoed in the third number, *Totenklage*, whereby we again see homage paid to the dead, mimicking the theme of *Totenmal*. Artur Michel offers an interpretation of *Totenklage* in 1935, noting that small groups of women – as well as individuals – move in singular expressions of lamentation (13). The women form a great circle with the common aim of honoring the dead. At the end, "[the women] all kneel down, and overwhelmed by the greatness of the sorrow they bend flatly onto the floor. One dancer passes into the middle of the circle, kneels down gently and bows her head" (Ibid.). The image of this dance shows Wigman *qua* medium in her desire to contact the dead. Again, she wears a dark, floor-length gown, taking center stage albeit encircled by the group. It is not clear whether she is the final dancer to enter the circle, however, we may assume that all of the women on the floor pass to their deaths.

The final two dances – *Tanz der Seherin* and *Hexentanz* – likewise revisit Wigman's earlier Weimar themes, such as mediumism. The prophetess, or spirit seer, is not unlike the medium in *Totenmal* insofar as both are in search of otherworldly experiences. In this solo performance (albeit accompanied by six other female dancers), Wigman and her entourage hold their hands on their foreheads as they peer into the future. With a fixed gaze, Wigman, set apart from the others, appears intent on teasing out the riddle of the unknown, Artur Michel describing her actions thus: "[the dance] develops in severe hieratic gestures to a great ecstasy. The prophetess sees the future; she tries to resist the horror of what she has seen; but she is crushed down. At last she goes to face the inevitable fate in a solemn and sublime dance" (Ibid.). Here, horror and prophesy commingle to capture the journey into the unknown.

Wigman's intensity is manifest in the final number *Hexentanz*, in which the women's group shakes, darts, and dissolves in jumps and somersaults (Ibid.). Here, the mass "gallops in all directions, joins for a wantoning circle dance and rushes off disappearing from view" (Ibid. 13–14). Wigman – now mistress of the witches – encourages the throng to return through an enactment of her own whirling dance. The dancing group shake and turn in a whirling motion until they land with heads, arms, and hands raised; a wild yet synchronized cluster of bodies. In the final image, Wigman's demonic expression appears egregious within the horde of otherwise smiling women, her grimace alone replicating the demonic quality of the medium.

This Witches' Sabbath in Wigman's 1934 *Hexentanz* fulfills the promise inherent in Goebbel's dance program; the abyss of Goethe's *Walpurgisnacht* surging with occult energy. Indeed, while tempered by the smiling throng at the performance's conclusion, Wigman's singular intensity recalls the occult force evinced in her earlier Weimar (and Wilhelmine) renditions. *Frauentänze* begins with a dark premonition, a device that constitutes a nod to Wigman's earlier *Hexentanz* costuming, thereby attaining the occultic heights of Wigman's playing of the spirit seer.

In utilizing various "archetypes of female experience" (e.g., bride and mother) in *Frauentänze* (Manning, *Ecstasy and the Demon* 177), Wigman manages to continue the tradition of the macabre through the medium of dance. Images and descriptions of her 1934 performances reveal an intensity of experience that outstrip the foregoing archetypes. Without even using a mask as in her earlier Weimar work, Wigman presents a vital *tour de force* in her solo work, which is far removed from all traditional notions of female servility and obeisance.

Wigman's theme of mediumism, as evidenced in her performance at the 1934 Dance Festival, would enjoy a renaissance the following year as she premiered her *Tanzgesänge* (Hymnic Dances). Wigman noted in the festival's program that this work was also informed by "dark threats (*Song of Fate*), to elemental rhythm (*Fire Dance*), to the experience of nature (*Moon Song*)" (qtd. in Manning, *Ecstasy and the Demon* 185), thereby suggesting an otherworldly source. In *Mondlied* (Moon Song), Wigman reproduces her whirling solos of the Weimar era with their transcendent qualities, redolent of the mystery of the whirling dervishes. Even Wigman's solo section of the work – entitled *Schicksalslied* (Song of Fate) – portrays her again as a seer of the future and medium, complete with eyes afire and a full-body cloak-dress, complete with headpiece and veil. Although she finally strikes a pose of resignation, her trip into the unknown is filled with dread and awe as she summons her hands above her head, fingers spread to conjure the illusion.

Wigman's final utilization of the occult theme came in her contribution to the 1936 Berlin Olympic Games' opening night spectacle. Working with the dancers Gret Palucca, Dorothee Günther, and Harald Kreutzberg, she produced *Olympische Jugend* (Olympic Youth), featuring 10,000 performers before a stadium of spectators (Manning, *Ecstasy and the Demon* 194). As in *Totenmal*, the fourth section of this Olympic production culminates in a *Totenklage* (Death Lament), whereby female dancers (led by Wigman) mourn the war dead. In this section, eighty women – together with Wigman – are left on the field at the end of the performance, Adolf Hitler apparently surveying the spectacle from the stands (Ibid. 199).

After 1936, Goebbels and his Cultural Ministry, with Hitler's support, rejected the "intellectual art" proffered by expressionist dancers such as Wigman. By as early as 1934, the Ministry had struck the name *Ausdruckstanz* from the education system, instead using the term German Dance (Deutsche Tanz). Instead of abstract or intellectual dance, the Cultural Ministry placed an emphasis on "classical" dance, thereafter (from 1936) prioritizing entertainment over "artistic challenge" (Ibid. 208).[32]

Conclusion

The occultic trance-dancer and conniving medium constitute a hypnotic pairing who crystallized Weimar anxieties about the New Woman and the threat she posed to male subjectivity. Just as the trance-dancer *qua* hypnotist is portrayed as an unexampled erotic menace, the New Woman is likewise adjudged a sexual incendiary; thwarting and endangering the dominant discourse. The irrepressible powers of the modern woman, while a formidable challenge of the Weimar period, became a problem

---

32 While Wigman ceased to receive financial support from the State after 1936, her work was not banned. Indeed, she was largely unthreatened by the Nazis. She was moreover able to keep her school afloat until 1942 with funds from her solo career. Her series of "beautiful solos" (1937–42) were likewise not entirely bereft of her Weimar and early-Nazi emphasis on the occult. One reviewer noted in 1938: "Not that [her lighter solos] lack charm and playfulness, but even in the intricate decoration of her movement Wigman remains tied to the demonic" (qtd. in Manning, *Ecstasy and the Demon* 211).

that was increasingly better "managed" under Hitler's categorical Reich. With the onset of Nazism, the challenges posed by Germany's New Woman were deflated, although she was still considered a blight on traditional values; a creature thereby proclaimed incompatible with the aspirations of a social and societal utopia. This being so, let us conclude by elaborating upon how the Nazis went about their negotiations with the occultic Neue Frau.

The Nazi regime was hostile to occult practice in general, and the occult woman in particular, as a "wave of official hostility engulfed the fifty-year-old occult movement" (Treitel 226). For the Nazis, occultism constituted a regression to the Middle Ages, a pox on the Nazi social body (Treitel 217). National Socialists tolerated certain occult organizations from 1933–36 insofar as individuals who practiced the occult were considered neither Marxist nor Jewish (Ibid. 224). An official decree in 1937, however, dissolved the majority of such groups, rendering occult and associated practices illegal.[33]

With respect to women and the occult in Nazi Germany, laws forbidding occult practices disproportionately affected women, such as Therese Neumann from Konnersreuth in Bavaria. Bleeding from the eyes, feet, and hands, while speaking multiple languages in a trance-like state, Neumann was greatly revered between 1926–28, courting around 2,000 visitors per week who came to solicit information about dead relatives or seeking cures for the sick (O'Sullivan 184). During the Third Reich, these visits became categorically curtailed by the Catholic church in an effort to minimize competition with a National Socialist regime, which spurned alternative worldviews (Ibid. 189–90). State censorship of the press, as well as continued monitoring by Nazi officials, further thwarted Neumann's "Friday night bleeding, her visions of the crucifixion [...] and revelations during a state of ecstasy," which had become commonplaces of the Weimar period (Ibid. 185).

Like the artists who had pluckily depicted the occult woman, female occult practitioners (such as Neumann) receded into oblivion during the Third

33   The persecution of practicing occultists rose to a "fever pitch" in 1941 with the defection of the deputy leader of the Nazi party, Rudolf Hess, himself an occult practitioner (Treitel 213).

Reich. Indeed, having been forced to join the *Reichskammer der bildenden Künste* (Reich Chamber of Fine Arts), many artists chose to go into inner and territorial exile, otherwise leaving the country altogether. Otto Dix, for instance, remained in Germany and was forced to paint landscapes under Nazi rule, while Paul Klee, whose images of female ghosts and witches utterly emblematized the heyday of the Weimar occult, lost his job in Germany, in 1934 having to emigrate to Switzerland. Other avant-garde artists were likewise forced to emigrate: some to the U.S., others elsewhere; their art being held up as negative exemplars in the Nazi *Entartete Kunst* (Degenerate Art) exhibition of 1937.

Literary artists did not fare much better than their paintbrush-wielding counterparts. In early 1933, books by alleged socialists, communists, pacifists, and "Jewish intellectuals" were burned by members of the German Student Union. Many writers were banned from writing, their works being expunged from libraries across the country. Hanns Heinz Ewers, an NSDAP member in 1931, saw much of his work banned in 1934. Although this ban was later revoked, Ewers desisted from employing horror themes in his writing. Gerhardt Hauptmann likewise had various works banned, ceasing to write on matters of the occult after 1933. Claire Goll, a Jewish German-French writer and journalist, was forced to flee Europe altogether in 1939.

After 1933, German cinema likewise saw a purging of themes that were deemed ideologically unworthy by the Nazis.[34] The sexualized occult woman, as evidenced in later Weimar titles such as *Alraune* (1930), *Vampyr* (1932), and Leni Riefenstahl's *Das Blaue Licht* (1932), got replaced during the Third Reich by the modern woman, held up as an asexual comrade. While the *femme fatale* character did not disappear completely in Nazi films – as seen in the classic propaganda film *Hitlerjunge Quex* (*Hitler Youth Quex*, 1933) – depictions of female comrades proliferated during this period, with Ulla (Helga Bodemer) in *Hitlerjunge Quex* and Hanne (Inge Kick) in *Ich für Dich, Du für Mich* (I for You, You for Me, 1934) being notable

---

34 The *Reichsfilmdramaturg* (the Reich's dramatic adviser for films) pre-censored scripts before they went into production, with films being censored once again upon completion by a central agency in Berlin. A ratings system lauded both artistic and political excellence, with financial incentives accruing to producers who made, and to cinemas who screened, highly rated movies.

examples.[35] Horror films furthermore became conspicuously absent, the Nazis instead preferring to produce "racially correct" films that eschewed an occult worldview.[36]

The New Woman – and by extension the occult woman – was ultimately a casualty of Hitler's Third Reich. Under Nazi rule, women would cease to be members of the public sphere, instead bearing the expectations of raising children, as befitted the German *Volk*. Indeed, the State persuaded women to procreate, with the Reichsbund der Kinderreichen (Reich Association for Multiple Offspring Families) and the creation of the Mutterkreuz (Mother's Cross of Honor) helping to remind women of their proper roles as mothers and wives. For the Nazis, the notion of women's emancipation was in fact "an invention of the Jewish intellect" (Hitler qtd. in Rabinbach and Gilman 311): the world of woman would again be circumscribed to "her husband, her family, her children, and her home" (Ibid. 312).

Thus, the occult woman – both real and imaginary – was an exclusively Weimar phenomenon, which could not continue after 1936. From perceived supernatural beings in the form of ghosts to the medium or card reader earning her salt in Munich, the occult woman served as a barometer for Weimar gender relations. Evincing a sexual emancipation in her relationship with men, and ever-powerful in the public sphere, the occult woman constituted a puissant, reckoning force. Her power was ultimately rooted in her access to knowledge of the unknown: her ability to traverse the bounds between this world and the next was as much prized as it was vilified. Just as the National Socialists took choices away from the New Woman, they also ensured that the occult woman was gone forever: buried deep beneath a National Socialist rhetoric of female sacrifice for the *Vaterland*.

35   Sensual characters, such as Astre in *La Habanera* (1936), are long-suffering and are punished for their sexual transgressions.
36   There were several science fiction films produced, notably *Gold* (1934). Such films revealed a world on the vanguard of scientific progress, where advances like artificially manufacturing gold had to be weighed against the interests of the community.

Works Cited

A., O. *8 Uhr-Abendblatt*. October 7, 1921, qtd. in *Film und Presse*, 37/38, 1921.

Agamben, Giorgio. *Stanzas: Word and Phantasm in Western Culture*. Minneapolis: University of Minnesota Press, 1993.

Aigner, Eduard. *Gibt es Geister?* Siegmar-Chemnitz: Verlag "Das Wissen dem Volke" Otto Uhlmann, 1921.

Aksakow, Alexander. *Animismus und Spiritismus*. Leipzig: Mutze, 1919.

Allen, Virginia M. *The Femme Fatale: Erotic Icon*. Troy, NY: Whitston Publishing, 1983.

Andriopoulos, Stefan. *Possessed: Hypnotic Crimes, Corporate Fiction, and the Invention of Cinema*. Translated by Peter Jansen and Stefan Andriopoulos. Chicago: University of Chicago Press, 2008.

Angel, H. "Das Blaue Licht." *Lichtbild-Bühne* 72, March 26, 1932.

Auerbach, Nina. *Our Vampires, Ourselves*. Chicago: University of Chicago Press, 1995.

Baerwald, Richard. *Okkultismus, Spiritismus und unterbewußte Seelenzustände*. Leipzig: B. G. Teubner, 1920.

Basham, Diana. *The Trial of Woman: Feminism and the Occult Sciences in Victorian Literature and Society*. London: Macmillan, 1992.

Baskin, Judith Reesa. *Midrashic Women: Formations of the Feminine in Rabbinic Literature*. Hanover: University Press of New England, 2002.

Bauer, Bernhard A. "Wie bist du, Weib?" *Querschnitt* 4, 1924, pp. 339–40.

Bäumer, Gertrud. *Die Frau in der Krisis der Kultur*. Schriftenreihe der Akademie für soziale und pädagogische Frauenarbeit in Berlin, Heft I. Berlin: F. A. Herbig Verlagsbuchhandlung, 1926.

Bebermeyer, Renate. "'Krise'-Komposita - verbale Leitfossilien unserer Tage, Muttersprache." *Zeitschrift zur Pflege und Erforschung der deutschen Sprache* 90, 1980, pp. 189–210.

Becker-Cantarino, Barbara. "Witch and Infanticide: Imaging the Female in *Faust I*." *Goethe Yearbook* 7, 1994, pp. 1–22.

Berber, Anita, and Sebastian Droste. *Die Tänze des Lasters, des Grauens und der Ekstase*. Wien: Gloriette Verlag, 1923.

Bergengruen, Werner. *Die Zigeuner und das Wiesel. Das Buch Rodenstein*. Frankfurt am Main: Iris- Verlag, 1927, pp. 46–60.

Berl, Emmanuel. "Die Anbetung der Jungfrau." *Der Querschnitt* 12.4, 1932, pp. 233–34.

Bertschik, Julia. "'Bluterguß der Seele': Diskursformen vampiristischer Ökonomie in der Zwischenkriegszeit." *Poetische Wiedergänger: Deutschsprachige Vampirismus-Diskurse vom Mittelalter bis zur Gegenwart.* Edited by Julia Bertschik and Christa Agnes Tuczay. Tübingen: Francke Verlag, 2005, pp. 233–46.

"Beseitigung der Kunstkritik: statt dessen Kunstbericht, Mindestalter für Kunstschriftleiter 30 Jahre, ein Erlaß des Propagandaministers." *Film Kurier,* November 28, 1936, p. 1.

Bever, Edward. "Witchcraft, Female Aggression, and Power in the Early Modern Community." *Journal of Social History* 35.4, 2002, pp. 955–88.

Blazan, Sladja. "Introduction." *Ghosts, Stories, Histories: Ghost Stories and Alternative Histories.* Edited by Sladja Blazan. Newcastle: Cambridge Scholars Publishing, 2007, pp. 1–8.

Boak, Helen. *Women in the Weimar Republic.* Manchester: Manchester University Press, 2013.

Böhm, Dr. "Der Spuk von Dietersheim (Mittelfranken)." *Psychische Studien* 48, 1921, pp. 76–80.

Bordwell, David. *The Films of Carl-Theodor Dreyer.* Berkeley: University of California Press, 1981.

Bovenschen, Silvia. "The Contemporary Witch, the Historical Witch and the Witch Myth: The Witch, Subject of the Appropriation of Nature and Object of the Domination of Nature." *New German Critique* 15, 1978, pp. 82–119.

Brandon, Ruth. *The Spiritualists.* New York: Alfred A. Knopf, 1983.

Breuer, Joseph, and Sigmund Freud. "Studies on Hysteria." *The Standard Edition of the Complete Psychological Works of Sigmund Freud.* Translated and edited by James Strachey. Vol. 2. London: The Hogarth Press, 1955, pp. 1–305.

Bridenthal, Renate, and Claudia Koonz. "Beyond *Kinder, Küche, Kirche*: Weimar Women in Politics and Work." *When Biology Became Destiny: Women in Weimar and Nazi Germany.* Edited by Renate Bridenthal, Atina Grossmann, and Marion Kaplan. New York: Monthly Review Press, 1984, pp. 44–53.

Brittnacher, Hans Richard. "Phantasmen der Niederlage über weibliche Vampire und ihre männlichen Opfer um 1900." *Poetische Wiedergänger: Deutschsprachige Vampirismus-Diskurse vom Mittelalter bis zur Gegenwart.* Edited by Julia Bertschik and Christa Agnes Tuczay. Tübingen: Francke Verlag, 2005, pp. 163–83.

Bronfen, Elisabeth. *Over Her Dead Body: Death, Femininity and the Aesthetic.* New York: Routledge, 1992.

Bronnen, Arnolt. "Die weibliche Kriegs Generation." *Die Frau von morgen wie wir sie wünschen: Eine Essaysammlung aus dem Jahre 1929.* Edited by F.M. Huebner. Frankfurt am Main: Insel Verlag, 1990, pp. 68–74.

Budd, Mike, editor. *The Cabinet of Dr. Caligari: Texts, Contexts, Histories.* New Brunswick, NJ: Rutgers University Press, 1990.

Carter, Josephine. "An Other Form of Ghost Story: Janet Frame's *The Adaptable Man.*" *Interdisciplinary Literary Studies* 13.1-2, 2011, pp. 45–60.

Cella, Ingrid. "'… es ist überhaupt gar nichts da.' Strategien der Visualisierung und Entvisualisierung der vampirischen Femme fatale." *Poetische Wiedergänger: Deutschsprachige Vampirismus-Diskurse vom Mittelalter bis zur Gegenwart.* Edited by Julia Bertschik and Christa Agnes Tuczay. Tübingen: Francke Verlag, 2005, pp. 185–215.

Christaller, Helene. *Zigeunertaufe. In Meine Waldhäuser. Bilder aus einem Dorfe.* Stuttgart: Strecker und Schröder, 1922, pp. 68–74.

Clément, Catherine B. "Charlatans and Hysterics." *The Cabinet of Dr. Caligari: Texts, Contexts, Histories.* Edited by Mike Budd. New Brunswick, NJ: Rutgers University Press, 1990, pp. 197–98.

Cohen, Selma Jeanne. "Modern Dance and Ausdruckstanz." *Ausdruckstanz, Eine mitteleuropäische Bewegung der ersten Hälfte des 20. Jahrhunderts.* Edited by G. Oberzaucher-Schüller. Wilhelmshaven: Florian Noetzel Verlag, 1992, pp. 161–65.

Corrinth, Curt. "Weltkrieg in der Prophezeiung." *Querschnitt* 12.12, December 1932, pp. 879–82.

Cowan, Michael. "The Heart Machine: 'Rhythm' and Body in Weimar Film and Fritz Lang's *Metropolis.*" *Modernism/Modernity* 14.2, 2007, pp. 225–48.

Creed, Barbara. *The Monstrous-Feminine: Film, Feminism, Psychoanalysis.* London: Routledge, 1993.

Dahlke, Günther, and Günter Karl, ed. *Deutsche Spielfilme von den Anfängen his 1933.* Berlin: Henschel Verlag, 1988.

[Daniel], Anita. "Die Vermännlichung der Frau." *Berliner Illustrirte Zeitung* 35, August 31, 1924, pp. 997–98.

"Das Blaue Licht." *Film-Kurier* 73, 26 March, 1932.

"Der Spruch der Kartenlegerin." *Querschnitt* 12.12, December 1932, pp. 893.

Dessoir, Max. *Vom Jenseits der Seele: die Geheimwissenschaften in kritischer Betrachtung.* Stuttgart: Verlag von Ferdinand, 1919.

Die Haarmann-Protokolle. Edited by Christine Pozsár and Michael Farin. Reinbek bei Hamburg: Rowohlt Verlag, 1995.

Dijkstra, Bram. *Evil Sisters: The Threat of Female Sexuality and the Cult of Manhood.* New York: Alfred A. Knopf, 1996.

Dix, Otto. *Der Schützengraben* (destroyed in the war). 1920–23.

———. *Drei Dirnen auf der Straße*, private collection, Hamburg. 1925.

———. *Mädchen vor dem Spiegel* (destroyed in the war). 1921.

Doane, Mary Ann. *Femmes Fatales: Feminism, Film Theory, Psychoanalysis.* New York: Routledge, 1991.

Döblin, Alfred. *Die beiden Freundinnen und ihr Giftmord.* Außenseiter der Gesellschaft 1. Edited by Rudolf Leonhard. Berlin: Verlag Die Schmiede, 1924.

Douglas, Mary. *Purity and Danger: An Analysis of the Concepts of Pollution and Taboo.* London: Routledge, 1966.

Dreyer, Carl Theodor, and Christen Jul. "*Vampyr*: The Screenplay." *Writing Vampyr.* New York: The Criterion Collection, 2008, pp. 1–93.

Duchamp, Marcel. *The Bride Stripped Bare by her Bachelors, Even/The Large Glass.* Glass, wire, lead foil, and dust. 1915–23.

"Each Month, Thousands of Witches Cast a Spell against Donald Trump." *VOX*, October 30, 2017, <www.vox.com/2017/6/20/15830312/magicresistance-restance-witches-magic-spell-to-bind-donald-trump-mememagic>.

Eisner, Lotte H. *The Haunted Screen: Expressionism in the German Cinema and the Influence of Max Reinhardt.* Berkeley: University of California Press, 1990.

——. *Murnau.* Berkeley: University of California Press, 1973.

Eldorado: Homosexuelle Frauen und Männer in Berlin 1850–1950 – Geschichte, Alltag und Kultur. Edited by Berlin Museum. Berlin: Fröhlich & Kaufmann, 1984.

Ellis, Havelock. *Studies in Psychology of Sex.* Vol. 3. Philadelphia: F. A. Davis. Co., 1927.

Elsaesser, Thomas. "Social Mobility and the Fantastic: German Silent Cinema." *Wide Angle* 5.2, 1982, pp. 15–25.

"Enough Is Enough! against the Masculinization of Women." *The Weimar Republic Sourcebook.* Edited by Anton Kaes, Martin Jay, and Edward Dimendberg. Berkeley: University of California Press, 1994, pp. 659.

Ewers, Hanns Heinz. *Alraune.* Translated by S. Guy Endore. New York: John Day Co., 1929.

——. *Das Mädchen von Shalott und andere Dramen.* Munich: Georg Müller, 1923.

——. *Nachtmahr: Seltsame Geschichten.* Munich: Georg Müller Verlag, 1922.

——. *Vampire.* Translated by Fritz Sallagar. New York: John Day Co., 1934.

"Exit Polls 2016." CNN, <www.cnn.com/election/2016/results/exit-polls/national/president>.

Fahnert, Margarethe. *Die Kunst des Kartenlegens.* Dresden: Rudolph'sche Verlagsbuchhandlung, 1926.

Ferris, Alison. "The Disembodied Spirit." *The Disembodied Spirit.* Edited by Alison Ferris. Brunswick, ME: Bowdoin College Museum of Art, 2003, pp. 32–43.

Ferro, Marc. *The Great War 1914–1918.* London: Routledge, 1993.

Fielding, Penny. "Reading Rooms: M.R. James and the Library of Modernity." *Modern Fiction Studies* 46.3, Fall 2000, pp. 749–71.

Figdor, Karl. "Die Männerfresserin." *Berliner Leben* 15, 1924, pp. 25–27.

———. *Carmen* review. *Erste Internationale Filmzeitung*, Nr. 6, 1920.

Figueira, Dorothy. "Cante Jondo: German Literary Gypsies and Theoretical Nomads." *The Comparatist* 27, May 2003, pp. 79–93.

Finck, Adele von. "Chirologie und Chiromantie." *Der Querschnitt* 8.6, June 1928, pp. 405–09.

———. "Zigeuner, Magie, Karten." *Der Querschnitt* 9.7, July 1929, pp. 473–76.

Fischer, Lothar. *Tanz zwischen Rausch und Tod: Anita Berber 1918–1928 in Berlin.* Berlin: Haude & Spener, 1996.

Flake, Otto. "Die alte Aufgabe – die neue Form." *Die Frau von morgen wie wir sie wünschen: Eine Essaysammlung aus dem Jahre 1929.* Edited by F. M. Huebner. Frankfurt am Main: Insel Verlag, 1990, pp. 135–40.

Forel, August. *Der Hypnotismus oder die Suggestion und die Psychotherapie: Ihre psychologische, psychophysiologische und medizinische Bedeutung mit Einschluss der Psychanalyse, sowie der Telepathiefrage.* Stuttgart: Verlag von Ferdinand Enke, 1919.

Freud, Sigmund. "Female Sexuality." *Freud: Sexuality and the Psychology of Love.* Edited by Philip Rieff. New York: Collier Books, 1963, pp. 194–211.

———. "The Uncanny." *The Standard Edition of the Complete Psychological Works of Sigmund Freud* 17. Edited and translated by James Strachey. London: Hogarth Press, 1955, pp. 217–52.

Frevert, Ute. *Women in German History: From Bourgeois Emancipation to Sexual Liberation.* New York: Berg Publishers, 1993.

Funkenstein, Susan Laikin. "Anita Berber: Imaging a Weimar Performance Artist." *Woman's Art Journal* 26.1, 2005, pp. 26–31.

Fustich, Katie. "Why Is Digital Witchcraft So Appealing." *The Social Justice Foundation.* October 28, 2016, psmag.com/news/why-is-digital-witchcraft-so-appealing-to-young-women.

Gauld, Alan. *A History of Hypnotism.* Cambridge: Cambridge University Press, 1992.

Giles, Steve. "Making Visible, Making Strange: Photography and Representation in Kracauer, Brecht and Benjamin." *New Formations* 61, 2007, pp. 64–75.

Goens, Fritz. *Der Sohn der Hexe.* Potsdam: Ernte-Verlag, 1929.

Goldwurm, Hersh, ed. Talmud Babli. Tractate Eruvin, Vol. 2 (FOLIOS 52B-105A). Trans. Yisroel Reisman. New York: Mesorah, 1991.

Goll, Claire. *Jedes Opfer Tötet Seinen Mörder (Arsenik).* Berlin: Edition der 2, 1977.

Grabinski, Bruno. *Spuk und Geistererscheinungen oder was sonst?* Hildesheim: Franz Borgmeyer, 1922.

Grellmann, Heinrich Moritz Gottlieb. *Historischer Versuch über die Zigeuner betreffend die Lebensart und Verfassung, Sitten und Schicksale dieses Volkes seit seiner Erscheinung in Europa, and dessen Ursprung.* Göttingen: Johann Christian Dieterich, 1787.

Groskopff, G. "Spiritismus oder Telepathie?" *Psychische Studien* 48, 1921, pp. 50–51.

Grossmann, Atina. "*Girlkultur* or Thoroughly Rationalized Female: A New Woman in Weimar Germany?" *Women in Culture and Politics: A Century of Change.* Edited by Judith Friedlander, et al. Bloomington: Indiana University Press, 1986, pp. 62–80.

——. "The New Woman and the Rationalization of Sexuality in Weimar Germany." *Powers of Desire: The Politics of Sexuality.* Edited by Ann Snitow, Christine Stansell, and Sharon Thompson. New York: Monthly Review Press, 1983, pp. 153–71.

Grossmann, Rudolf. "Besuche in der vierten Dimension." *Querschnitt* 12.12, 1932, pp. 870–75.

——. "Wahrsager." *Querschnitt* 8.6 (1928): 410–13.

Grosz, George. "Among Other Things, a Word for German Tradition." *The Weimar Republic Sourcebook.* Edited by Anton Kaes, Martin Jay, and Edward Dimendberg. Berkeley: University of California Press, 1994, pp. 499–506.

Gunning, Tom. "Der frühe Film und das Okkulte." *Okkultismus und Avantgarde: Von Munch bis Mondrian 1900–1915.* Edited by Veit Loers. Frankfurt am Main: Schirn Kunsthalle, 1995, pp. 558–61.

——. *The Films of Fritz Lang: Allegories of Vision and Modernity.* London: BFI, 2000.

——. "Haunted History, Uncanny Modernity: Ghosts, Photography and the Modern Body." *The Disembodied Spirit.* Edited by Ferris. Brunswick, ME: Bowdoin College Museum of Art, 2003, pp. 8–19.

——. "Phantom Images and Modern Manifestations: Spirit Photography, Magic Theater, Trick Films, and Photography's Uncanny." *Fugitive Images: From Photography to Video.* Edited by Patrice Petro. Bloomington: Indiana University Press, 1995, pp. 42–71.

——. "To Scan a Ghost: The Ontology of Mediated Vision." *Grey Room* 26, 2007, pp. 94–127.

Hans, Anjeana. *Gender and the Uncanny in Films of the Weimar Republic.* Detroit: Wayne State University Press, 2014.

——. "The *Zigeunerdrama* Reloaded: Leni Riefenstahl's Fantasy Gypsies and Sacrificial Others." *Continuity and Crisis in German Cinema 1928–1936.* Rochester, NY: Camden House, 2016, pp. 151–66.

Hansen, Miriam. "With Skin and Hair": Kracauer's Theory of Film Marseille 1940." *Critical Inquiry* 19, Spring 1993, pp. 437–69.

Hatvany-Winsloe, Christa. "Zigeuner." *Der Querschnitt* 9.7 (July 1929): 471–73.

Hauptmann, Gerhart. *Spuk.* Berlin: G Fischer Verlag, 1930.

Hellwig, Albert. "Gibt es nachweisbar echte Fälle von Kriminaltelepathie?" *Kriminalistische Monatshefte* 6.2, 1928, pp. 121–23.

——. "Hellsehen als strafbare Gaukelei." *Archiv für Strafrecht und Strafprozess* 71.2, April 1927, pp. 124–30.

——. "Hypnotismus und Kinematograph." *Zeitschrift für Psychotherapie und medizinische Psychologie* 6, 1916, pp. 310–15.

Henderson, Linda Dalrymple. "Die Moderne Kunst und das Unsichtbare." *Okkultismus und Avantgarde: Von Munch bis Mondrian 1900–1915*. Edited by Veit Loers. Frankfurt am Main: Schirn Kunsthalle, 1995, pp. 13–31.

Herrmann-Neiße, Max. *Kabarett: Schriften zum Kabarett und zur bildenden Kunst*. Frankfurt am Main: Zweitausendeins, 1988.

Herzfeld, Fränze. "Vierte Dimension." *Querschnitt* 11.3, 1931, pp. 168–70.

Herzog, Todd. *Crime Stories: Criminalistic Fantasy and the Culture of Crisis in Weimar Germany*. New York: Berghahn Books, 2009.

Hesse, Hermann. *Narziß und Goldmund*. Berlin: Fischer Verlag, 1930.

Hille, Almut. *Identitätskonstruktionen: Die "Zigeunerin" in der deutschsprachigen Literatur des 20. Jahrhunderts*. Würzburg: Königshausen & Neumann, 2005.

——. "'Manche Esmeralda endete am Galgen oder auf dem Scheiterhaufen.' 'Hexen' und 'Zigeunerinnen' in Tanja Kinkels Roman *Die Puppenspieler*." *Horizonte verschmelzen. Zur Hermeneutik der Vermittlung*. Edited by Hans Richard Brittnacher, Matthias Harder, Almut Hille, and Ursula Kocher. Würzburg: Königshausen & Neumann, 2007, pp. 69–74.

Hirschfeld, Magnus. *Geschlecht und Verbrechen*. Leipzig: Verlag für Sexualwissenschaft Schneider & Co., 1930.

——. "Tötung zweier Kinder während der Menstruation: Zum Fall der Käthe Hagedorn." *Medizinische Welt* 27, 1927, pp. 845–47.

Hitler, Adolf. "Speech to the Meeting of the National Socialist Women's Organization." *The Third Reich Sourcebook*. Edited by Anson Rabinbach and Sander L. Gilman. Berkeley: University of California Press, 2013, pp. 311–14.

Hollander Walther von. "Autonomie der Frau." *Die Frau von morgen wie wir sie wünschen: Eine Essaysammlung aus dem Jahre 1929*. Edited by F. M. Huebner. Frankfurt am Main: Insel Verlag, 1990, pp. 38–46.

Horkheimer, Max, and Theodor W. Adorno. *Dialektik der Aufklärung. Philosophische Fragmente*. Frankfurt am Main: S. Fischer Verlag, 1969.

Horsley, Richard A. "Further Reflections on Witchcraft and European Folk Religion." *History of Religion* 19.1, 1979, pp. 71–95.

Horsley, Ritta Jo, and Richard A. Hosley. "On the Trail of the 'Witches': Wise Women, Midwives and the European Witch Hunts." *Women in German Yearbook* 3, 1986, pp. 1–28.

Howe, Dianne S. "The Notion of Mysticism in the Philosophy and Choreography of Mary Wigman 1914–1931." *Dance Research Journal* 19.1, Summer 1987, pp. 19–24.

Huyssen, Andreas. "The Vamp and the Machine: Fritz Lang's Metropolis." *After the Great Divide: Modernism, Mass Culture, Postmodernism*. Bloomington: Indiana University Press, 1986, pp. 65–81.

Ickes, Paul. *Film-Kurier*, 236, October 10, 1921.

Jacob, Heinrich Eduard. "Haarschnitt ist noch nicht Freiheit." *Die Frau von morgen wie wir sie wünschen: Eine Essaysammlung aus dem Jahre 1929*. Edited by F. M. Huebner. Frankfurt am Main: Insel Verlag, 1990, pp. 111–16.

Jaschke, Willy K. *Maria. Eine Stimme aus dem Jenseits? Experimentelle Sitzungsergebnisse mit den Medien Luise Weber und Karl Schneider*. Bamberg: Kommissionsverlag W.E. Hepple'sche Buchhandlung (P. Treuner), 1928.

Jensen, Paul M. *The Cinema of Fritz Lang*. New York: A. S. Barnes & Co., 1969.

Jung, C. G. *Dream Analysis: Notes of the Seminar Given in 1928–1930*. Edited by William McGuire. Princeton: Princeton University Press, 1984.

Jung, Uli, and Walter Schatzberg. *Beyond Caligari: The Films of Robert Wiene*. New York: Berghahn Books, 1999.

Kaes, Anton. "Modernity and Its Discontents: Notes on Alterity in Weimar Cinema." *Qui Parle* 2/5, Distractions, 1992, pp. 135–42.

——. *Shell Shock Cinema: Weimar Culture and the Wounds of War*. Princeton: Princeton University Press, 2009.

Kaiser, Isabelle. *Bilda, Die Hexe*. Regensburg: Verlag von Jos. Kösel & Friedrich Pustet, 1921.

Kandinsky, Wassily. *Über das Geistige in der Kunst*. Munich: Piper, 1912.

Kant, Marion, and Lilian Karina. *Hitler's Dancers: German Modern Dance and the Third Reich*. New York: Berghahn Books, 2003.

Karpman, Benjamin. "Obsessive Paraphilias (Perversions)." *Archives of Neurology and Psychiatry* 32.3, September 1934, pp. 577–626.

Kaul, Stephanie. "Whose Fault Is the Long Dress?" *The Weimar Republic Sourcebook*. Edited by Anton Kaes, Martin Jay, and Edward Dimendberg. Berkeley: University of California Press, 1994, p. 671.

Keegan, John. *The First World War*. New York: Vintage Books, 2000.

Kemmerich, Max. *Die Brücke zum Jenseits: Erweiterte Neubearbeitung von "Gespenster und Spuk."* Munich: Albert Langen, 1927.

Klee, Paul. *Brauende Hexen*. Oil transfer drawing and watercolor on paper mounted on cardboard, Staatliche Museen zu Berlin, Nationalgalerie, 1922.

——. *Tanzende Hexe*. Pen and Indian ink on paper mounted on cardboard, Privatsammlung, 1922.

Kleinschmidt, Paul. *Bei der Kartenlegerin*. Etching, 1922.

Koegler, Horst. *In the Shadow of the Swastika: Dance in Germany 1927–1936*. New York: Dance Perspectives Foundation, 1974.

Kollontai, Alexandra. "Die neue Frau." *Neue Frauen: Die zwanziger Jahre*. Edited by Kristine von Soden and Maruta Schmidt. Berlin: Elefanten Press, 1988, pp. 6–7.

Kontou, Tatiana, ed. *Women and the Victorian Occult*. London: Routledge, 2013.

Kort, Pamela, ed. *Paul Klee: In der Maske des Mythos*. Haus der Kunst, Munich: Museum Boijmans Van Beuningen, Rotterdam, 1999.

Koselleck, Reinhart, and Michaela Richter. "Crisis." *Journal of the History of Ideas* 67.2, April 2006, pp. 357–400.

Kracauer, Siegfried. "Die Photographie." *Das Ornament der Masse*. Frankfurt am Main: Suhrkamp, 1977, pp. 21–39.

——. *From Caligari to Hitler: A Psychological History of the German Film*. Princeton: Princeton University Press, 1947.

——. "Photography." *Critical Inquiry* 19, Spring 1993, pp. 421–36.

Kramer, Heinrich, and James Sprenger. *Malleus Maleficarum*. Translated by Montague Summers. New York: Dover Publications, 1971.

Kuhn, Annette. *The Power of the Image: Essays on Representation and Sexuality*. London: Routledge & Kegan Paul, 1985, pp. 48–74.

"Kunst und Natur sei eines nur." *Film-Kurier* 14–74, March 29, 1932.

Kupschinsky, Elke. "Die vernünftige Nephertete." *Die Metropole: Industriekultur in Berlin im 20. Jahrhundert*. Edited by Jochen Boberg, Tilman Fichter, and Eckhart Gillen. Munich: Beck Verlag, 1986, pp. 164–73.

Kurtz, Rudolf. *Expressionismus und Film*. Verlag der Lichtbildbühne, 1926.

Lämmel, Rudolf. Der moderne Tanz. Eine allgemeinverständliche Einführung in das Gebiet der Rhythmischen Gymnastik und des Neuen Tanzes. Berlin: P.J. Oestergaard, 1928.

Lavin, Maud. "Androgyny, Spectatorship, and the Weimar Photomontages of Hannah Höch." *New German Critique* 51, Fall 1990, pp. 63–86.

"The Legacy of War." *The Weimar Republic Sourcebook*. Edited by Anton Kaes, Martin Jay, and Edward Dimendberg. Berkeley: University of California Press, 1994, pp. 5–6.

Lehmann, Alfred. *Aberglaube und Zauberei: von den Ältesten Zeiten an bis in die Gegenwart*. Aalen: Scientia Verlag, 1985.

Lehmann, Wilhelm. *Die Schmetterlingspuppe. Sämtliche Werke in drei Bänden*. Vol. I. Gütersloh: Mohn, 1962, pp. 173–255.

Lessing, Theodor. *Haarmann: Die Geschichte eines Werwolfs und andere Gerichtsreportagen*. Munich: DTV, 1995.

Lewis, Beth Irwin. "*Lustmord:* Inside the Windows of the Metropolis." *Berlin: Culture Metropolis*. Edited by Charles W. Haxthausen and Heidrun Suhr. Minneapolis: University of Minnesota Press, 1990, pp. 111–40.

Lichtbild-Bühne, Nr. 37, 11.9.1920.

Linse, Ulrich. *Geisterseher und Wunderwirker: Heilssuche im Industriezeitalter.* Frankfurt am Main: Fischer Taschenbuch Verlag, 1996.

Löbel, Dr. J. "Die verstandene Frau." *Die Dame* 8.1, 1927, pp. 34–36.

Lomnitz, Alfred. *Gespenstersonate.* Original woodcut, *Das Kunstblatt.* Berlin: Verlag Gustav Kiepenheuer, 1920.

Löns, Hermann. "Der Vampir." *Die Toten sind unersättlich. Gespenstergeschichten.* Edited by Hans Joachim Kruse. Berlin/Weimar: Aufbau-Verlag, 1988, pp. 260–66.

Lungstrum, Janet. "*Metopolis* and the Technosexual Woman of German Modernity." *Women in the Metropolis: Gender and Modernity in Weimar Culture.* Edited by Katharina von Ankum. Berkeley: University of California Press, 1997, pp. 128–44.

"#MagicResistance: The Rise of Feminist Witchcraft." *Breitbart*, December 17, 2017, <www.breitbart.com/tech/2017/12/17/rise-feminist-witches/>.

Malten, Thea. *Die Hexe Lil.* Oldenburg & Co. Verlag, 1922.

Manning, Susan A. *Ecstasy and the Demon: Feminism and Nationalism in the Dances of Mary Wigman.* Berkeley: University of California Press, 1993.

——. "Feminism, Utopianism, and the Incompleted Dialogue of Modernism." *Ausdruckstanz, Eine mitteleuropäische Bewegung der ersten Hälfte des 20. Jahrhunderts.* Edited by G. Oberzaucher-Schüller.Wilhelmshaven: Florian Noetzel Verlag, 1992, pp. 105–15.

——. "Ideology and Performance between Weimar and the Third Reich: The Case of *Totenmal.*" *Theatre Journal* 41.2, May 1989, pp. 211–23.

März, Roland, and Rosemarie Radeke, ed. *Von der Dada-Messe zum Bildersturm: Dix & Berlin.* Berlin: Museumspädagogik/Besucherdienst der Staatlichen Museen zu Berlin Preußischer Kulturbesitz, 1991.

Matthias, Leo. "Sei nicht tüchtig!" *Die Frau von morgen wie wir sie wünschen: Eine Essaysammlung aus dem Jahre 1929.* Edited by F. M. Huebner. Frankfurt am Main: Insel Verlag, 1990, pp. 60–67.

McCormick, Richard W. "Desire versus Despotism: The Politics of *Sumurun* (1920), Ernst Lubitsch's 'Oriental' Fantasy." *The Many Faces of Weimar: Rediscovering Germany's Filmic Legacy.* Edited by Christian Rogowski. Rochester, NY: Camden House, 2010, pp. 67–83.

——. *Gender and Sexuality in Weimar Modernity: Film, Literature, and "New Objectivity."* New York: Palgrave, 2001.

Michel, Artur. "The Development of the New German Dance." *The Modern Dance.* Edited by Virginia Stewart and Merle Armitage. New York: E. Weyhe, 1935, pp. 3–17.

Miegel, Agnes. *Der Gaukler. Märchen und Spiele. Gesammelte Werke* Vol. IV. Düsseldorf / Köln: Diederichs, 1955a, pp. 61–79.

———. *Die schöne Malone. Märchen und Spiele. Gesammelte Werke* Vol. IV. Düsseldorf / Köln: Diederichs, 1955b, pp. 23–41.

Mihaly, Jo. "Ein Kommentar zur Zigeunerfrage." *Landstrasse, Kunden, Vagabunden.* Edited by Klaus Trappmann. Berlin: 1980, pp. 296–300.

Moll, Albert. *Der Spiritismus*. Suttgart: Franckh'sche Verlagshandlung, 1924.

———. *Hypnotism*. New York: Charles Scribner's Sons, 1902.

———. *Psychologie und Charakterologie der Okkultisten*. Stuttgart: Ferdinand Enke, 1929.

Mosse, George L. "National Cemeteries and National Revival: The Cult of the Fallen Soldiers in Germany." *Journal of Contemporary History* 14.1, January 1979, pp. 1–20.

"Most Americans 18–29 Years Old Believe in Demon Possession." *Huffington Post*, October 25, 2013, <www.huffingtonpost.com/bruce-wilson/most-americans-1829–years_b_4163588.html>.

Müller, Hedwig. *Mary Wigman: Leben und Werk der Großen Tänzerin*. Weinheim: Quadriga Verlag, 1986.

Müller, Hedwig, and Patricia Stockemann. *"… jeder Mensch ist ein Tänzer": Ausdruckstanz in Deutschland zwischen 1900 und 1945*. Gießen: Anabas-Verlag, 1993.

Müller, Oskar A. *Albert von Keller: 1844 Gais/Schweiz-1920 München*. Munich: Verlag Karl Thiemig, 1981.

Musil, Robert. "Die Frau gestern und morgen." *Die Frau von morgen wie wir sie wünschen: Eine Essaysammlung aus dem Jahre 1929*. Edited by F. M. Huebner. Frankfurt am Main: Insel Verlag, 1990, pp. 85–93.

Nash, Mark. *"Vampyr* and the Fantastic." *Screen: The Journal for the Society of Education in Film and Television* 17.3, 1976, pp. 29–67.

"'Nasty Woman': Trump Attacks Clinton during Final Debate." *The Guardian*, October 20, 2016, <www.theguardian.com/us-news/.../nasty-woman-donald-trump-hillary-clinton>.

Neale, Stephen. *Genre*. London: BFI, 1980.

Negri, Pola. *Memoirs of a Star*. Garden City, NY: Doubleday, 1970.

Noll, Richard. "Introduction." *Vampires, Werewolves, and Demons: Twentieth Century Reports in the Psychiatric Literature*. Edited by Richard Noll. New York: Brunner/Mazel Publishers, 1992, pp. 3–25.

Oesterreich, Traugott Konstantin. *Der Okkultismus im modernen Weltbild*. Dresden: Sibyllen Verlag, 1921.

Oinas, Felix. "East European Vampires and Dracula." *Journal of Popular Culture* 16.1, 1982, pp. 108–16.

Ostwald, Hans. *Sittengeschichte der Inflation: Ein Kulturdokument aus den Jahren des Marksturzes*. Berlin: Neufeld & Henius Verlag, 1931.

O'Sullivan, Michael E. "Therese Neumann of Konnersreuth, National Socialism, and Democracy." *Revisiting the "Nazi Occult": Histories, Realisties, Legacies.* Edited by Monica Black and Eric Kurlander. Rochester, NY: Camden House, 2015, pp. 181–201.

Peirse, Alison. "The Impossibility of Vision: Vampirism, Formlessness and Horror in *Vampyr.*" *Studies in European Cinema* 5.3, 2008, pp. 161–70.

Perhold, Sabine. "Die monströse Darstellung weiblicher Vampire in der 'Verzahnung' von Religion, Mythologie, Literatur, Medien und Film." *Rote Küsse.* Edited by Sabine Perhold. Tübingen: Konkursbuchverlag Claudia Gehrke, 1990.

Petro, Patrice. *Joyless Streets. Women and Melodramatic Representation in Weimar Germany.* Princeton: Princeton University Press, 1989.

——. "The Woman, The Monster, and *The Cabinet of Dr. Caligari.*" *The Cabinet of Dr. Caligari: Texts, Contexts, Histories.* Edited by Mike Budd. New Brunswick, NJ: Rutgers University Press, 1990, pp. 205–17.

Peukert, Detlef J. K. *The Weimar Republic.* Translated by Richard Deveson. New York: Hill and Wang, 1993.

Piper, Otto. *Der Spuk: Zweihundertundfünfzig Geschehnisse aller Arten und Zeiten.* Munich: R. Piper & Co., 1922.

Poiret, Paul. "Die Mode in 30 Jahren." *Der Querschnitt* 7.1, 1927, pp. 30–33.

Powrie, Phil, et al. *Carmen on Film: A Cultural History.* Bloomington: Indiana University Press, 2007.

Prel, Karl du. "Röntgens Strahlen und der Occultismus." *Die Zukunft* IV.14, 1896, pp. 316–24.

——. *Der Spiritismus.* Leipzig: Reclam, 1893.

Presber, Rudolf. *Die Hexe von Endor.* Stuttgart und Berlin: Deutsche Verlags Anstalt, 1932.

Preston-Dunlop, Valerie, and Susanne Lahusen. *Schrifttanz: A View of German Dance in the Weimar Republic.* London: Dance Books, 1990.

Princenthal, Nancy. "Willing Spirits Art of the Paranormal." *Art in America* 94.2, February 2006, pp. 104–15.

Prins, Herschel. "Vampirism: A Clinical Condition." *Vampires, Werewolves, and Demons: Twentieth Century Reports in the Psychiatric Literature.* Edited by Richard Noll. New York: Brunner/Mazel Publishers, 1992, pp. 74–80.

——. "Vampirism: Legendary or Clinical Phenomenon?" *Medicine, Science, and the Law* 24.4, 1984, pp. 283–93.

Purkiss, Diane. *The Witch in History: Early Modern and Twentieth-Century Representations.* London: Routledge, 1996.

Pytlik, Priska. *Okkultismus und Moderne. Ein kulturhistorisches Phänomen und seine Bedeutung für die Literatur um 1900.* Paderborn: Ferdinand Schöningh, 2005.

Querschnitt, Der. Issue on the occult. 12.12, December 1932.

Rapaport, Herman. "Spectres of Benjamin." *Textual Practice* 19.4, 2005, pp. 415–43.

Rentschler, Eric. "Mountains and Modernity: Relocating the Bergfilm." *New German Critique* 51, Fall 1990, pp. 137–61.

——. *The Ministry of Illusion: Nazi Cinema and Its Afterlife.* Cambridge: Harvard University Press, 1996.

Riefenstahl, Leni. *Leni Riefenstahl-A Memoir.* New York: St. Martin's Press, 1992.

Riviere, Joan. "Womanliness as a Masquerade." *Formations of Fantasy.* Edited by Victor Burgin, James Donald, and Cora Kaplan. New York: Methuen, 1986, pp. 35–44.

Rosalie, A. *Rache einer Zigeunerin oder Der Mensch denkt und Gott lenkt!* Neu-Ulm: Schwäbische Verlagsanstalt, 1928.

Roth, Joseph. "Die Frauen Nebbe und Klein." *Werke.* Edited by Klaus Westermann. Köln: Kiepenhauer & Witsch, 1989, pp. 952–54.

Rowe, Dorothy. *Representing Berlin: Sexuality and the City in Imperial and Weimar Germany.* Aldershot: Ashgate, 2003.

Ruthner, Clemens. "Sexualität Macht Tod/t: Prolegomena zu einer Literaturgeschichte des Vampirismus." *Kakanien revisited,* 2002, pp. 1–16.

Sannwald, Daniela. "Überlebenskünstlerinnen. Frauenrollen im Film der zehner und zwanziger Jahre." *City Girls. Frauenbilder im Stummfilm.* Edited by Gabriele Jatho und Rainer Rother. Berlin: Bertz & Fischer, 2007, pp. 14–51.

Schenzinger, Karl Aloys. *Der Hitlerjunge Quex.* Berlin: Zeitgeschichte Verlag, 1932.

Schertel, Ernst. "Erotik, Tanz und Okkultismus." *Zeitschrift für Menschenkunde* 4, 1929, pp. 306–09.

——. "Gibt es hypnotischen Tanz?" *Die Umschau* 30.2, January 1926, pp. 31–35.

Schneickert, Hans. *Das Weib als Erpresserin und Anstifterin.* Abhandlungen aus dem Gebiete der Sexualforschung Band I/Heft 6. Bonn: A. Marcus & E. Webers Verlag, 1918/19.

Schur, Ernst. *Der moderne Tanz.* Munich, 1910.

Schwab, Friedrich. "Teleplasma, eine mysteriöse Substanz." *Der Querschnitt* 12.12, 1932, pp. 859–61.

Schwabe, Toni. "Der Vampir." *Das Gespensterbuch. Ein Jahrbuch für die unheimliche Geschichten.* Edited by T. S. Jena, 1920, pp. 288–94.

Sharp, Lynn L. "Women in Spiritism: Using the Beyond to Construct the Here and Now." *Proceedings of the Annual Meeting of the Western Society for French History* 21, 1994, pp. 161–68.

Siebenpfeiffer, Hania. *Böse Lust: Gewaltverbrechen in Diskursen der Weimarer Republik.* Köln: Böhlau Verlag, 2005.

Silverman, Kaja. *Male Subjectivity at the Margins.* New York: Routledge, 1992.

Simmel, Ernst. "War Neuroses and 'Psychic Trauma.'" *The Weimar Republic Sourcebook*. Edited by Anton Kaes, Martin Jay, and Edward Dimendberg. Berkeley: University of California Press, 1994, pp. 7–8.

Sorell, Walter. *The Mary Wigman Book*. Edited and translated by Walter Sorell. Middletown: Wesleyan University Press, 1975.

Stein, Leonhard. "Der Vampyr." *Das Ballett des Todes*. Jena: Landhausverlag, 1918, pp. 5–29.

Stoker, Bram. *Dracula*. *Three Vampire Tales*. Edited by Anne Williams. Boston: Houghton Mifflin, 2003, pp. 149–460.

Strauss, Daniel. "Anti-Gypsyism in German Society and Literature." *Sinti and Roma: Gypsies in German-Speaking Society and Literature*. Edited by Susan Tebbutt. Oxford: Berghahn Books, 1998, pp. 81–90.

Süddeutsche Monatshefte. Issue on astrology. June 1927.

——. Issue on alternative medicine. November 1932.

Talhoff, Albert. *The Call of the Dead*. Translated by M. A. Moralt. Stuttgart: Deutsche Verlags-Anstalt, 1930.

——. *Totenmal: Dramatisch-chorische Vision für Wort, Tanz, Licht*. Stuttgart: Deutsche Verlags-Anstalt, 1930.

Tatar, Maria. *Lustmord: Sexual Murder in Weimar Germany*. Princeton: Princeton University Press, 1995.

"The Legacy of War." *The Weimar Republic Sourcebook*. Edited by Anton Kaes, Martin Jay, and Edward Dimendberg. Berkeley: University of California Press, 1994, pp. 5–6.

Thiess, Frank. "Krise der neuen Freiheit." *Die Frau von morgen wie wir sie wünschen: Eine Essaysammlung aus dem Jahre 1929*. Edited by F. M. Huebner. Frankfurt am Main: Insel Verlag, 1990, pp. 141–50.

Thurschwell, Pamela. "Refusing to Give Up the Ghost: Some Thoughts on the Afterlife from Spirit Photography to Phantom Films." *The Disembodied Spirit*. Edited by Ferris. Brunswick, ME: Bowdoin College Museum of Art, 2003, pp. 20–31.

Toepfer, Karl. *Empire of Ecstasy: Nudity and Movement in German Body Culture, 1910–1935*. Berkeley: University of California Press, 1997.

Treitel, Corinna. *A Science for the Soul: Occultism and the Genesis of the German Modern*. Baltimore, MD: The Johns Hopkins University Press, 2004.

Tretzel-Groschlattengrün, Fritz. "Mediumistische Erscheinungen." *Psychische Studien: Vorzüglich der Untersuchung der wenig gekannten Phänomene des Seelenlebens gewidmet* XLVIII, 1921, pp. 42–46.

"Trump Draws Outrage after Megyn Kelly Remarks." *CNN*, August 8, 2015, <www.cnn.com/2015/08/08/politics/donald-trump-cnn-megyn-kelly-comment/index.html>.

Trumpener, Katie. "The Time of the Gypsies: A 'People without History' in the Narratives of the West." *Critical Inquiry* 18.4, Summer, 1992, pp. 843–84.

Vaerting, Mathilde. "Die heutige Rolle der Virginität im Seelenleben des jungen Mädchens." *Der Querschnitt* 12.4, 1932, 246–49.

Vanden Bergh, Richard L., and John. F. Kelly. "Vampirism: A Review with New Observations." *Vampires, Werewolves, and Demons: Twentieth Century Reports in the Psychiatric Literature.* Edited by Richard Noll. New York: Brunner/ Mazel Publishers, 1992, pp. 27–36.

Vollmer-Heitmann, Hanna. *Wir sind von Kopf bis Fuß auf Liebe eingestellt: Die Zwanziger Jahre.* Hamburg: Ernst Kabel Verlag, 1993.

Von Ankum, Katharina. "Introduction." *Women in the Metropolis: Gender and Modernity in Weimar Culture.* Edited by Katharina von Ankum. Berkeley: University of California Press, 1997, pp. 1–11.

Von der Vring, Georg. "Offensive der Frau." *Die Frau von morgen wie wir sie wünschen: Eine Essaysammlung aus dem Jahre 1929.* Edited by F. M. Huebner. Frankfurt am Main: Insel Verlag, 1990, pp. 55–59.

Von Gulat-Wellenburg, W. Carl Graf Von Klinckowstroem and Hans Rosenbusch. *Der Physikalische Mediumismus.* Berlin: Ullstein, 1925.

Von Keller, Albert. *Madeleine Guipet als Kassandra* (Madeleine Guipet as Cassandra, 1904a), oil on panel. Kunsthaus Zürich.

——. *Madeleine Guipet als Traumtänzerin* (Madeleine Guipet as Dream Dancer, 1904b), oil on panel. Kunsthaus Zürich.

Von Klinckowstroem, Carl Graf. "Der Unfug des Mediumismus." *Der Querschnitt* 12.7, 1931, pp. 473–77.

——. "Taschenspieler und Medien." *Der Querschnitt* 12.12, 1932, pp. 862–66.

Von Krafft Ebing, Richard. *Psychopathia Sexualis.* Philadelphia: F. A. Davis Co., 1895.

Von Schrenck-Notzing, Freiherr A. "Der Spuk in Hopfgarten. Eine gerichtliche Feststellung telekinetischer Phänomene." *Psychische Studien* 48, 1921, pp. 529–52.

——. *Die Physikalischen Phänomene der Grossen Medien.* Stuttgart, Berlin, und Leipzig: Union Deutsche Verlagsgesellschaft, 1926.

——. *Die Traumtänzerin Magdeleine G. Eine psychologische Studie über Hypnose und dramatische Kunst.* Stuttgart, 1904.

——. *Phenomena of Materialisation.* Translated by E. E. Fournier d'Albe. London, 1920.

——. *Phenomena of Materialisation: A Contribution to the Investigation of Mediumistic Teleplastics.* Translated by E. E. Fournier d'Albe. London: Kegan Paul, Trench, Trubner & Co., 1923.

——. *Physikalische Phänomene des Mediumismus.* Munich: Verlag von Ernst Reinhardt, 1920.

Von Vegesack, Siegfried. "Deutscher Okkultismus." *Die Weltbühne* 21.1, 1925, p. 559.

Von Weisl, Wolfgang. "Querschnitt durch ein okkultes Zeitalter." *Querschnitt* 12.12, 1932, pp. 846–51.

Wallace, Peggy. "'The Most Important Factor War the Spirit': Leni Riefenstahl during the Filming of *The Blue Light*." *Image* 17.1, March 1974, pp. 17–29.

Weiß, Ernst. *Der Fall Vukobrankovics*. Außenseiter der Gesellschaft 4. Edited by Rudolf Leonhard. Berlin: Verlag Die Schmiede, 1924.

Werner, Paul. *Die Skandal Chronik des deutschen Film von 1900–1945*. Frankfurt: Fischer, 1990.

The William Davidson Talmud. Shabbat 151b, <www.sefaria.org/Shabbat.151b?lang=bi>.

Williams, Linda. "When the Woman Looks." *Re-Vision: Essays in Feminist Film Criticism*. Edited by Mary Ann Donne, Patricia Mellencamp, and Linda Williams. The American Film Institute Monograph Series, Vol. 3. Frederick, MD: University Publication of America, 1984, pp. 83–99.

Winter, Jay. *Sites of Memory Sites of Mourning: The Great War in European Cultural History*. Cambridge: Cambridge University Press, 1995.

Witzmann, Pia. "'Dem Kosmos zu gehört der Tanzende': Der Einfluß des Okkulten auf den Tanz." *Okkultismus und Avantgarde: Von Munch bis Mondrian 1900–1915*. Edited by Veit Loers. Frankfurt: Schirn Kunsthalle, 1998, pp. 600–45.

Woche, Die, 34. Issue on occultism. September 24, 1932.

Wolffram, Heather. "Parapsychology on the Couch: The Psychology of Occult Belief in Germany, c. 1870–1939." *Journal of the History of Behavioral Sciences* 42.3, 2006, pp. 237–60.

Wulffen, Erich. *Irrwege des Eros*. Hellerau bei Dresden: Avalun-Verlag, 1929.

——. *Woman as a Sexual Criminal*. Translated by David Berger. New York: American Ethnological Press, 1934.

Wünsch, Stefan. "Käthe Hagedorn: Ein historischer Beitrag über das unsichtbare Phänomen der pädophil-begehrenden Frau." *Plurale* 7, 2008, pp. 241–72.

Zanger, Anat. "Romanies, Women, and Other Smugglers in Carmen." *Framework: The Journal of Cinema and Media* 44.2, Fall 2003, pp. 81–93.

Zweig, Stefan. "The Monotonization of the World." *The Weimar Republic Sourcebook*. Edited by Anton Kaes, Martin Jay, and Edward Dimendberg. Berkeley: University of California Press, 1994, pp. 397–400.

Index

Women, Gender & Sexuality in German Literature & Culture

Helen Watanabe-O'Kelly, University of Oxford
Series Editor

Women, Gender and Sexuality in German Literature and Culture continues the mission of the book series *Women in German Literature,* which launched twenty years ago. Originally focused primarily on women writers, the series is now expanding its remit to cover German cultural production more broadly and to include studies relating to gender and sexuality.

The series welcomes proposals for monographs and rigorously edited essay collections focusing on the work of women and LGBTQ+ creators as well as the representation of women, gender and/or sexuality in literature, media and culture from the Middle Ages to the present day. The series contributes to efforts to broaden the German canon by publishing pioneering studies of relatively unknown writers, artists and filmmakers and cutting-edge assessments of more established figures. Studies of the history of women in German-speaking culture, such as the participation of women in German intellectual life and the struggle for equal rights, as well as historical considerations of gender and sexuality in German-speaking countries, are also encouraged.

Editorial Board: Helga Druxes (Williams College), Georgina Paul (University of Oxford), Helmut Puff (University of Michigan) and Yasemin Yildiz (University of California, Los Angeles)

14　Alexandra Merley Hill, *Playing House: Motherhood, Intimacy, and Domestic Spaces in Julia Franck's Fiction.* 192 pp. 2012. ISBN 978-3-0343-0767-3

15　Christa Spreizer (ed.), *Discovering Women's History: German-Speaking Journalists (1900–1950).* 428 pp. 2014. ISBN 978-3-0343-0747-5

16　Abigail Dunn, *Virtuous Victim or Sexual Predator? The Representation of the Widow in Nineteenth- and Early Twentieth-Century German Fiction.* 256 pp. 2013. ISBN 978-3-0343-0776-5

17　Beatrix M. Brockman, *"Nur fliegend fängt man Worte ein". Eva Strittmatters Poetik.* 265 pp. 2013. ISBN 978-3-0343-0948-6

18　Terrill John May, *Popular Fiction in the Age of Bismarck: E. Marlitt and her Narrative Strategies.* 391 pp. 2014. ISBN 978-3-0343-0950-9

19　Birgit Mikus, *The Political Woman in Print: German Women's Writing 1845–1919.* 268 pp. 2014. ISBN 978-3-0343-1736-8

20　Edward Timms, *Anna Haag and her Secret Diary of the Second World War: A Democratic German Feminist's Response to the Catastrophe of National Socialism.* 273 pp. 2016. ISBN 978-3-0343-1818-1

21　Lauren Selfe, *Representations of Muslim Women in German Popular Culture, 1990–2015.* 274 pp. 2019. ISBN 978-1-78707-997-7

22　Corinne Painter, *Writing Lives: A Female German Jewish Perspective on the Early Twentieth Century.* 178 pp. 2019. ISBN 978-1-78874-155-2

23　Barbara Hales, *Black Magic Woman: Gender and the Occult in Weimar Germany.* 210 pp. 2021. ISBN 978-1-78997-681-6

www.ingramcontent.com/pod-product-compliance
Lightning Source LLC
Chambersburg PA
CBHW071107100726
47908CB00008B/2290